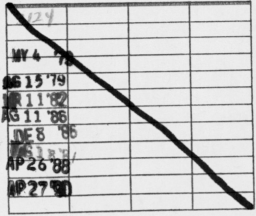

THE JOB OF THE CONGRESSMAN

THE JOB OF THE CONGRESSMAN

An introduction to service in the U. S. House of Representatives

DONALD G. TACHERON *and* MORRIS K. UDALL, *Member of Congress, Second District of Arizona*

SECOND EDITION

THE BOBBS-MERRILL COMPANY, INC. *Indianapolis and New York*

FIRST EDITION, Copyright © 1966
SECOND EDITION, Copyright © 1970
BY THE BOBBS-MERRILL COMPANY, INC.
Printed in the United States of America
ISBN–0–672–51416–8 (pbk)
Library of Congress Catalog Card Number 77–140113
Second Printing

Preface

WITH ITS relatively large membership and intricate power structure, the U.S. House of Representatives is a difficult place in which to establish an identity and to assume a constructive role. This gives rise to the adage: It takes a freshman Congressman at least one full session to learn the fundamentals of his job.

Many members of Congress and students of government have commented on the isolation of congressional newcomers. Woodrow Wilson, writing in the 1880's, said, "Possibly the members from his own state know him and receive him into full fellowship, but no one else knows him, except as an adherent of this or that party, or as a newcomer from this or that state. He finds his station insignificant, and his identity indistinct." Commenting on his first year in the House, in the 1920's, Emanuel Celler of New York said, "A freshman Congressman is a lost soul. He cannot find his way. . . . He doesn't know the rules and nobody bothers explaining them."

Fifty years ago it was not so important for the newcomer to become equipped for constructive legislative service early in his career. Then, as George B. Galloway has pointed out, the national legislature sat only nine months out of twenty-four; members spent the rest of the time at home practicing law or attending to their

v

private affairs. The mail they received referred mostly to free seed, rural routes, Spanish War pensions, and occasionally a legislative matter. The situation is different in the modern House; most Congressmen are in daily contact with a host of constituent problems —and the legislative business that the individual member must help to conduct has increased enormously in volume and complexity.

Recognizing the need for some form of orientation for incoming members, a bipartisan House group began in 1959 to conduct seminar sessions describing House operating procedures and making suggestions for effective service. The American Political Science Association joined as a co-sponsor of the Seminar for Freshman Congressmen in 1963, and the Legislative Reference Service of the Library of Congress participated in a similar fashion in 1969.

The Job of the Congressman: An Introduction to Service in the U.S. House of Representatives was prepared for use as a supplement to such orientation seminars. It is not intended as an analysis of congressional organization or functions, nor does it attempt to describe the power structure or workings of the House itself. Rather, the purpose of *The Job of the Congressman* is to provide, in a single source, basic information about operating problems of particular concern to the newly elected member—setting up and managing a congressional office, conducting legislative business, and serving and informing a constituency.

Many individuals contributed to the preparation of this volume. Its organization and content follow closely the agendas of the 1959 and 1963 orientation seminars; a substantial portion of the material it contains was compiled from transcripts of these two programs, published by Congressional Quarterly, Inc. Thus, in a sense, the authors of *The Job of the Congressman* are the more senior House members who have been willing to devote valuable time and thought to the problems of their newly elected colleagues. In this context, particular credit is due Representative Morris K. Udall of Arizona, whose initiative led to the establishment of the seminars on a continuing basis, and to the other House sponsors over the years—the late John F. Baldwin, of California; Representatives Glenn R. Davis, of Wisconsin; Dante Fascell, of Florida; Gerald R. Ford, Jr., of Michigan; Peter Frelinghuysen, Jr., of New Jersey; James G. Fulton, of Pennsylvania; William S. Mailliard and John E. Moss, both of California; James G. O'Hara, of Michigan; Melvin Price, of Illinois; Albert H. Quie, of Minnesota; and former Representatives Frank M. Coffin, of Maine; Carl Elliott, of Alabama; Charles Goodell, of New York; Donald Rumsfeld, of Illinois; and Stewart L. Udall, of Arizona.

In their collaboration, Mr. Udall and Donald G. Tacheron had the invaluable assistance of Richard P. Conlon in the preparation of a first draft of *The Job of the Congressman*. The Bibliography was prepared by John F. Manley of the University of Wisconsin. Others whose comments and suggestions contributed substantially to the volume include congressional staff members Warren Butler, William P. Cochrane, Roger K. Lewis, Richard C. Olson, and Kent Watkins; Dean Stephen K. Bailey, of Syracuse University; Robert L. Peabody, of The Johns Hopkins University; John S. Saloma III, of the Massachusetts Institute of Technology; and Walter E. Beach, A.P.S.A. Staff Associate. Lois Forbes (and Joyce I. Horn, for the second edition) went well beyond the call of duty in organizing successive draft manuscripts for typing, and Mette Tacheron read galley proofs as a labor of love.

In addition to the 1959 and 1963 seminar transcripts, and data provided by the Library of Congress and various Executive departments and agencies, the following sources were used for reference purposes: Clarence Cannon, *Cannon's Procedure in the House of Representatives* (U.S. Government Printing Office, 1963); Lewis Deschler, *Constitution, Jefferson's Manual and Rules of the House of Representatives* (U.S. Government Printing Office, 1965); Charles L. Clapp, *The Congressman: His Work as He Sees It* (The Brookings Institution, 1963); Floyd M. Riddick,

The U.S. Congress: Organization & Procedure (National Capital Publishers, Inc., 1949); Charles Zinn, *How Our Laws Are Made* (U.S. Government Printing Office, 1965); Charles B. Brownson, ed., *1965 Congressional Staff Directory* (Congressional Staff Directory, 1965); and *Congressional Secretaries Club Handbook: 1964 Edition* (Congressional Secretaries Club, 1964).

In addition, acknowledgment and thanks are due many observers of the congressional scene who permitted the authors to reprint published material or who made research results available for publication in this volume, as indicated in the text or footnotes.

The Job of the Congressman owes a great deal to members first elected to serve in the 89th Congress, who used the initial draft as a supplementary text during the 1965 Seminar for Freshman Congressmen. More than sixty of these members responded to a subsequent request for suggestions for making the first edition, published in 1966, a more useful introduction to the job of the legislator. Similarly, participants in later seminars held in 1967 and again in 1969 have contributed many useful comments, which have been incorporated in this revised edition. To these individuals and to those who will follow them—the conscientious newcomers—this book is respectfully dedicated.

Finally, it is customary to attribute any merit a volume may have to those whose criticisms and guidance prevented the authors from going intellectually astray. To the authors, of course, is reserved the responsibility for any glaring errors of fact or interpretation. In keeping with this tradition, and under the circumstances of this collaboration, it seems reasonable to share the wealth. Accordingly, Mr. Tacheron is to blame for those sections that are impolitic, Mr. Udall for those that are unscientific.

EVRON M. KIRKPATRICK, *Executive Director*
The American Political Science Association

WASHINGTON, D. C.
May 1970

Contents

★ 1 ★

The congressional setting

AS CONGRESSMAN JIM WRIGHT tells the story,* six members were sitting around a table in the Capitol Dining Room just below the House chamber. It was seven o'clock in the evening, and they were tired. Moreover, each had a "mountain of mail" in his office awaiting his signature. But they could not leave because a vote was imminent in the chamber, and eventually one of them expressed annoyance at this state of affairs:

I came here to make laws, and what do I do? I send baby books to young mothers, listen to every maladjusted kid who wants out of the service, write sweet replies to pompous idiots who think a public servant is a public footstool, and give tours of the Capitol to visitors who are just as worn out as I am.

Six years of this, and my net worth has gone down by $45,000 while my blood pressure has gone up eight points. And what contribution have I made? Take today. I wanted to hear this debate, because I'm

* In *You and Your Congressman* (New York: Coward-McCann, Inc., 1965), pp. 13–14. Reprinted by permission of the publisher.

1

not real sure on this bill. Since noon I've had five long-distance calls, and seven different groups of tourists have called me off the House floor to show them the Capitol. Two of them insisted on seeing the President. Today! They couldn't understand why I didn't just pick up the phone and tell him they were coming over. I'm just about fed up!

Others around the table, continues Wright, "murmured sympathetic comments and general assent" until finally Congressman Jack Brooks of Texas said wryly:

You fellows are just exactly right. Not one of us ever *asked* for this job. It was *forced* on us. And in my case I have no intention of making it a career. Thirty or forty years will be entirely long enough!

Of course, both parties to this exchange had a point. The job of the Congressman *is* demanding and multifaceted. The average House member, as described in preliminary findings of the American Political Science Association's Study of Congress Project, works about sixty hours in a typical week.* A little over half his time is devoted to legislative matters; about a third is spent answering the mail, coping with constituent problems, meeting office visitors and the like; and the remainder is distributed among party functions, writing chores, and press or radio and television work. (A detailed breakdown of time spent on various functions, as well as the volume of work performed, appears in the Appendix, pages 303–311).

Yet, despite the heavy work load, the incessant demands of constituents and others, the often frenetic pace and occasional frustration, few members leave Congress unless they are in trouble

---

* Based on a Revised Interim Report of 158 offices surveyed during the 89th Congress by John S. Saloma III, of the Massachusetts Institute of Technology, under auspices of the American Political Science Association's Study of Congress Project. Cited hereafter as *Interim Report on Congressional Offices,* this report and its findings are analyzed in Saloma's *Congress and the New Politics* (Boston: Little, Brown and Company, 1969), pp. 183–195.

with the electorate or are advancing in years and in poor health.*

Why do Congressmen continue to run? At least in part the answer lies in the challenges and rewards of public service. The nature of these intangibles is indicated in the following section, which describes the role of Congress and the functions it performs for our democratic society. Subsequent sections of this chapter deal with various aspects of House organization and operation, including the division of labor and dispersion of power in the committee system; the potential for and exercise of influence by committee and party leaders; the nature of consultation between rank-and-file members and committee and party leaders; and informal standards of conduct believed to be conducive to effective legislative service and the attainment of influence in the House. All the materials in these sections are excerpts from the writings of Congressmen or former Congressmen, political scientists, and other close observers of the congressional scene.

Congress in perspective

From Congressional Distinguished Service Awards presentation speech by Ralph K. Huitt, American Political Science Association Annual Meeting, September 10, 1965, Washington, D.C. Formerly Professor of Political Science at the University of Wisconsin, Mr. Huitt was Assistant Secretary (for legislation) in the Department of Health, Education, and Welfare, 1965–1968.

* The table below indicates the number of House members leaving for reasons other than general election losses, 86th–90th Congresses:

Congress	Primary defeats	Deaths	Retired-Resignations	Total
86th	5	12	27	44
87th	12	8	41	61
88th	8	10	41	59
89th	8	5	43	26
90th	5	4	26	35

The Congress of the United States presents a paradox. On the one hand, it probably is the most criticized public institution in America. When it is slow to act it is called do-nothing, obstructionist, and archaic. When it moves swiftly to pass a large program of legislation, as it has this year, it still is criticized.

But today I heard a variation on the old theme. A member of Congress was explaining why he supported the President's veto on the military construction bill. He said, "This has been a productive and creative Congress. We have passed dozens of bills and sent them down to the White House. The President has signed every one of them. He's a rubber-stamp President. Now that he has taken a little initiative I think we ought to encourage him."

The paradox is that while Congress is roundly criticized it is without question one of the most successful political institutions in the world. Today Congress exercises all the powers intended for it by the framers of the Constitution. . . . Consider what has happened to other legislative bodies in the period of life of Congress. The House of Commons in England has conquered the Crown, reduced the House of Lords to impotence, and in turn has fallen victim to its own creature, the Prime Minister. In the same time, the French legislature has had to adapt itself, if my count is right, to three kings, two emperors, five republics, and one Charles de Gaulle.

Meanwhile, Congress has held its own. It is today the most powerful and respected representative assembly in the world. This is not to say that Congress has not been tested. On the contrary, it has met the great tests of American history. In its lifetime, we have absorbed forty million immigrants and made them Americans. We have expanded from a tiny cluster of states on the eastern seaboard to a great continent-wide empire. From the day when the only federal official most people ever saw was the postman, we have built a national government which regulates and promotes the welfare of our people from the cradle to the grave. We have fought wars, survived depressions, and weathered the worst test a political system can sustain, a civil war. . . .

The basis of congressional power rests, I think, on two basic principles in the American Constitution.

The first is the principle of separation of powers. It is true that powers are not really separated in our system. Congress, the President, and the Courts all share in legislation and administration in a way that defies explanation. The powers of the federal government are commingled among the three great branches.

What we have is not a separation of powers but a separation of institutions, of personnel. The Constitution clearly says that no member of Congress may serve in the Executive establishment and vice versa. This means that if Congress is to maintain its position as a co-equal branch it must have a mechanism for independent consideration of legislation and its own sources of information. . . .

The result has been the standing committee with specialized jurisdiction. But the standing committees have come to be much more than agents for information gathering and independent consideration. They are bastions of power. They cannot be captured by the party leadership or anyone else. . . . It is true that the results of decentralized power in Congress are somewhat erratic, but what is enormously important to the working of the American system is the strengthening of diversity and the provision of many points of access to people who want to try to influence their government.

The second basic principle affecting the power of Congress is federalism. Federalism provides a local base of power for the individual congressman. No national party leadership can hurt him very much if his constituents are happy with him, nor help him if they are not. The great experiment in responsible party government in our time was tried not by academic theorists but by Franklin Roosevelt, the most popular vote-getter of his time. Mr. Roosevelt presented to Democrats the reasonable proposition that if they wanted him to enact his program they should send him Democrats who would support it. He tried to purge eight members of Congress. You remember the result: Only one was defeated and there is no proof that Mr. Roosevelt caused that.

This is a lesson no practical politician in the country can fail to understand. So it is that the member courts his constituency. The baby books, the congratulatory letters, the favors go out in a steady stream. . . . The source of the strength and independence of the individual member is the tie he has with the people at home.

How good is Congress? The truth is, no one can tell. It is not possible to extract Congress from the political system of which it is a part. It performs many of the same functions for the American people that the other branches do and these tasks are shared with political parties, interest groups, the press, and other American institutions. Moreover, we cannot devise tests to determine how effective a political institution is until we can say with confidence what services the institution performs for the whole political system. But there are political functions which Congress shares which it seems especially fitted to perform.

Like the other branches of government, it helps to resolve conflict. But sometimes it is at its best when it avoids conflict, when it postpones or evades an issue which the society is not yet ready to face. The legislature is particularly suited to give a half loaf or to avoid action while seeming to take action. Again, Congress furnishes catharsis for those members of society who are disaffected and cannot otherwise find relief. Individuals in the larger society whose causes cannot prevail identify with their heroes on the floors of Congress.

The "errand boy function," which has received so much criticism, actually provides a vital link between the great government in Washington and people in society. It is important for an individual to believe that he can have ready access to his government, and that he can get a speedy reply which he understands.

All this suggests, I think, that while Congress is known as a law-making body the actual enactment of legislation may be a relatively small function in comparison with others which it performs. And in any final casting-up, it is well to remember that the representative assembly is one of the great creations of free men and that its historic mission is not efficiency in government but the maintenance of freedom. Measured against the tests of American experience, Congress has performed this mission very well.

FUNCTIONS OF CONGRESS

From commencement speech by then Vice-President Hubert H. Humphrey, Syracuse University, June 6, 1965. The complete text may be found in the CONGRESSIONAL RECORD, *June 7, 1965, pp. A2910–A2912. Reprinted with the permission of the author.*

Few persons can deal directly with either a President or a Supreme Court. But any person can communicate with his elected representatives in Washington.

The members of Congress provide a direct link between the national government and the almost 195 million persons who comprise this republic. Surely this connection is vital in keeping our national government responsive to the needs and opinions of the American people.

I have found congressional service to be a remarkable form of higher education. My teachers have been Presidents and department heads, constituents and the press, and, above all, a group of wise and distinguished colleagues in both Houses. I cannot in a few minutes convey to you all that I have learned from these teachers. But perhaps I can suggest some lessons in democratic theory and practice which I have gained from my collegial experiences in Congress.

The first lesson has to do with the creative and constructive dimension of the process of compromise.

There are 100 members of the U.S. Senate; 435 members of

the House. They come from states and districts as diverse as Nevada and New York, Alaska and Alabama. No two states or regions of the United States have identical interests or prejudices. One of the jobs of Congress is to reconcile such differences through the process of compromise and accommodation. What sometimes seem to the untutored eye to be legislative obstructionisms are often no more than the honest expressions of dedicated representatives—trying to make clear the attitudes and interests of their states and regions. As Sir Richard Grenfell once observed: "Mankind is slowly learning that because two men differ neither need be wicked."

From the earliest days of this republic—at the Constitutional Convention of 1787—the leaders of this nation have maintained an unwavering commitment to moderation. If our Founding Fathers had not understood the need to overcome extremes in drafting our Constitution, this noble experiment in the art of self-government would have surely foundered on the rocks of dissension and discord.

As in the deliberations of the Constitutional Convention, the heart of congressional activity are skills of negotiation—of honest bargaining among equals. My willingness to compromise—and I have done so more times than I can count—is the respect I pay to the dignity of those with whom I disagree.

Through reasonable discussion, through taking into account the views of many, Congress amends and refines legislative proposals so that once a law is passed it reflects the collective judgment of a diverse people. Surely this is a remarkable service. Surely, the habits of accommodation and compromise are of universal consequence. These are the skills and attitudes so desperately needed on the larger stage of world conflict. . . .

A second lesson I have learned from my congressional teachers is the importance of the congressional role of responsible surveillance. There are roughly 70 separate departments and agencies of the federal government. Some are small; some are large. All are engaged in carrying out the will of the people as expressed through Congress.

In the interests of efficiency, economy, and responsiveness, these departments and agencies need a continuing critical review by the committees and Houses of Congress. The genius of our Founding Fathers is nowhere more in evidence than in those sections of the Constitution which provide for checks and balances. Through its review of the Executive budget, in the appropriations process, through committee investigations, through advice and consent on appointments and treaties, and through informal discussion, Congress seeks to improve and to support the Executive branch of the government.

This exercise in freedom protects and extends freedom. If legislative voices are occasionally strident, citizens should take stock of what their world would be like if no legislative voices were heard at all. We know what happens in countries without independent and constructively analytical legislatures. Mankind invented a word for such systems centuries ago. The word is "tyranny."

But there is a final lesson I have learned from my congressional teachers: the creative joy of politics. Each Congress is devoted in substantial measure to the development of new public policies designed to promote the general welfare and the national security of this nation. Congress is not a battlefield for blind armies that clash by night. It is a place where national objectives are sought—where Presidential programs are reviewed—where great societies are endlessly debated and implemented.

If, as Emerson once wrote, Congress is a "standing insurrection," it is a standing insurrection against the ancient enemies of mankind: war, poverty, ignorance, injustice, sickness, environmental ugliness, economic and personal insecurity.

Few careers open such remarkable opportunities for translating dreams into reality. A new bill, a creative amendment, a wise appropriation, may mean the difference between health and sickness, jobs and idleness, peace and war for millions of human beings. Stemming from ancient parliamentary origins, the main job of Congress is to redress grievances, to right wrongs, to make freedom and justice living realities for all. What higher calling exists? This is the essence of politics: To translate the concerns and the creative responses of a vast citizenry into effective and humane laws.

I cannot conclude without a personal note. For almost twenty years, Congress has been my home. As Vice President, my relationships with my former colleagues are inevitably more formal and more intermittent than in past years. Yet I can say unashamedly that I cherish them dearly. I have seen their weaknesses as they have seen mine.

I have on occasion been restive of delays and procedural anachronisms—and so have they. But I have seen in the halls of Congress more idealism, more humaneness and compassion, more empathy, more understanding, more profiles in courage than in any other institution I have ever known. Like many of you today, I find it in my heart to praise and to thank my teachers.

Power in the House

From CONGRESS AND THE PRESIDENCY, *by Nelson W. Polsby, Professor of Political Science, University of California at Berkeley (Englewood Cliffs, New Jersey: Prentice-Hall, Inc., 1964), pp. 47–49. Copyright 1964. Reprinted by permission of the publisher.*

On April 3, 1964, Everett G. Burkhalter, a Democratic representative in Congress from California, announced that he would not be a candidate for re-election. In an illuminating statement to the press, the California congressman explained why: "I could see I wasn't going to get any place. Nobody listens to what you have to say until you've been here 10 or 12 years. These old men have got everything so tied down you can't do anything. There are only about 40 out of the 435 members who call the shots. They're the committee chairmen and the ranking members and they're all around 70 or 80." Mr. Burkhalter correctly saw that as a 67-year-old freshman in the House, the likelihood of his becoming a leader —or indeed of getting much of anywhere at all—was extremely slim.

His plight contrasts sharply with the position of the freshman senator. The newly-elected senator enters immediately into the big whirl of Washington social and political life. He and his brethren sit four notches up the table from their colleagues in the House according to the strict protocol of Capitol society. His comings and goings are likely to be chronicled by the society pages. The press releases prepared by his sizeable staff often find their way into print. After holding his peace for a decorous period, he may join in the well-publicized debates on public policy that the Senate stages from time to time. He is a member of several committees, and is consulted when the business of the Senate touches concerns of his own, as, for example, when a presidential appointment from his party and his state is scheduled for confirmation. If he chooses, he can block the appointment by merely saying that the prospective appointee is personally unacceptable to him. . . .

. . . Collectively, the House is quite as powerful as the Senate. Both houses share fully the power to legislate; bills must pass each house in order to become laws. The Senate alone has the power of confirmation, giving it the right to advise and consent to major presidential appointments. And the Senate alone ratifies treaties. But the House has other advantages; under the Constitution, it originates all bills raising revenue—which means all tax bills, tariff bills, and bills pertaining to the social-security system (in spite of the dubious revenue-raising aspect of the latter types of legislation). By an extension of this constitutional privilege, bills appropriating money to run the federal government also start in the House. The mere privilege of initiating bills does not mean they cannot be changed in the Senate. But the power of initiation does set the terms of legislation, often suggesting limits beyond which the Senate cannot go if it wishes bills on a given subject to pass at all. The House enjoys another advantage. Because of its size, it can apportion work among more hands than can the Senate. One result is that the House has developed over the years a corps of members who are devoted subject-matter experts to a degree quite unusual in the Senate. Busy senators, due at three meetings at once, must rely to a much greater extent on their staffs. House members can dig into subject matter themselves. . . .

Taken individually, rank and file representatives must on the whole be regarded as somewhat less powerful than individual senators. Internally, power in the House is held by a small group. . . . But this group is seldom united, and its members generally concern themselves only with sharply limited areas of public policy. On such a matter as making up the schedule of activity on the floor, Senate Majority and Minority Leaders customarily touch bases with all senators who ask to be consulted on given questions. In the House, on the other hand, only those members who because of their committee assignments are legitimately concerned with a piece of legislation are normally consulted when the schedule for debate is arranged. We also may contrast the unlimited debate of the Senate with the sharply restricted debate in the House. In the House, the most senior committee members allocate among themselves and other members strictly limited segments of time, as suits their preferences and strategies, usually according to a formula dividing time equally between the parties, with driblets of time going to majority and minority members of the relevant committee. As far as the preferences of individual members are concerned, floor action resembles a car pool in the Senate, a bus line in the House. The Senate runs by unanimous consent; the House, by a codified set of rules.

It would be foolish to conclude [however] that the Senate is the more powerful body because the average senator is likely to have more powers than the average representative. Buses, are, after all, capable of moving passengers as far and as fast as car pools.

SPEAKER OF THE HOUSE

> *From* MY FIRST FIFTY YEARS IN POLITICS, *by Joe Martin, Speaker of the House in the 80th and 83rd Congresses (New York: Mc-Graw-Hill Book Company, Inc., 1960), pp. 180–183. Copyright 1960 by Joseph W. Martin, Jr. Reprinted by permission of the publisher.*

Next to the President, the Speaker is the most powerful elective official in the United States. In some respects he is less powerful than he was years ago, but in others he is more so.

His power over committees, for example, is less than it was. In the 1890s Speaker Thomas B. Reed, a Republican from Maine, usurped the authority of the Rules Committee by making himself a member and taking control of it. He thus installed himself in a position from which he could dictate which legislation would reach the floor and which would not. This comes close to being the ultimate power in a legislative body. From the autocracy of Reed the House passed to the despotism of Speaker Joseph G. (Uncle Joe) Cannon, a Republican from Illinois, who adopted tactics similar to Reed's but prosecuted them with tyrannical force. . . .

In 1910 the House revolted against Cannon's tyranny and stripped the Speakership of most of its powers. The rebellious members took particular care to enlarge and liberate the Rules Committee. The Speaker lost his absolute power to appoint and remove members of this and other standing committees. The seniority system was strengthened, and the committee on committees in each party took over the function of selecting new members for standing committees.

During the half-century since that revolt against Cannon's

rule Speakers have succeeded in rebuilding a great deal of the power that "Uncle Joe" lost. While the committee on committees may formally select members for committees, for example, the Speaker does in fact exercise a strong influence over these choices from among the ranks of his own party. Thus members must look to him for a chance of advancement. In the four years that I served as Speaker no Republican went on an important committee without my approval. In the case of select committees created for certain limited but important tasks the Speaker does appoint the members from his own party. The Speaker is in a position to expedite or delay legislation and to encourage or shut off debate. Another element that goes to make up his authority is his power of recognition. Merely by ignoring a member he can deprive him of the floor. I believe, however, that many tend to exaggerate this power. In order to maintain his effectiveness a Speaker has to be fair. He is no longer a Reed or a Cannon. His rulings can be overturned by the House.

The thing that makes the Speaker's influence greater in a way than it used to be is the much broader role the House plays in the government than it did in Cannon's day. Until World War II, for example, the House had scant voice in foreign affairs, as contrasted with the Senate, which has the constitutional responsibility for ratifying treaties. In the post-war world, however, United States foreign policy has rested on programs which, like Greek-Turkish aid, the Marshall Plan, and Mutual Security, require large sums of money. Since the Constitution provides that all appropriations must originate in the House, the House has come to have a large influence over the scope and nature of these instrumentalities of foreign policy. As the role of the House has grown, the Speaker's influence has increased.

For one who has as little taste for public speaking as I have always had the title of Speaker was a trifle incongruous. But the Speaker does a good deal more than speak. Presiding over the House is his chief function, but only one of a great many duties.

He is, for example, the manager of a very sizable estate including . . . office buildings and a power plant. The police force and the page boys in the House are under his jurisdiction. . . .

An effective Speaker needs to hold the good will of members of the Rules Committee, which controls the flow of legislation to the Floor. I never had any trouble on this score, partly perhaps because I had been a member of that committee since before most of the members then sitting ever came to Congress.

In addition to all his other duties the Speaker remains the leader of his party in the House. The details of leadership are handled by the chosen floor leader, who in my two terms as Speaker was [Charles] Halleck, but the Speaker himself is the grand strategist and guiding spirit. Each Speaker, of course, exercises his leadership according to his own character and the prevailing political situation. For my own part I was never dictatorial. . . . In fact I often counseled members against taking positions on legislation that could cost them the next election.

One instance I particularly remember occurred during consideration of the Taft-Hartley bill. Among the Republicans in the House was Representative Louis E. Graham, who came from a district in Pennsylvania where labor was strong. We did not need Graham's vote to put the bill through, and I sauntered over to his desk to tell him so.

"I am going to stay with you," he assured me.

"We've got plenty of votes," I replied. "If I were you, I'd think it over. You've got a bad district. If you decide to go the other way, I'm not going to hold it against you."

When the roll was called Graham loyally voted for the Taft-Hartley bill. On election day he retained his seat, though he was to lose it later on.

While I was not iron-handed with members, I nevertheless expected the Republicans to keep me informed about their moves in the House, and I sometimes showed my annoyance when they failed to do so. Without my knowledge, for example, one of our men rose one day and delivered a long, controversial, rambling speech on foreign affairs. When it was over he came to me with light in his eyes.

"How did I go, Joe?" he asked.

"You didn't go anywhere," I replied.

PARTY LEADERSHIP

> *From* FORGE OF DEMOCRACY: THE HOUSE OF REPRESENTATIVES, *by Neil MacNeil, chief congressional correspondent for* Time *(New York: David McKay Company, Inc., 1963), pp. 87–95. Reprinted by permission of the publisher.*

The Speaker, if he has always held the great seat of power, has never run the House of Representatives without help. . . .

The principal aide of the Speaker long has been the majority floor leader, and he in turn has been helped by the party whip and assistant whips, and, often, by the chairmen of the influential House committees. The Speaker frequently has had other lieutenants, picked from among the ablest men of the House and the members of powerful committees. These lieutenants normally have chaired the political and party organizations in the House—the party caucus, oldest of all; the Rules Committee, long the great "arm" of the Speaker, although in recent years tending to operate independently of the party leadership; the Steering Committee, a group used to regulate the flow of legislation; the Policy Committee, whose function has been to help set party positions;* the Committee on Com-

---

* Among the party organizations, only the Republican Policy Committee has been active in recent years in *stating* party positions on public policy issues. The Democratic Steering Committee has been inactive, and the Caucus—although formally empowered to make policy decisions binding on all House Democrats—had not met in recent years to discuss policy questions until the 91st Congress. Then, with the change to a Republican administration, the Caucus began meeting monthly to discuss, among other items, pending legislative business. The GOP equivalent of the House Democratic Caucus is the House Republican Conference.

mittees, which has allocated committee assignments to party members; the Patronage Committee, which has dispensed Capitol jobs to the party faithful; and the Campaign Committee, whose purpose has been to help members win reelection. Each organization has proved useful to create party harmony and unity, the source of party power. . . .

The first lieutenant of the Speaker, the man on whom he has normally depended most, long has been the majority party floor leader, a technically unofficial officer of the House, for he has been selected by either the Speaker or the party caucus and not been elected by the House. The floor leader has had over-all management of the majority party on the floor, and has had command of the House's formal agenda. He has been his party's principal spokesman on the floor; it has been he who normally has responded to the minority floor leader; it has been he who, by both word and deed, has had the responsibility of rallying his own party members to his party's cause. On him also has fallen the responsibility of keeping the House busily at work. He has had to make plans to call up legislation for action in a systematic way, so as to avoid unnecessarily jamming the final days of each session. To do so, he has had to consult frequently with all committee chairmen, to learn from them when they expected to report their major bills to the House, and to urge them to keep their bills on schedule so that the House itself could proceed under an orderly timetable. On the majority leader also has rested the responsibility of keeping both his own party members and the minority fully informed of the coming legislative program, normally announcing this program a week in advance. To do so effectively, the majority leader normally has held private consultations with the minority leaders, and to fail to do so would have risked antagonizing the whole membership of the House. Traditionally the floor leader has scrupulously accommodated members of both parties in scheduling bills and votes on the floor. The majority leader, for example, has carefully

avoided roll-call votes for days on which any state has held a
primary—Representatives from that state quite naturally have
wanted to be free of House responsibilities on such a day so that
they could return to their Congressional districts and vote in the
primary.

As his party's floor leader, John McCormack frequently used
the House restaurant as a rendezvous for his friends and allies in
the House. Every morning McCormack used to stop off at a table
where the Massachusetts Representatives gathered for coffee. On
hand normally were Thomas "Tip" O'Neill, William Bates, Edward Boland; normally Joseph Martin, the Republican leader, was
there, too. McCormack would settle much of the House's routine
business over the morning coffee with Martin. With O'Neill and
James Delaney of New York, who also stopped by for coffee,
McCormack was kept up to date on the operations of the Rules
Committee of which both were members. Boland served on the
Appropriations Committee, one equally important. At lunch, Mc-
Cormack normally ate in the members' private dining room at a
large table reserved for the liberal Democrats. There he picked up
much of the gossip of the House, the problems and the complaints
of the members, and he set forth his own views on pending ques-
tions. He used the lunch table as a communications center. . . .

The Floor leader, according to Champ Clark of Missouri, who
served as his party's floor leader before he became Speaker, "must
possess tact, patience, firmness, ability, courage, quickness of
thought, and knowledge of the rules and practices of the House"
if he was to succeed as a leader. The modern House leader has had
but little power to enforce his will on his fellow members and he
has had to depend on his wits and his power of persuasion to woo
followers to his cause. "I have never asked a member to vote
against his conscience," said John McCormack. "If he mentions his
conscience—that's all. I don't press him any further." Joseph Martin had much the same philosophy of leadership. "I didn't give the

Democrats hell enough," he said, just after the House Republicans removed him as their leader in 1959 and replaced him with Charles Halleck. "Well, I had a program to get through and you don't give a fellow a crack on the jaw to make him agree with you. I believe in persuasion and conciliation." Martin cited an instance when undue partisanship by Halleck had cost the Republicans a bill. Martin, as his party's floor leader, had worked out an arrangement with the Democrats not to fight a bill President Eisenhower wanted. Halleck made a fiery floor speech against the Democrats, and the Democrats responded by voting down the bill. "Joe," said McCormack to Martin after the vote, "we were going to give you that bill—until Halleck damned us all." Halleck has privately acknowledged that on occasion he has pressured his colleagues too severely. "Some guys say I drive too hard," said Halleck, "that I push too hard. You can't push them too hard. You've got to know when to let up. You can go too far, however, and I have a few times. . . ."

Halleck, however, knew the limitations of a leader. "You get pressure from guys who have come along with you on a tough vote about the fellows who went off the reservation," Halleck once said. "Some of them want to read these guys out of the party. But, hell, there may be a vote next week when you need a fellow who has strayed real bad and you can catch him on the rebound." Carl Albert of Oklahoma, Halleck's opponent on the House floor, had much the same view that rough tactics by the floor leader could cost him more votes than such tactics could gain. "If you can't win them by persuasion, you can't win them at all," Albert said. "If you whip them into line every time, by the time you reach the third vote you're through." There have been, in recent years, minor ways of disciplining party members—by denying them choice committee assignments, patronage jobs in the Capitol to hand out to friends, or perhaps more luxurious offices—but these punishments have given the party leaders but little help in controlling their party members. "I can't fire another member of the House," said Halleck. "They're all elected just like me by about the same number of people and they all draw the same pay."

Martin followed a much gentler course than Halleck. "For my own part, I was never dictatorial," he wrote in his autobiography. "I worked by persuasion and drew heavily on long-established personal friendships. Unless it was absolutely necessary I never asked a man to side with me if his vote would hurt him in his district. Whenever I could spare a man this kind of embarrassment I did so and saved him for another time when I might need him more urgently." Carl Albert had a similar view, but acknowledged that the leaders resented Representatives who resisted all unpopular positions. "If a fellow keeps begging off," said Albert, "we tell him that it's his turn to take the heat the next time. . . ."

COMMITTEE CHAIRMEN

> *From an essay, "The Internal Distribution of Influence: The House," by Richard F. Fenno, Jr., Professor of Political Science, University of Rochester; in* THE CONGRESS AND AMERICA'S FUTURE, *edited by David B. Truman (Englewood Cliffs, New Jersey: Prentice-Hall, Inc., 1965), pp. 53–59. Copyright 1965 by The American Assembly, Columbia University, New York City. Reprinted by permission of the publisher.*

Individually and collectively, House members are called upon to make decisions, sometimes within the space of a few hours, on matters ranging from national security to constituency service. In short, a body of 435 men must process a work load that is enormous, enormously complicated and enormously consequential. And they must do so under conditions in which their most precious resources, time and information, are in chronically short supply. The need for internal organization is obvious.

Committees, division of labor and specialization. To assist them in making their constituency-related decisions, members hire an office staff and distribute them between Washington and "the district." To meet the more general problems the House has developed a division of labor—a system of standing committees. To this they have added a few *ad hoc* select committees and, in conjunction with the Senate, a few joint committees. The 20 standing committees plus the Joint Committee on Atomic Energy provide the backbone of the House's decision-making structure. They screen out most of the bills and resolutions introduced in the House— 10,412 out of 11,296 in 1963. On a small fraction, they hold hearings. In fewer cases still the committee will send a modified bill out to the floor of the House for final action. With a few important exceptions, the full House accepts the version of the bill produced by the committee. Decisions of the House for the most part are the decisions of its committees.

The authority of the committees in the chamber rests on the belief that the members of a committee devote more time and possess more information on the subjects within their jurisdiction than do the other congressmen. Specialization is believed to produce expertise. For the non-committee member, reliance on the judgment of the experts on the committee is a useful short-cut in making his decision. For the committee member, the deference of others is a source of influence. . . .

The conditions of committee influence vary. Members are likely to defer to a committee, for example, when the issues are technical and complicated, when large numbers do not feel personally involved, or when all committee members unite in support of the committee's proposal. Some or all of these conditions obtain for committees such as Armed Services and Appropriations, and doubtless help to account for the fact that their recommendations are seldom altered on the floor. Conversely, members are less likely to defer to the judgment of a committee when the issue is of a broad ideological sort, where national controversy has been stirred, or where the committee is not unanimous. These latter

conditions frequently mark the work of the Committees on Education and Labor and on Agriculture. Under such circumstances
committee influence may be displaced by the influence of party, of
constituency, or of a member's social philosophy. Yet even here
the committee can determine the framework for later decision-
making, and members not on the committee may still be influenced
by the factional alignments within the committee. . . .

   Committee leadership and its conditions. Acceptance of the
division of labor as a necessity by House members makes it likely
that committee leaders will have major shares in the making of
House decisions. Who, then, are the committee leaders and how do
their shares vary? In describing the committee-based leaders, it is
easy to mistake form for substance. The most common pitfalls are
to assume that invariably the most influential committee leaders
are the chairmen and to infer that the vital statistics of these twenty
individuals characterize committee leadership. Each committee
chairman does have a formidable set of prerogatives—over procedure, agenda, hearings, subcommittee creation, subcommittee
membership, subcommittee jurisdiction, staff membership, staff
functions—which gives him a potential for influence. His actual
influence in the House, however, will depend not only upon the
prestige of his committee, but also upon his ability to capitalize on
his potential and to control his committee. Consequently, many
important committee leaders do not hold the position of chairman.
They may be subcommittee chairmen, ranking minority members
of committees or subcommittees, and occasionally members who
hold no formal committee position.

   Because House committees differ tremendously in power and
prestige, committees like Ways and Means, Rules and Appropriations necessarily are more influential than committees like Post
Office and Civil Service, House Administration, and District of
Columbia. . . . Circumstance may, of course, alter the relative
importance of committees, but at any point in time influential

House leaders must be sought among the most influential House committees.

House leaders must be sought, too, among the subcommittee leaders of important House committees. The Committee on Appropriations, for example, divides its tasks among thirteen largely autonomous subcommittees, whose chairmen have as large a share in House decision-making as all but a few full committee chairmen. . . .

The influence of a committee leader in the House depends not only upon the relative power of his committee, but also upon how each committee or subcommittee makes its decisions. To be influential in the House a committee leader must first be influential in his committee. The patterns vary from autocracy to democracy. A chairman who is the acknowledged expert in his field, whose skill in political maneuver is at least as great as that of his colleagues, and who exploits his prerogatives to the fullest can dominate his committee or subcommittee. But his dominance may well proceed with the acquiescence of a majority of the committee. They may, and usually do, expect him to lead. Since a majority of any committee can make its rules, it is impossible for a chairman to dictate committee decisions against the wishes of a cohesive and determined majority of its members—at least in the long run. The acquiescence of his subcommittee chairmen will be especially crucial. On the other hand, since timing is of the essence in legislative maneuver, a shortrun autocracy may be decisive in shaping House decisions. A successful chairman, however, must retain the support of his committee, and most chairmen are sensitive to pressures which may arise inside the committee for a wider distribution of internal influence. Long-term resistance to such pressure may bring about a revolt inside the committee which permanently weakens the influence of its chairman. . . .

It is wrong to assume that most chairmen—even if they could—would monopolize decision-making in their committees. In most cases the creation of subcommittees means a sharing of influence inside the committee. Sharing can be kept to a minimum by designating subcommittees (sometimes simply by numbers) and giving them no permanent jurisdiction of any kind. . . . Or the same result can be produced by withholding jurisdiction over certain bills for the full committee, as is sometimes done by the chairman of the Armed Services and the Interstate and Foreign Commerce Committees. But where subcommittees are allowed a maximum of autonomy (Government Operations, Public Works, Appropriations, for example) the chairman may willingly provide leaders of his subcommittees with a base of influence in the House. . . .

Characteristics of committee leaders. The chairman and ranking minority members of the standing committees attain their formal leadership positions through seniority. A variety of rules exist for determining seniority in the case of simultaneous appointments to a committee, but the rules of advancement from that time on are simple to understand and can be applied automatically. A chairman or ranking minority member who retains his party designation and gets re-elected is not removed from his leadership position.

Seniority, however, only partially governs the selection of subcommittee leaders. These positions are filled by the committee chairman (and by the ranking minority member for his side), and he retains sufficient authority over the subcommittee structure to modify the impact of seniority if he so desires. Once a committee member has been appointed to a subcommittee, he usually rises via seniority to become its chairman or ranking minority member. But the original assignment to subcommittees may not be made in accordance with seniority on the parent committee. It may be made on the basis of constituency interests (as is the case with the crop-oriented Agriculture subcommittees), on the basis of prior experience, or on the basis of the chairman's design for influencing subcommittee decisions.

Since the chairman may control subcommittee leadership by his power to determine their jurisdiction and to create or abolish subcommittees, his actions may infuse an important element of flexibility into the rigidities created by strict adherence to seniority. . . .

Normal adherence to the rule of seniority means that by and large committee leaders have had long experience in dealing with their subject matter. Committee-based leadership is founded on subject-matter specialization, and committee-based influence in the House operates within subject-matter areas. Along with information and knowledge, the accumulated experience of committee leaders normally produces practical political wisdom on such matters as how to retain the support of a committee, when to compromise on the contents of a bill, when to take a bill to the floor, how to maneuver in debate, and how to bargain with the Senate in conference—all in a special subject-matter area. . . .

Rules and the distribution of influence. What we have called the House structure of influence (as distinguished from the party structure) results not only from the division of labor by committees but also from the body of formal rules which superintend decision-making. One obvious requirement for the House is a body of rules sufficiently restrictive to prevent unlimited delay and to permit the members to take positive action. Such a set of rules must recognize both a majority's right to govern and a minority's right to criticize. Each is necessary if the rules are to be accepted by both. The accomplishment of this kind of balance is best evidenced by the extraordinary devotion to established rules and to procedural regularity which characterize every aspect of House action.

Increments of influence accrue to those leaders who understand House rules and can put them to use in their behalf. As they exist in the Constitution, in Jefferson's Manual, in the eleven volumes of Hinds's and Cannon's precedents, and in the forty-two

Rules of the House, the procedures of the chamber represent as technical and complex a body of knowledge as any subject-matter area. Influence inside a committee may carry over to the House floor, but success on the floor requires additional skills. Primary among these are the ability to sense the temper of the House and the ability to use the Rules of the House to advantage. . . .

Influence among equals

From CONGRESSMAN FROM MISSISSIPPI, *by Frank E. Smith, Member of the House, 1950–1962 (New York: Pantheon Books, 1964), pp. 128–146. Copyright 1964 by Frank E. Smith. Reprinted by permission of Random House, Inc.*

House leaders on both sides are constantly occupied with the problem of persuading members to vote in ways that will be unpopular at home. The general theme of the whips is, "Vote with us if you can, but don't vote against your district."* The most successful leader is the one who brings in the votes of members who feel they are voting against majority sentiment in their districts, yet does it in such a way that the individual vote does not appear to be anomalous, and thus does not lessen the member's influence on other issues.

There are issues which come before the Congress of such overriding importance as to justify a member's losing his seat if that is the price to be paid for voting his conscience. Fortunately, there are leaders willing to take members down to this position when the legislation demands it, and there are individual members willing to take their political lives in their own hands at these times. Part of the measure of a member is where he places this point of departure from self-interest. I found that the longer my period of service, the easier the decision became. . . .

When I came to the House of Representatives, I wanted to be

* For a detailed description of the functions of the whips, see Randall B. Ripley, *Party Leaders in the House of Representatives* (Washington, D.C.: The Brookings Institution, 1967), pp. 33–41.

a responsible member, with both a voice and a vote in historic decisions made by the Congress. If my constituents were to give me this freedom, I felt that I had to render them special service in areas of major concern to the district. This called for specialization in flood control and water resource development, which in turn required membership on the House Public Works Committee. . . .

The interests of my district dictated my field of specialization in the House, but the decision to specialize in some legislative field is automatic for the member who wants to exercise any influence. The members who are respected in the House are the men who do their committee chores and become able exponents of the legislative programs in which they have specialized.

Speaker Sam Rayburn liked to comment that House members had two constituencies—the voters back home and the other members of the House. There are three groups of members who either cannot or will not recognize their House constituency. The first group are the nonentities, the members who make no effort to acquire or exert influence in the House. They could be expected to have rather brief House careers, but some last a surprisingly long time. The second group are the demagogues. The term may be strong, but it is the one commonly applied in the House to the member who plays to the press gallery and the home folks on every possible occasion, in full knowledge that everything he says and does is recognized, and discounted, by his colleagues for exactly what it is. The third group who ignore the House constituency are the "pop-offs." Their behavior may occasionally be demagogic, but most of the time it is based on the sincere but greatly exaggerated notion that their colleagues and the world in general need their good advice. Their opinions are quite often sound, but because of their attitude, the "pop-offs" have no influence on the House at large. They are not good allies to have in a legislative fight, but the publicity they receive often brings them advancement. I served with several who were elected to the Senate, where they have much greater value. A talking senator has a certain influence in shaping public opinion that a House member seldom achieves.

Over the years, House members come to know how most of the other members will react to any given issue, and it is natural that the closest relationships, working and personal, are developed among those men who face common problems and have compatible points of view. The influential member is not the man who limits himself to these natural associations; he is, rather, the man who takes the time to study the problems of other groups of members, to seek among them the areas of compatible short-term interest, and who capitalizes on those interests by working with such groups in temporary alliances to mutual benefit.

Ability as a speaker is helpful to any member of the House, but it is not usually the outstanding characteristic of effective House leaders. The most talented orators, for sheer historic and vocal ability, were usually among the least influential during my years in the House. Perhaps one reason is that a gifted orator finds things so relatively easy in other political trials that he tends to take the easy way out when faced with the hard chores of legislative participation. With 435 members, the House learns to confine its listening to the man who has something to say, not the man who says little or nothing, though beautifully.

Integrity (or the lack of it) is one of the favorite catchwords members of the House use in assessing one another. News commentators are fond of it, too. Unfortunately, there are almost as many definitions of integrity as there are members. For some, the man of integrity is the member who votes as they vote. For others, it is the man who opposes the party leadership. The member of the opposing party who has integrity is usually the one who votes against his party. Perhaps the most valid index of integrity is the degree of reliance that can be placed on the unofficial commitments every member must make from time to time. The legislative process involves many areas of negotiation, compromise, and informal agreement which never become evident in the formal procedures through which legislation moves to enactment. On both major and minor issues, the individual member must at times enter into unofficial, unrecorded commitments to other members if progress is to be made. This kind of responsibility falls most often on the leadership, and on committee and subcommittee chairmen, of course, but it is a position in which every active member finds himself at one time or another. And it is here that his integrity counts most, and is most easily—and lastingly—assessed by his fellow members. His word is not enforceable, and he knows it is not. Can he be relied upon to honor it, regardless of pressures to the contrary? If he can, he will have the respect of his colleagues, even though they may disagree with everything he stands for; if he can't, none of them will respect him, however brilliant or able he may otherwise be. . . .

Personal relationships in the House transcend party divisions, but the interparty friendships seldom become close ones, unless there is some tie other than membership in the House (living in the same Washington neighborhood, friendships among wives, school or professional ties antedating congressional service, to mention a few). By common consent, it is against the rules to attack another member publicly, unless there has been extreme provocation. It is simply accepted that you have to live and work with other members on another day, and that all members of the House are honorable. A classic example of preserving the amenities came from then Majority Leader McCormack, in the face of repeated insults from a Republican gadfly: "I have a minimum high regard for the gentleman," McCormack said.

PERIOD OF APPRENTICESHIP

From MY FIRST FIFTY YEARS IN POLITICS, *by Joe Martin, pp. 47– 64.*

I entered the House of Representatives in some awe of the great names all about me. . . .

The men who were loaded with the coin of seniority were rather more aloof in those days than they are now.* They were less reticent about letting a newcomer know that they were running the show. The large round table which is still an important meeting place in the House restaurant was reserved for the Speaker, the chairmen of the various committees, and perhaps a few senior members of the Rules Committee. Anyone serving his first term would have been completely out of place. I had been in Congress three years before I dared pull up a chair.

In spite of the great reputations, I soon discovered, as new members probably still do, that whenever a particular subject came up, there was always one or perhaps two members who were expert on it and could address themselves to it far more intelligently than anyone else. And very often these were members that one had never heard of until he came to Congress. . . .

In older days, I was told, a member would not wish to make more than two speeches in a session. The country might be better off if we returned to that custom. During my own time in Congress I have witnessed a deterioration in political oratory. Speakers are less eloquent nowadays. More personal effort used to go into the writing of speeches. I remember one year, when we were holding a big meeting in Massachusetts, I went to the North Shore several days beforehand to call on former Senator Albert J. Beveridge of Indiana, who was vacationing, to ask him to speak. "I would not make a speech," he said, declining the invitation, "unless I had two weeks to prepare it. . . ."

The great difference between life in Congress a generation ago and life there now was the absence then of the immense pressures that came with the Depression, World War II, Korea, and the cold war. Foreign affairs were an inconsequential problem in Congress in the 1920's. For one week the House Foreign Affairs Committee debated to the exclusion of all other matters the question of authorizing a $20,000 appropriation for an international

* Representative Martin began serving in the House in 1925.

poultry show in Tulsa. This item, which we finally approved, was about the most important issue that came before the committee in the whole session.

From one end of a session to another Congress would scarcely have three or four issues of consequence besides appropriation bills. And the issues themselves were fundamentally simpler than those that surge in upon us today in such a torrent that the individual member cannot analyze all of them adequately before he is compelled to vote. In my early years in Congress the main issues were few enough so that almost any conscientious member could with application make himself a quasi-expert at least. In the complexity and volume of today's legislation, however, most members have to trust somebody else's word or the recommendation of a committee. Nowadays bills which thirty years ago would have been thrashed out for hours or days go through in ten minutes. . . .

In contrast to present salaries of $22,500 a year [increased to $42,500, effective in March 1969],* members of Congress received $7,500 then and had a single clerk and a one-room office. Mail was light. I doubt that I received in the beginning twenty-five letters a day until veterans' pension cases started piling up. It was not until the New Deal that the blizzard struck. Then letters rolled in at the rate of 200 a day and the total reached 500 at the height of big controversies.

My first office was in the basement of the Old House Office Building almost next door to my friend, Representative La Guardia, soon to become New York's most famous mayor. He once said to me, "I wish you were a liberal. If you were, you'd be a great leader for us." Although we were poles apart politically, I liked and admired La Guardia. Many people complained that he was a radical; perhaps he was. That does not alter the fact that he did a great deal of good.

Except for him, I was surrounded almost entirely by south-

---

* For congressional pay increases—and decreases—since 1789, see Appendix, pages 297–299.

erners in the House Office Building. This got me off to a good
start in making friends from the South who were to prove useful in
the days ahead when, as Republican leader, I needed some Democratic votes to block New Deal spending. . . .

In the Republican ranks of the House I got off to a good
start, and as time passed and I achieved seniority by being re-
elected every two years, I progressed steadily, if slowly, toward a
position of leadership.

As a newcomer in 1925 I supported Longworth in his bitter
but successful fight for Speaker against Representative Martin B.
Madden of Illinois, also a Republican. I did so at the request of
Coolidge and his friends. This was the first step in the right direction, for it pays to be on the winning side in a contest for the
Speakership, particularly since the Speaker has a great influence on
appointments to committees. But almost more important to my
progress was my good standing, not only with the President himself but with the powerful figures from Massachusetts who surrounded him. . . .

By a trick of circumstances, more or less, I landed in my first
year on the House Foreign Affairs Committee. My predecessor,
the late Representative Greene, had been a member of the Committee on Merchant Marine and Fisheries, but someone other than
myself had been picked to fill this vacancy. Several Massachusetts
newspapers had urged my appointment to the Post Office Committee, and I decided that I would ask for this assignment. On one of
my first days in Washington, however, I happened to inquire of
Frank Foss, who had come to Congress with me, what committee
he aspired to.

"Post Office," he said. "How about you, Joe?"

I did not wish to stand in the way of my friend, the man who
had recently been the Republican chairman in my state, so I replied that I was going to make a play for the Committee on Interior and Insular Affairs, the only other one I could think of on the

spur of the moment. Foss made the Post Office Committee all right, but I never became a member of Interior and Insular Affairs. Instead, to my surprise, the Committee on Committees selected me for Foreign Affairs. Somewhere along the line a decision had been made to give the vacancy on this committee to Massachusetts. There were no other powerful contenders, a circumstance due partly to the fact that foreign policy did not seem so important then as it does now, and I was chosen by a margin of one vote. . . .

In spite of the dearth of great issues, I found that being on the Foreign Affairs Committee gave me a good deal of prestige. Borah was one of the respected voices in the country on foreign questions then, and although he was on the Senate Foreign Relations Committee, the public tended to confuse our committee with his, and people assumed that I sat at his right hand.

Much more important to my advancement than the Foreign Affairs Committee was my appointment to the powerful House Rules Committee in 1929. A seat had become vacant through the death of a member from Massachusetts, Representative Louis A. Frothingham. It was agreed that it should be filled from our state. The Massachusetts delegation was polled and I was selected. "I was awfully glad to see you get on this committee, Joe," Speaker Longworth told me. It was a long step forward. I was on the escalator now, so to speak, and I continued to move as Longworth picked me as a member of his "cabinet," as his steering committee was called. We have no such body in the House now as this small, informal but nevertheless influential group. It was made up of leading Republicans in the House from each section of the country. The "cabinet" always met in the Speaker's office. It functioned extremely harmoniously as an organ of programming and high policy.

I had become a good friend of Longworth's. In the Congressional campaign of 1930 the Republicans won control of the House by a very narrow margin. Under the old rules, the Seventy-second would not meet until December 1931, more than a year away. In so long an interval a number of members would be expected to die, and with so slight a majority deaths could change the balance in such a way that the Democrats would get control and Longworth would be replaced as Speaker. Needless to say this was very much on his mind when, suddenly, one of our Republican members, who was in his seventies, married a woman of thirty. When the bridegroom entered the House one morning Longworth beckoned me to the Speaker's desk and whispered, "Say, Joe, you don't think that old boy is going to do me out of my job, do you?" Fate wrote a different ending. Several members of the Seventy-second did die before it met, and one of them was Nick Longworth. The seventy-year-old man with the thirty-year-old wife lived on. Longworth's fear had been justified, however. Because of the deaths, the Democrats were able to organize the new Congress and to elect Representative John Nance Garner of Texas as Speaker.

VOTE FOR HAPPINESS

> *From* MEMBER OF THE HOUSE: LETTERS OF A CONGRESSMAN, *by Clem Miller, Member of Congress, 1958–1962 (New York: Charles Scribner's Sons, 1962), pp. 39–41. Copyright 1962 Charles Scribner's Sons. Reprinted by permission of the publisher.*

There are all sorts of ways to get things done in Congress. The best way is to live long enough to get to be a committee chairman, and resilient enough to be a good one. Chairmen complain to me that they are frustrated too, but this is really beside the point. If things can be done, they can do them; we are very sure of that.

However, there are other ways, and one of the most effective persons is a congressman from Florida. I first met him at a congressional children's party where he was joyously and enthusiastically larruping up the crowd with imitations of frogs, pigs, and other noisy animals.

I soon learned that this is the man's trademark—the joyful and enthusiastic acceptance of life. His brief appearances on the House Floor are always heralded with high good humor. The somber aspect of the Chamber takes on a lighter hue. Members stream in from the cloakroom. "———— is on," is the word. "Did you hear what he told them?"

After one of his speeches, everyone feels better and usually the Member from Florida feels the best of all. This congressman rarely speaks without a purpose, larded as it is with friendliness and cheer.

He has an angular face with a turned up chin, giving it a puckish cast. His voice is melodious enough, but when he calls out, he can be heard through a six-inch mahogany door. As he talks he leans into his audience (most of our good talkers are leaners) and cocks his head to one side like a mocking bird.

And this man can charm the birds out of the trees. Partisan lines soften, and political gunboats cease cannonading, and the hardbitten Appropriations chairmen vie with one another for the nicest things to say.

To tackle the Appropriations Committee on the Floor of the House is a major decision, frequently the most important decision a Member will make that term of Congress. Here is a choice. If he is silent, perhaps the Senate will restore the item to the bill. If he speaks up and is beaten, he will *never* get it back. And the chances of winning are better than five hundred to one against. These odds mean silence to most congressmen, but not to the Florida representative.

First, he sets the stage in the hearing on the Rule by telling everyone what he is going to do.

"Mr. Chairman, at the appropriate time, I intend very humbly and very prayerfully to offer an amendment. I hope the gentleman from Texas, my distinguished, intellectual leader and my athletic leader, will help me a little bit with it and if he would I would bestow upon him the highest accolade of all and call him my spiritual leader, if he will help me to correct an injustice that I know he does not want to be meted out upon the gentleman from Florida. . . . I know that this Committee will not be unfair to the gentleman from Florida and deny him his laboratory when some of you have received so much."

Everyone is put in a receptive mood by being told with what fear and trepidation he approaches the task. Everyone trembles before the Appropriations Committee so that his well-planned fright is shared by all, and vastly appreciated. He casts an apprehensive eye at the Committee Chairman.

He spins out his dilemma. He knows he can get this entomological laboratory if he will wait till January, 1961, but for this, that, and the other reason he wants to get started in 1960. We all understand these dilemmas. We share the explicit and implicit direction of his remarks; our empathy adds savor to the whole performance.

Then he goes to work on the main redoubts. He offers an amendment. He cocks his head. The Committee Chairman, on his feet in an instant, says, "Mr. Chairman, I reserve a point of order." Ruefully, but with the utmost grace, the Florida congressman backs away: "I ask unanimous consent to withdraw the amendment and offer another one." No one objects.

"Mr. Chairman, I appreciate the courtesy of my beloved chairman." When this congressman says "beloved" the word has substance and meaning. He really likes people; and usually, in politics, among professionals, this is hard to get across.

There follows a lightning-quick description of what the amendment would do. He ripples over it like a dancer. No waste motion, no bogging down in boring detail. Enough, but not too much. Then he disarms the opposition with his nimble tracery.

"I want to apologize to many of my friends because I told you this amendment would not cost you any more money. If my first amendment had been in order it would not have. Please forgive that error. I would like you to vote against me if you think I have misled you."

There follows a neat fencing match with the Floridian tripping a light step between the ranking Republican and the Committee Chairman, the master, who realizes he has a past master on his hands. He begs his friend from Florida to hold off until January, to which the latter responds:

"Sir, I am put in an embarrassing situation. Mr. Chairman, may I say I would be grateful if I could have action now; and if I am not successful I know my dear friend would not hold it against me for making this attempt. Then if I am not successful in this attempt, I can come back in January."

His five minutes expire; but the delighted House, by unanimous consent, permits him to proceed for three more minutes. In the general levity which followed, I admitted we have bugs in my district and we want them eradicated. He beamed his broadest and repeated with comical inflection: "Bugs in California? I thank the gentleman. . . ." The House roared in enjoyment.

A Member from Ohio rose to suggest that we delete some funds from a monument and use it to get rid of insects.

Another congressman from Iowa suggested we not only want to get rid of bugs but we want to return this wonderful person to Congress next year.

Our Florida colleague beamed and bobbed at the Speaker's lectern, telling us he would be overjoyed to yield to Members who would say such nice things about his laboratory.

The Committee Chairman threw up his hands and sat down. The amendment was agreed to by voice vote.

Everyone was happy.

★ 2 ★

Office organization and operation

CONGRESSIONAL NEWCOMERS ARE not invited to play the "musical offices game," which takes place at the beginning of each Congress. At stake are suites in the three House office buildings vacated by death, retirement, and resignation. First claim on these goes to members with prior House service, and newly elected Congressmen draw lots for offices remaining vacant after all their elders are settled.

Once assigned space, however, the Congressman is free to organize and operate his office as he sees fit. Each member is provided allowances for staff salaries, office supplies and equipment, long-distance telephone service, and the like. These allowances are expressed in different ways—clearly and specifically in dollar amounts, or in a roundabout fashion, as in the case of the telephone allowance, which does not indicate actual sums available for payment of long-distance tolls.

Members who represent more than 500,000 people receive

somewhat higher allowances than those representing fewer people. The funds available are reviewed and increased periodically.* During the Second Session of the 91st Congress, a representative of 475,000 people was entitled to:

★ About $125,000 per year for salaries of up to twelve staff employees

★ $5,500 worth of new or used office equipment

★ $3,000 per year for purchase of stationery, supplies, and printing

★ 35,000 minutes of long-distance telephone time per two-year term

★ 480,000 heavy-duty brown envelopes per year

★ $700 worth of stamps per year

★ $2,400 per year for rental of district office space

★ $2,400 per year for district office supplies, equipment, and telephone expense.

In addition, members of Congress are entitled to free and unlimited "franked" first-class postage; and a number of services are performed free or at cost. In 1970 each member was entitled to reimbursement for one round trip to his district per month while Congress was in session, plus three additional trips—one for himself and two for his staff employees.

* Representatives were first provided a clerk-hire allowance in 1893, when they were authorized $100 per month during the time Congress was in session. They were authorized up to two staff employees from 1919 to 1939, when the maximum was raised to three. In recent years increases have been authorized as follows:

Year	Population of District Less than 500,000	More than 500,000
1955–56	8	9
1961	9	10
1965–66	11	12
1969	12	13

Only the allowances for stationery and district office supplies may be withdrawn in cash for use as needed. Funds in the other allowance categories are earmarked for reimbursement of specific expenditures or, as in the case of the salary allowance, are paid directly to whoever supplies the equipment or service. Funds may not be transferred from one of these allowance categories to another.

Use of the funds available varies from office to office and from year to year, of course, depending on the member's political situation, the kind of district he represents, and his personal inclinations. Some permit unused portions of their allowances to revert to the Treasury. Others use them fully—and Congressmen can and do, from time to time, pay for additional supplies and services out of their own pockets.

Each congressional office is, for all practical purposes, a self-contained unit, operating independently of other member's offices. There is no central repository of management information, and congressional newcomers rely on their experienced colleagues for guidance in setting up their offices.* Nor does Congress itself exercise any central administrative control apart from limitations placed on the use of the various allowances. Office hours, staff size, utilization of employees and conditions of employment, arrangement of furniture and decoration—all are determined by the individual member, reflecting his particular needs, talents, interests, and temperament.

---

* After 11 days of debate over a two-month period, the House on September 17 passed the Legislative Reorganization Act of 1970, which had been developed after extensive study and hearings by a special subcommittee of the House Rules Committee. Approved by the Senate on October 6, the Act includes numerous changes in House organization and operation—and provides for the establishment of an Office of Placement and Office Management. A summary of H.R. 17654, the Legislative Reorganization Act of 1970, appears in the Appendix of this volume, pages 401–418.

Assignment of space

Members are assigned space in one of the three House office buildings—the Old House Office Building, or Cannon Building, the New House Office Building or Longworth Building, and the newer Rayburn Building. The most important consideration in determining who gets which suite of offices is length of congressional service. All applications for offices are made in writing to the Superintendent of the House Office Buildings. The schedule for submitting them and the assignment procedures are:

★ *Re-elected members and former members,* returning after a break in congressional service, apply for vacant offices from noon of the first Monday after election day until noon on December 1. The order of choice is: (1) to members with the longest continuous service, and (2) in cases of equal service, to the member whose application was received first. If both service and timing of application are identical, the choice is determined by lot.

★ *Newly elected members,* or their designated representatives, draw numbers during the morning of December 5, from 9 A.M. to noon, to determine the order of their choice of remaining offices. An individual may draw for several members as long as he submits written authorization from each one to the Superintendent of the House Office Buildings. For example, at the beginning of the 89th Congress the Doorkeeper of the House drew for about fifty incoming members. Offices are assigned at 1 P.M. the day of the drawing.

The rules for office selection and assignment provide for a change of date whenever application deadlines fall on a Sunday. They also establish procedures for assignment of offices that become vacant during the session and for assignment of offices to members who miss the regular drawings. Finally, they fix the checkout time for outgoing members. (For the official rules, as adopted by the House Office Building Commission, see Appendix, page 300.)

FURNITURE AND DECORATION

All House offices are completely furnished, but exchange or moving of individual items can be arranged with the House Property Custodian, who is also responsible for maintenance of desks, chairs, bookcases, desk lamps, and other office furniture. Maintenance of built-in equipment, such as filing cabinets, safes, and bookcases in the Longworth and Rayburn buildings, is the responsibility of the House Office Building Superintendent.

Members may decorate their offices as they please, in keeping with good taste. Some favor a relatively severe decorating scheme, using only government-issue furniture and hanging only official-looking photographs, honorary degrees, and the like. Others display collections or hobbies, hang paintings, or add antique furniture to create a more relaxed setting. Of course, the decorating scheme may be changed from time to time, to show objects from the Congressman's district. An exhibition of watercolors or oils by constituents can be particularly effective, and some members have sponsored one-man shows in their offices, inviting their colleagues to meet a "well-known artist from my district."

Housekeeping services and supplies for decorating offices are available to members through the Building Superintendent's Office and other agencies (see Appendix, pages 317–318).

House office staffing*

Staffing practices vary widely from office to office. In some offices each staff employee is given a title and well-defined responsibilities.

* This section follows closely Charles L. Clapp, *The Congressman: His Work as He Sees It* (Washington, D.C.: Brookings Institution, 1963), pp. 56–64.

At the other extreme are offices in which all employees are on the same level, and work is parceled out to whoever is not overly busy at the time. Some members have their most highly paid employees, and most of their clerical staff, in the Washington office, whereas others assign their top aide and several assistants to the district offices. Some ranking employees perform only routine tasks; others are trusted advisers who are given important responsibility or broad authority to act on the member's behalf.

The individual character of congressional offices is reflected in staff titles. In 1965 an unofficial publication, the *Congressional Staff Directory,* listed twenty-six different kinds of secretaries and eighteen different kinds of assistants.* One office had an "Executive Secretary-Administrative Assistant." Another had one person who was simply "In Charge." There was a "Departmental Assistant and Secretary," a "Home Secretary," a "Fiscal Adviser," and, simply, an "Aide." (A compilation of titles in use during the 89th Congress appears in the Appendix, page 314.)

Despite individual variations in organization and operation, however, employees who have certain capabilities are considered by experienced members to be valuable in maintaining an effective congressional office. These are:

★ At least one top assistant—either in the Washington or district office—who is well acquainted with the district.

★ At least one employee who is qualified to assist with legislative matters, if only on a part-time basis.

---

* Compiled by a former member of the House, Charles B. Brownson, the *Congressional Staff Directory* is published annually for each session of Congress. It contains names and telephone numbers of House and Senate committee staff employees, and of staffs of the officers and members of both Houses, as well as listings of state delegations, key personnel of Executive departments and agencies, and other useful information. The office of publication is 300 New Jersey Ave., S.E., Washington, D.C.

★ At least one employee who is able to write well—clearly, succinctly, and under pressure.

★ At least one employee who is experienced in congressional casework, which involves assistance to constituents in their dealings with various Executive departments and agencies.

STAFF ALLOWANCE

Within limits set in the clerk-hire authorization, salaries paid staff employees are determined by the individual member. The clerk-hire allowance in effect during the 91st and previous Congresses did not specify actual dollar amounts available. This complex system—scheduled* for conversion and simplification in January 1971—provides:

★ Members who represent fewer than 500,000 people receive a *basic* allowance of $34,500 and are entitled to employ up to twelve persons on their staff at any one time.

★ Members whose districts are certified by the Bureau of Census as having an estimated population of more than 500,000 are entitled to a basic allowance of $37,000 and may employ up to thirteen persons. (In 1970, 123 districts were so certified.)

The basic clerk-hire allowance was established in 1944. Since then, congressional employees have received numerous pay increases according to various formulas, each of which must be applied to the employee's basic pay rate in order to determine his gross annual pay. Only the basic rate is indicated on the em-

---

* In 1967, the Senate abandoned the basic-rate method of identifying salary allocations. A gross-rate system was adopted in its place, and the actual dollars authorized (1969) each Senator for clerk hire ranged from $239,805 to $401,865 annually, depending on the population of his state. A similar system for the House, written into the draft Legislative Reorganization Act of 1970, was eliminated prior to the House Rules Committee's reporting the bill in May. The bill was amended on the floor, however, and the Act as finally approved provides for a *gross* salary system instead of the existing *basic* system.

ployee's official certification of employment. But in setting up the office payroll the basic rate of an employee is important only as it relates to budgeting the over-all clerk-hire allowance. Examples of basic rates and their equivalents in gross annual pay in 1970 follow:

If the employee's basic rate is—			*His actual gross annual salary is—*
(Minimum permitted)	$	5	$ 1,287
		1,020	4,681
		2,040	7,724
		3,060	11,227
		4,020	14,670
		5,040	18,522
		6,060	22,208
(Maximum permitted)		7,500	27,343

As the table indicates, the maximum basic rate is $7,500, or a gross annual salary of $27,343.* At any one time, only one employee of a member may be paid at the maximum rate. The minimum rate permitted is $5 basic. Aside from these limitations a member may use his allowance to pay his employees whatever he desires. Complete information on the clerk-hire allowance, including current tables of basic rates and gross salary equivalents, is available to members in the House Disbursing Office.

1971 PAYROLL CONVERSION

Many members do not use all their staff allowance; few distribute it so as to employ the maximum number of full-time persons. During the first session of the 91st Congress, according to information prepared for a House Appropriations subcommittee, about three-

* As approved by the House Committee on Rules, the Legislative Reorganization Act of 1970 authorized members to designate one staff employee as an Administrative Assistant with salary comparable to the highest rate a Senator may pay his top aide (about $31,000). But this provision was eliminated in floor action prior to House passage of the Act on September 17.

fifths of the members employed ten or more persons. Somewhat more than a quarter of the members employed eight or nine persons, and forty-four employed fewer than eight persons.*

These figures do not necessarily represent total employment, which includes use of temporary consultants and part-time clerical help. And there are extra hands available outside the office salary system. For instance, committee and subcommittee chairmen and other more senior members may make use of committee staff personnel from time to time for chores not directly related to committee operations, and some offices are able to attract volunteer helpers of one kind or another. Or, if he has private means, a member can hire any number of assistants at his own expense.

There is no uniform salary schedule for congressional office employees; staff salaries are determined by the individual member. (For a description of a suggested initial staff salary schedule, see Appendix, page 312.) Keeping part of the staff allowance in reserve permits the hiring of temporary help whenever needed, as well as allowing for other payroll adjustments. Salary and payroll changes may be made each month; the schedule ordering the change must be filed with the House Disbursing Office by the tenth of the month in which the change is to become effective. Referring to budgeting of the staff allowance, a discussion leader during the 1963 Seminar for Freshman Congressmen urged congressional new-

---

* As of April 30, 1969, according to information furnished the Legislative Appropriations Subcommittee by the Clerk of the House, the members were employing 4,301 clerks at a gross monthly salary of $4,421,083, although under the law 4,912 could be employed. The table below shows the number of offices employing staff at selected levels, 1967–1969:

Number of Clerks	1967	1968	1969
12	18	31	37
11	84	123	137
10	82	98	91
9	82	69	73
8	57	54	54
Under 8	113	61	44

comers to proceed with care in committing their clerk-hire allowance:

You cannot set all of your employees at a maximum because from time to time you are going to have the need for incentive increases. You may also find it desirable, where you have employees from your district, to occasionally adjust salary to reflect the extra expense incurred by them in traveling to and from Washington.

Gross Salary System. Under terms of the Legislative Reorganization Act of 1970, a change from the complex *basic* clerk-hire allowance to a *gross* salary system becomes effective on January 3, 1971, at the start of the 92nd Congress. The new system provides:
★ Members who represent fewer than 500,000 people are authorized up to $133,500 per year for payment of staff salaries.
★ Members whose districts are certified by the Bureau of Census as having an estimated population of more than 500,000 are authorized up to $140,500 per year.

Conversion to this system eliminates the roundabout *basic* rates that made it difficult for outsiders to determine the actual amounts being paid staff employees. The new system is less flexible, however; under the basic system, part-time help could be employed at little cost to the total clerk-hire allowance (because a low basic rate brought a far greater actual annual salary return by itself than it did as part of a high basic rate). For example, the minimum basic rate of $5 produced an actual monthly salary of about $107—sufficient to pay a part-time employee. And even if the basic allowance was fully committed, it was possible to shift $5 basic from an employee receiving the maximum rate—an adjustment that cost him little more than $1 per month in actual pay.

In any event, the new system maintains most existing limitations on the use of the clerk-hire allowance. The allowance is not cumulative, because the Act specifies that the monthly office payroll may not exceed one-twelfth of the total annual allowance. Thus, the monthly payroll of a member who represents fewer than 500,000 people may not exceed $11,125 (the maximum monthly payroll for those representing larger districts is $11,708). Existing limitations on the number of staff employees remain in effect (twelve at any one time for those who represent fewer than 500,000; thirteen for those who represent more).

The maximum salary a member may pay his top aide also remains unchanged at $27,343 per year. Otherwise, as in the past, the member decides the pay levels of his employees, certifying staff rearrangements or salary changes in writing to the Clerk of the House. The member may also establish—by written notice to the Clerk—titles for his staff employees as he sees fit.

STAFF RECRUITMENT

Some Congressmen recruit their staff entirely from their own district or state. But evidence suggests that place of residence is becoming less important as a condition of employment for both professional and clerical help. Basing his findings on a series of round-table discussions and interviews with Congressmen conducted from 1959 to 1963, Charles L. Clapp, a political scientist who has had considerable Capitol Hill experience, concluded that

> . . . the complexity and volume of work in a congressional office have placed a premium on experience and expertise, and there has been a relaxation of the residence requirement. Secretaries move easily from one office to another, their new employer often representing another state, and perhaps another political party, from that of their former boss. Congressmen generally believe it is advantageous—both politically and personally—to have at least part of their staff from their own district (though some caution that it is more difficult to discharge someone from home), but professional competence is a more important criterion of selection than it used to be.*

* Clapp, *The Congressman*, p. 63.

For the newly elected member, employment of at least one experienced aide is considered especially important. Senator J. Caleb Boggs, describing his experience as a newcomer to the House, made this point during hearings of the Joint Committee on the Organization of the Congress in 1965:

> I went through that in 1947 as a new member of the House. Mr. Martin, of Massachusetts, then Speaker, gave some valuable advice to me. He said, "Boggs, why don't you try to find yourself a good career person around here to take into your office for a little while."
>
> I brought three staff people over from my state, and I was very fortunate in finding one here who met the Speaker's qualifications. I found her a tremendous help, and this fine lady stayed with me for about a year. She is still here on Capitol Hill, on the House side, in a very responsible position. I don't know what I would have done without taking in a person of her experience.

Retirements and election casualties make a number of experienced staff people available for employment at the beginning of each Congress, and although there is no central personnel office,* their availability ordinarily is widely known in the House office building complex. Also, the United States Employment Service operates a Capitol Hill branch, with offices in the Old Senate Office Building and the Longworth House Office Building. The service reports filling from ten to twenty jobs per week at the beginning of each session. But for the most part, particularly at the professional level, job shopping continues to be done by word of mouth.

Volunteer help. Political internship programs, which bring

---

* In June 1966, House Republican leaders announced the creation of a Minority Personnel Office directed by William R. Bonsell, House Minority Doorkeeper. This office was to maintain job applications and placement records for the GOP members and to "provide immediately to each member, upon request, a list of qualified personnel for a particular job which a member desires to fill."

students and other professionally trained people to Capitol Hill, are another source of assistance. Lawyers, newspapermen, and undergraduate and graduate political science students are among participants in such programs, and they are made available for varying periods of time—often at no cost to the member for whom they work. The only special treatment most interns expect is time off to attend certain committee hearings and sessions of the House or Senate, in keeping with the educational nature of their program. Otherwise, they serve as a part of the regular staff, doing whatever tasks are assigned to them.

Most extensive of the internship programs is the Congressional Fellowship Program conducted each year by the American Political Science Association. Congressional Fellows include newspapermen, political science teachers, federal executives on leave from their civil service jobs, and teachers and government officials from various foreign countries. About thirty Fellows are included in the program each year. They work half the session in House offices, half in Senate offices. Each Fellow receives a stipend from A.P.S.A. to take care of his living expenses. Office assignments are by mutual agreement between the Fellow and the member.

Many colleges and universities conduct programs under which students—most of them undergraduates—are placed in congressional offices during the summer months. Some college programs are funded and pay their interns varying amounts. Others do not, and members may put the intern on the payroll for a nominal amount to meet living expenses. From 1965 to 1967, each member of the House was authorized to employ a college or university student during the summer, without charge to the regular staff allowance. Under this authorization, the member could pay a Student Congressional Intern up to $75 per week during a ten-week period between June 1 and August 31. Funds were not provided for this purpose in 1968–1969 but were approved by the House Appropriations Committee for 1970.

Allowances and services

In addition to their clerk-hire allowance, Congressmen are provided with funds to equip and operate Washington and district offices. Included are the allowances for postage for airmail and special delivery letters (members are entitled to free first-class postage under the franking privilege), office supplies and equipment, telephone and telegraph, and travel.* Various services also are performed for members free or at cost; the most important of these is the handling of bulk mailing projects.

EQUIPMENT ALLOWANCE

Orders are placed with the Clerk of the House for approved types of electrical and mechanical equipment—addressing machines, manual and electric typewriters, copying machines, duplicating or mimeographing machines, automatic letter opening and sealing machines, and recording machines for dictation and transcription. Members determine the type of equipment they need, but a limitation is placed on the amount they may have at any one time; the current value of the equipment may not exceed $5,500 regardless of the size of the district. In addition, each member is entitled to one automatic typewriter for the production of form letters without charge to his equipment allowance.

All office equipment furnished to members is registered in the office of the Clerk. It remains the property of the House and may not be removed from the office to which it is assigned.

The newcomer inherits the equipment in the Office to which he is assigned and must live with it for sixty days. During the next thirty days thereafter he may file a letter of intent with the Clerk

---

* Office fund allowances and regulations for their use are adjusted periodically. The figures and other information in this section are from *Regulations: Travel and Other Expenses of Committees and Members,* issued January 1, 1970, by the Committee on House Administration.

of the House indicating which items he wishes to dispose of. Equipment is depreciated on a yearly schedule, and the newcomer may contact the Clerk's office for information on the current value of equipment he has inherited as well as other assistance in planning for acquisition of additional new or used equipment. Maintenance and repair of equipment also is ordered through the Clerk's office.

TELEPHONE AND TELEGRAPH

For the one-year Congressional session, each member has an allowance of 70,000 "units" for long-distance telephone calls, telegrams, and cables. These units are applied as follows:

★ Telephone—1 minute equals 4 units

★ Telegram—1 word equals 1 unit

★ Radiogram—1 word equals 1 unit

★ Cablegram—1 word equals 1 unit

★ Night letter—1 word equals ½ unit

If an identical telegram is sent to several persons, the number of words in the message is multiplied by the number of addresses to determine its cost in units. For long-distance telephone calls, the charge against the allowance is the same whether the call is station to station, person to person, or a conference call; and the cost in units is the same regardless of the distance involved. A three-minute call from Washington to Baltimore, for example, costs twelve units; a three-minute call from Washington to Honolulu costs the same. Members are issued telephone and telegraph credit cards for official use when they are away from their offices.

Budgeting the allowance. Most members find it necessary to budget their telephone and telegraph allowances carefully. An emergency situation in the district can exhaust the entire allowance within a few months, at which point the member must either pay for long-distance telephone and telegraph service or mortgage his future allowance. Regulations applied to the allowance permit carrying over unused units—not in excess of 140,000 units—from session to session. Moreover, should the allowance be exhausted before the end of a session, unpaid bills for this service may be charged to units that will become available to the member at the beginning of the next session of Congress.

The total allowance provides for an average monthly use of 5,833 units, and it is possible to check periodically to see whether the allowance is being depleted too rapidly. The Chesapeake & Potomac Telephone Company and Western Union send monthly bills in duplicate to each member, listing items charged to his account during the previous month. One copy is certified and sent to the Clerk of the House for payment; the other is for the member's files. From time to time the Clerk notifies each member of the status of his allowance.

Making units count. Because long-distance calls cost the same number of units regardless of distance, many members use their telephone allowance only for calls involving longer distances, paying personally for less expensive calls over shorter distances. This may be accomplished either by charging the call to a personal account at the time it is made or by charging it to the congressional account and then marking it off as a personal call on the monthly billing. A personal check covering the cost of calls bought back is sent along with the certified bill to the Clerk of the House. Billing of telegrams on a personal account is accomplished simply by including the word "personal" on them.

FTS Telephone Service. In addition to long-distance service under the unit-allowance system, members are entitled to use the Federal Telecommunications System free of charge from 5 P.M. to 9 A.M. weekdays and on weekends and holidays. Patience is both a virtue and a necessity in placing long-distance calls through this direct-dial system; dialing procedures are complex, circuits are limited and busy, and the uninitiated user often strays wildly from his calling destination. Accordingly, many find that FTS is best used when there is no particular reason to complete a call in a hurry.

STATIONERY AND POSTAGE

Each member is allowed $3,000 per session for purchase of stationery and other office supplies. The allowance is credited to his account in the House Stationery Room. A newly elected member's account is set up and may be used as soon as his certification of election is received from the state secretary.

The stationery allowance may be withdrawn in cash or left on deposit for purchase of office supplies. Unused portions carry over from session to session, but whenever a member's allowance is exhausted he must pay for additional supplies with a personal check or money order. Cash purchases are not permitted, and the Stationery Room cannot extend credit. For convenience, a member whose allowance has been exhausted may deposit a check or money order to be used for future purchases.

Heavy-duty brown envelopes are excluded from the allotment that covers all other stationery supplies. Each member is allotted 40,000 of these envelopes per month. Orders specifying size and printing are placed with the Congressional Record Clerk. Advance withdrawals of up to three months' supply are permitted. Unused allotments are canceled at the end of each Congress.

Tax records. Portions of the stationery allowance withdrawn in cash are reportable income, so members who choose to handle their own office-supply funds must keep records of purchases for tax purposes.* Because the allowance is part of the member's emol-

---

* For a description of the basic method of reporting portions of the stationery allowance as well as computing other income and deductions relating to Congressional service, see Appendix, pages 376–379.

uments of office, any amount remaining to his credit is payable to him upon his resignation, or to his estate in the event of his death. No stationery allowance is available for the office of a resigned or deceased member.

Printing of stationery. The official congressional letterhead, with the member's name, his Washington and district office addresses, committee assignments, names of staff members, and other official items, is printed without charge to the member. Maps, state centennial emblems, and similar items also may be printed on stationery or envelopes. Those whose districts have been recently reapportioned find it particularly useful to include on their stationery or envelopes a state map outlining the new district. Any extra cost for such work—which can be done by the majority and minority rooms or by private firms—must be borne by the member. Copy for the official letterhead items and envelope printing is sent to the Stationery Room at the time the order is placed.

Postage allowance. In addition to the franking privilege, which covers regular mail only, each member is allowed $700 worth of stamps each calendar year. Like the frank, these stamps are for official use only. They are issued by the House Clerk's office on written request, and the allowance may be withdrawn all at once or as needed. Any postage not withdrawn by the end of the year is lost to the member; the allowance does not accumulate from year to year.

DISTRICT OFFICES AND TRAVEL

Congressmen may establish offices in their districts either in federal buildings or in space rented for this purpose. Under an optional allowance system, the Sergeant at Arms is responsible for securing office space at one or two locations in federal facilities *acceptable* to the member. If such space is not available on federal property, the member is entitled to an allowance of $2,400 per year for rental of space elsewhere. Assignment of space in a federal building does not preclude renting space in a second building, perhaps in another city, with the $2,400 allowance. Vouchers covering statements of amounts due for rental of such space are submitted to the Clerk of the House for payment.

Office expenses. Members who have district offices are allowed $1,200 per year to cover expenses for supplies, equipment rental, and the like, plus $1,200 per year to cover long-distance telephone costs.* Equipment in a member's Washington office may not be moved to his district offices. Employees assigned to the district offices are included in the twelve (or thirteen) staff members he is allowed to employ at any one time, and their salaries are charged to his over-all staff allowance.

Landlord problems. Experienced members suggest that it pays to choose landlords wisely. Referring to the inadvisability of using one's own or a relative's dwelling or building as a district office, one of the discussion leaders during the 1963 Seminar for Freshman Congressmen said:

I would suggest that you not rent any front porches, unless you want an interesting type of publicity which is not always productive of confidence on the part of your constituents.

* As of April 30, 1969, 221 members were being reimbursed for *rental* of non-Federal office space for district offices, with only fifty-eight of these using the full $200 per month allowed. But most members use their full allowances for district office equipment and long-distance telephone expenses. According to data prepared for 1968 by the Clerk—

For district office equipment expenses:

* 409 members were paid the full $1,200,
* 20 members were paid less than $300 per quarter,
* 11 members were paid no allowance;

For District telephone expense:

* 276 members were reimbursed for four quarters,
* 111 members were reimbursed for one to three quarters,
* 53 members were paid no allowance.

Subsequently, the speaker was asked to expand on his comment:

Q. Were you serious regarding use of a dwelling as a district office? *A.* I was trying to be a little bit facetious. We had a front porch rented on one occasion, and it created considerable interest, nationally. The gentleman is not now a member of the House.*

Pro and con. Even though most members operate district offices, there is little agreement as to their effectiveness. Some find that a year-round district office keeps them in closer touch with constituent needs and, at the same time, reduces the work load in the Washington office by taking care of many problems locally. Others maintain that such facilities actually increase the work load; that most problems eventually have to be handled twice, once in the district office and once in the Washington office, increasing the possibility of error; and that the benefits of closer staff contact with constituents are outweighed by the costs.

Whatever the merits of the cases for or against, in 1965, according to lists contained in the *Congressional Staff Directory,* 301 members assigned one or more staff employees to year-round offices in their districts. This total includes thirty-three members who operated two year-round offices with staff employees assigned to each of them, and six members who maintained three such offices. Only thirty-two members had no district offices listed; 102 were listed as operating part-time offices of one kind or another— "when home," "on adjournment," "when home and on adjournment," or simply "district office," without staff or specific schedule indicated.

Travel allowances. Each member is entitled to compensation for one round trip to his district per month, plus one additional

* Unless otherwise attributed, all quotations of comments by members are from transcripts of the 1959 orientation and 1963 Seminar for Freshman Congressmen programs, published by Congressional Quarterly, Inc., Washington, D.C.

trip to cover costs of travel to and from Washington at the beginning and end of each session. Thus, if Congress is in session nine months during the year, the member is entitled to reimbursement for ten round trips between the Capitol and his district. The allowance for one of these is determined at the rate of twenty cents per mile via the most direct highway route. The allowance for the other round trips is twelve cents per mile or the price of commercial travel. No compensation is allowed for transportation of family or household goods.

Members representing districts near Washington, D.C., are entitled to a lump sum of $750 per session in lieu of payment for individual trips. And, in addition to his own allowance, the Congressman may authorize two additional round trips per year for a member or members of his staff. These are reimbursed at actual cost or, if by auto, at twelve cents per mile.*

PUBLICATION ALLOWANCES

Selected government publications are made available to Congressmen in quantity for distribution to constituents. (See Appendix, pages 325–327, for a list of these publications and the number allotted to each member.) It is possible to build up a credit account with the Government Printing Office by turning back unused portions of allotments of these publications. Then, instead of having to pay cash for some other publication he may wish to purchase from

---

* In 1968, according to the Clerk of the House, travel was reimbursed as follows:

Members	Trips
175	10
130	less than 10
127	$750 in lieu of reimbursement
8	none

Members staff	Trips
297	2
89	less than 2
54	none

the GPO, the member may charge it against his exchange account.

Only publications specified by the Superintendent of Documents are accepted for exchange account purposes; no book or publication is accepted if a member's name has been stamped on it. The GPO's Division of Public Documents provides information on which books and publications are acceptable for exchange.

Binding and map services. Members may have any public document published during their term of office placed in a permanent binding by the Government Printing Office. Included are House and Senate documents, committee hearings and prints, and special reports. There are several sources for maps, which may be obtained for member's personal use or for sending to constituents and schools. (Sources, and the various kinds of maps they supply, are listed in the Appendix, page 328.) The Map Information Office of the Geological Survey and the Map Division of the Library of Congress provide detailed information on availability of specialized maps.

GENERAL SERVICES AVAILABLE

The majority and minority rooms, in the basement of the Cannon Office Building, maintain print-shop facilities for use by members of their parties. Among services available are the printing of newsletters, questionnaires, and other bulk mailing items; automatic typewriting; preparation of addressing machine plates; and addressing envelopes in bulk. These services are billed at cost and on a monthly basis; bills may be paid directly or charged against the member's stationery account.

Services provided by the House Folding Room are free to members of both parties. These include folding, inserting, and sealing envelopes for bulk mailings; book- and package-wrapping service; delivery and other miscellaneous services; and storage of various books and documents allocated to members.* (For details of Folding Room services, see Appendix, page 338.)

Radio-television studios. The Clerk of the House maintains studios in the Rayburn House Office Building where transcriptions and films for use on radio and television are made at cost. Members who plan to make regular radio or television recordings may reserve the studios for a certain time each week or month, whichever is desired. There is no specific allowance earmarked for use of these facilities and the cost of producing tapes and films is billed to the member monthly.

ADVICE ON FILING

Various agencies provide information and assistance on establishment of files, an important first step in setting up House officekeeping. A handbook on systems for congressional offices is available from the Office of Records Management, Archives and Records Division, General Services Administration. The Secretary of the Library of Congress is available for consultation on filing problems and also has prepared material on setting up and maintaining files. (A filing system developed especially for congressional office correspondence is described in detail in the Appendix, pages 319–324). The National Archives provides storage for members

---

* In recent years the House Folding Room has reported receiving from twenty to sixty *million* items for processing per *month*. The workload is heaviest during election years, as the table—prepared for the Legislative Appropriations Subcommittee for the month of October, 1963–1968—indicates:

Year	Items
1963	11,581,043
1964	44,745,495
1965	21,503,076
1966	42,500,938
1967	18,942,955
1968	58,456,298

outdated files. On request, the Archives will pack and index files and remove them for storage to the Federal Records Center, Alexandria, Virginia.

The Archives also has a full-time staff member available on request to assist with filing problems and procedures.

Subject filing is the system most commonly used in congressional offices. However, to avoid confusion in cases where a single letter refers to several topics, the subject file usually is supplemented by either a name or a date file. In these, an extra copy of all outgoing correspondence is filed either alphabetically or chronologically.

Methods of filing by subject, name, and date can be combined in a central filing system. In this system, materials placed in the name and date files include a cross reference indicating where the original incoming letter and all related items may be found in the subject file. An index-card file may be substituted for the name file. All incoming and outgoing correspondence is simply noted on individual cards, which are filed alphabetically. Each card may contain several entries, including the date and subject under which materials involving the individual correspondent are filed.

Special files. Many offices also maintain special files. Of these, the most common is a suspense file for keeping track of correspondence referred to Executive departments and agencies and for filing reminders of one kind or another. A simple method of setting up this file is to use large manila envelopes for the file folders, one for each day of the year. Another useful special file lists various legislative service highlights—introduction of a bill, brief explanation of a vote, solution of a constituent's problem, advice to the White House, and the like—on a systematic, daily basis. These achievement files are maintained on index cards, in chronological order, and are the responsibility of a single staff member.

★ 3 ★

Working for the district

CALIFORNIA'S 38TH DISTRICT, a two-county, 12,000-square-mile area with a rapidly increasing population, sent John V. Tunney to Congress in January 1965. Six months later, the new Representative was hard-pressed for staff time. "I could solve the problem," he told the Joint Committee on the Organization of the Congress, "by transferring some of my staff to purely legislative work and [leaving] district and constituent problems unattended." But, he added,

> I think most of you would agree that this is hardly an equitable solution. Very often, an individual constituent seeking solution of a problem has no other recourse than to request his Congressman's help. I, for one, should like to continue to give that help whenever and wherever I can.
>
> . . . my office gets 200 letters a day from the district and I think these letters have to be answered. This requires the untiring efforts of maybe three to four people working full time just to answer my mail, let alone do any creative work.

Neither the size of Representative Tunney's work load nor his reluctance to give it up is remarkable. For, as viewed by most Congressmen, job security and constituency service are like love and marriage—you can't have one without the other.

A typical congressional office with a small volume of mail receives from one hundred to three hundred letters weekly, and one with a large volume receives five hundred to a thousand letters weekly. On occasion, if the mail drops off sharply, some members actively encourage constituent requests for information and assistance. About twenty-five per cent of the letters received, on the average, contain constituent opinions or requests for the Congressman's views on legislation. About twenty per cent contain requests for help in getting jobs, in dealing with Executive agencies, or in securing government publications and other information.* In addition, the Congressman must meet with home-town delegations interested in various federal programs or legislation, and he is often asked to assist Washington visitors in other ways.

Processing the mail and responding to constituent requests does tax the time and ingenuity of most Congressmen and their office staffs. The average House member spends about one-third of his time on such service work. A substantially greater portion of his staff's time—probably more than one-half in a majority of offices—is taken up with district matters.†

Depending on the individual member's outlook, some tasks inspired by constituent requests may seem to be less rewarding—or necessary to the survival of the republic—than others. Because

* These figures are based on the *Interim Report on Congressional Offices,* as are estimates appearing elsewhere in this chapter on time spent on various functions, mail count, visitors, etc. For excerpts of this report, see the Appendix, pp. 303–311.

† The time spent on selected activities in an "average staff work week," as described in the following table prepared by political scientist John S.

of competing demands on a member's time and energy, some requests may be given short shrift or ignored altogether. But generally Congressmen value their service work, not entirely because of its contribution to job security, but also because, as Representative Tunney suggested, the aggrieved citizen may have no other place to look for help.

Casework for constituents*

Help given constituents in their dealings with Executive agencies is customarily called "casework," and it is the most time consuming

Saloma III, is illustrative (from *Congress and the New Politics,* page 185, copyright 1969 by Little, Brown and Co., Inc. Reprinted by permission of the publisher):

Activity	Hours per week (average)	Percentage
With the member in committee	1.1	0.5%
Handling constituent problems (casework)	40.6	18.7
Visiting with constituents in Washington	12.9	6.0
With lobbyists and special interest groups	4.9	2.3
On press work, radio, and television	13.9	6.4
Writing speech drafts, floor remarks	11.2	5.2
On legislative research, bill drafting	13.6	6.3
On pressure and opinion mail	34.2	15.8
On opinion ballots (preprinted by organizations)	4.4	2.0
On requests for information	14.6	6.7
On letters of congratulation, condolence	9.2	4.2
On correspondence other than described	26.2	12.1
Mailing government publications	8.5	3.9
Other	21.4	9.0
TOTAL	216.7	100.0

* This section follows closely the comments of Representative Gerald R. Ford, Jr., of Michigan, during the 1963 Seminar for Freshman Congressmen. For a description of the findings of political scientists and others who have studied congressional casework, see Walter Kravitz' *Casework by Members of Congress: A Survey of the Literature* (Legislative Reference Service multilith report, January 22, 1968).

of the service functions. It also receives the highest priority in most offices. Expressing a view that is widely shared by experienced members, Representative Gerald R. Ford, Jr., advised congressional newcomers in 1963 to adopt a positive attitude toward requests for such assistance. The constituent is not always right, Representative Ford suggested, but his problem deserves a hearing:

. . . you will find that your constituents will evaluate your merit or lack of it, based on how well or how badly you handle the cases which they submit to you. I won't pass judgment on whether this is right or wrong. I am simply saying that as a matter of fact [this is]true.

. . . I think it's important for you to determine at the outset whether cases are a chore or an opportunity. In our office, we adopt this attitude —and sometimes I must confess that it is a little difficult—but you will receive numerous communications from constituents, and at first reading you will feel that the inquiry is a bit senseless. And you wonder why he or she will have bothered you with this inquiry. [However,] in our office we always look at the inquiry from the point of view of the person who wrote it, not from our point of view, sitting in Washington. As a consequence, I think it has been helpful and beneficial in the evaluation of my service back home.

Further . . . we try to make our office the human link between a vast federal government and the individual at home. If your office becomes this human link, I think you will render excellent service to your constituents.

REQUESTS AND THE AGENCIES

Requests for help come in all shapes and sizes. Some are unusual. For instance, in 1966 one member reported receiving the following letter:

Dear Congressman:

Some ninny working for the government has informed me that under the law, oats are not a feed grain. Would you please explain that to my mule. I sure can't.

                                                            Sincerely yours,

Occasionally, casework brings to light shortcomings in the administrative process or results in legislation of general consequence. But more often than not it involves essentially personal matters, affecting one person or family. Some of the more common kinds of requests are listed by Representative Ford:

You will get a number of inquiries concerning veterans' affairs: How to establish a claim, how to increase benefits, how to prevent a decrease in a benefit. You will get inquiries about how to expedite hospitalization for a veteran. In the area of servicemen you will get a great many inquiries. How to get Johnny in or Johnny out of service. You will get a number of questions about health and morale problems. . . . You will get questions that refer to the Internal Revenue Service.

Starting about June or July you will start getting some letters, I am certain, which ask: "Why have I not received my [tax] refund? My next door neighbor got his two months ago." You will also get some inquiries about the merit or lack of merit in a tax matter. If I could pass along a bit of advice in these two areas, I believe it's a proper function of a member of the House to help expedite the refund. Surprisingly enough, in our office we have run into a number of instances where an income tax refund has been lost somehow in the Internal Revenue Service. And unless the member of Congress is helpful, you will find that many taxpayers will be long delayed in getting a proper refund from the Internal Revenue Service. I believe this is a proper function for us. . . . On the other hand, at least in our office, we are scrupulously careful never to get into the merits of a tax problem. I am certain from my reading of certain instances that those members that do, run into some problems. . . .

Many people will write, "How do I get a job?" and so forth. This refers to some extent to the Post Office Department, and I might say to my Republican colleagues, don't worry about that problem. On the other hand, I look with some sympathy at my Democratic friends. This is a chore which I am sure, after a reasonable period of time, you will be glad to shed, if you haven't already come to that decision. Passports: the passport division of the State Department, in my judgment, does a fabulously good job. They do urge you to follow the proper procedures, but if you do, you will get excellent service.

Use of liaison offices. Because of the volume of problems constituents bring to the attention of their Congressmen, some thirty-five federal agencies and the three military services have established liaison offices to assist members. The Army, Navy, and Air Force, and the Veterans Administration maintain liaison offices in the House office building complex itself. Other agencies and departments send their liaison personnel around to congressional offices periodically, offering the services that they are set up to render. Representative Ford continues:

Now what can you actually get from a liaison office? You can expedite action (and I mean in the most legitimate way). You can obtain vast amounts of information. These liaison offices do an excellent job, in my judgment, in obtaining information for you for the benefit of your constituents.

Last, but not least, every member of Congress in his or her term of office will find instances, few in number, but important nevertheless, where an error has been perpetrated by the Executive branch of the federal government. There are instances where this happens. Omission or commission is immaterial. There are cases where an individual has been wrongfully treated by his government. And about the only way, unless the individual resorts to court—and even in some cases the courts are not able to give proper relief—the only area or avenue open to the individual is through his Representative.

When you find a bona fide error has been made, I suggest that you make a maximum effort to remedy it. This I feel is a very vital and important function of those of us in the House of Representatives.*

* More than three-fourths of a sample of House members interviewed during the 88th Congress agreed that "going to bat" for constituents in their dealings with Executive agencies should be an important part of the Congressman's job. See material prepared by Roger Davidson, David Kovenock, and Michael O'Leary, in *Hearings Before the Joint Committee on the Organization of the Congress*, Pt. 5, U.S. Government Printing Office, Washington, D.C., 1965: pages 775–776.

Use of regional offices. Some agencies—for example, Civil Service, Internal Revenue, and the Veterans Administration—also have regional offices. Making a direct inquiry there sometimes brings quicker results than going through the liaison office and agency headquarters in Washington. Whether to advise a constituent initially to direct his inquiry to the regional or to the Washington agency office depends on the situation, according to Representative Ford:

You will get inquiries primarily from small businessmen who have no agent or no relationship down here. They will ask you, "Whom do I go to?" We try to urge the small businessman in my area to go to Detroit or to go to Chicago, where there are regional offices, and these respective offices do have information facilities for the small businessmen.

However, I must confess that many small businessmen, after going to these regional offices, don't feel that they get a sense of satisfaction out of it. If that happens and you are confident that the constituent has a good product or a good factory, I would urge him to come down here. Then you can see that he gets in to see people who have a broader view and who maybe can be more helpful. But I would start at the regional level in the first instance.

Acute or sensitive cases. In some cases, a problem may be so acute or sensitive as to require direct contact with the head of a particular agency. But as a rule, Representative Ford finds, it is best to operate through the regional or Washington liaison offices:

I think if you establish the right liaison with the regional office it is better to go to the regional office than it is to get tied down in the morass here in Washington. One other comment: You have, if an inquiry comes in, to make a decision as to the approach you will take. Should you go to the top, should you go to the boss in the agencies or the department, or should you deal with the liaison office? This is a matter of judgment. We normally try to deal with the liaison officer, and then if we are unsuccessful and it is a meritorious matter we then proceed higher up. On the other hand, where an emergency is in question then, on occasion, you will go directly to the top man in the department.

CASEWORK TECHNIQUES

In most offices, responsibility for day-to-day handling of casework is delegated to staff employees. Some districts generate a large number of requests of a particular kind, and one staff employee may be assigned to all such cases. Similarly, in an increasing number of offices, one professional-level employee is assigned to work primarily with district firms, civic groups, municipalities, or other administrative units in securing information about federal grant-in-aid programs, defense contracts, and the like.

Contacting the Executive agency. Except in unusual circumstances, the initial contact with the agency involved is made by a staff employee. In matters requiring immediate action, or in simple requests for information, Representative Ford recommends using the telephone and thereby avoiding paperwork:

> Can you call a liaison office or some official in the agency and get the information by telephone, or should you send the [constituent's] letter down to the liaison office or to the department? It's my observation that in many instances you get most of the information by telephone once you have established a rapport with the proper people in the department. We believe in our office that speed is vital. For that reason I would suggest that you don't send too many letters down and that you get more information by telephone.

Another member, in the 1969 Seminar, suggested that the department's desire to be helpful and to respond quickly may be dampened somewhat by a steady flow of requests for trivia from a particular congressional office:

> Work with your staff to establish priorities and procedures for referrals. Do not bother the agencies with routine inquiries—or make unreasonable demands for results on an "I want this or that yesterday"

kind of schedule. I have reason to believe that some members and staff people who bug the agencies this way get to be pretty well known downtown. And they don't always get the best, the quickest, the most complete service.

On more complicated problems, or in situations in which it is necessary to have a record of the matter and the action taken, the constituent's problem is customarily referred to the agency in writing. This may be done either by sending the constituent's letter itself or by restating his problem in a letter signed by the member. Restating the problem or including selected paragraphs from the constituent's letter is considered the better part of wisdom, for example, in cases where the constituent expresses his annoyance too colorfully or in excessive detail.

Whichever method of conveyance is used, the agency is expected to reply to the Congressman with a letter signed by the agency head. An extra copy of the agency's reply is included for the member's files in case he wishes to forward the original to the constituent. Sending the original of the agency letter—not the file copy—to the constituent is customary when the agency's decision is unfavorable or a constituent's job application is rejected. Many members make a practice of sending all agency replies to the constituent—whatever the outcome—to save time and as a way of demonstrating that his problem has received the attention of a top federal official.

Asking for agency reconsideration. On occasion it may become necessary to insist that an agency reconsider a decision a member feels is wrong. Most members avoid becoming too personally involved, however, because such interest may be misinterpreted as seeking special favor. Many members define and limit their request, in effect, by asking the agency to deal with the problem in a manner consistent with existing rules. As Representative Ford puts it:

I caution you to use a phrase like this one or the same. This is what we use in writing to various agencies where a constituent has asked for help. Our phrase, and others may have a different one, is: "Consistent with existing rules, will you take a look at this problem." I emphasize the phrase, "consistent with existing rules and regulations. . . ."

Representative Ford also suggests that members avoid giving the impression that they can solve any problem simply by reaching for the telephone:

. . . I think it's dangerous to encourage a constituent in the belief that if he or she writes you that all you have to do to get relief is to call downtown. Unfortunately, a number of people at home do believe that all a member of Congress has to do is make a telephone call and his or her problem will be resolved. If you start the constituent out in the opposite frame of mind, perhaps discouraging the person making the inquiry, when you are successful in being helpful I think you will be applauded quite readily.

Problems of military personnel. In handling requests for transfer, discharge, or promotion of military personnel, most offices take no action until they hear directly from the serviceman himself. Representative Ford explains why:

You will find that the services, the Army, Navy, and Air Force, will not do anything until Johnny has made an application for early discharge, or for transfer or for any one of a number of other things. This is good. It's good because [sometimes] the mother or the wife will contact you and, lo and behold, Johnny doesn't really want to get transferred or Johnny doesn't want to get out of the service. And so it's mandatory, at least we insist on it, and the services do likewise, that a request be made in writing in the hand of the military personnel.

. . . and we always caution an individual who writes us and asks, "Why didn't I get promoted?" or "Why was I treated differently from somebody else?"—we always caution these people that whether it's right or wrong, it seems to happen that if a member of Congress makes an inquiry, particularly about career people, that there is a notation made on the service record of the individual.

Now this is always denied by the services. I have never personally looked at a service record to know, but I have some friends and they tell me that somehow a [notation] gets on the career service record of an individual, if an inquiry comes to the department about his record. Now we always tell the individual that this is the possibility. We let him make up his mind, in light of this circumstance, whether he should make the inquiry or have us make the inquiry on his behalf. This is a practical thing, and I think it's important for the individual to know.

Avoiding legal tangles. Many members are wary of serving as advocate for a single constituent by personally pleading his case. For example, veterans who have cases before the Veterans Appeal Board often request their Congressman to appear at the hearing in their behalf. One experienced member describes the reasons behind his standing policy of refusing such requests:

I have followed the practice from the time I got here of never, under any circumstances, ever consenting to that kind of request. In the first place, the types that come up on appeals are difficult cases. They have been rejected time and time again, so you might as well recognize the fact that four out of five of them are going to be turned down. Therefore, if you are the one that represents them you are going to be accused of having it turned down if you go there personally. Secondly, you won't be able to brief yourself adequately.

Once you accept one of them then you haven't any means of drawing a line as to others that you can accept, and the only way to handle those properly is just to say that you are here elected by your constituents to serve as a legislative representative. This is not within the province of the duties of a legislative representative; that your assignment that you have been given by your constituents is full-time, and you therefore recommend that they take other steps to see that their case is properly presented.

Coordination with Senators. Individuals often address requests for assistance to all members of a state's congressional delegation.

Recognizing the possibilities for duplication of effort, some members of the House make it a practice to coordinate casework with their state's Senators. Similarly, requests received from individuals residing in another congressional district are called to the attention of the proper member. Representative Ford describes how this kind of cooperation sometimes occurs despite party differences:

> In our own case we have a good liaison with our two Senators, even though they are Democrats and we are Republican. If we are told in advance by the writer that he has written Senator McNamara or Hart, we immediately make contact with their offices to see that we don't duplicate what they are doing. Where we get an inquiry which we think is only to us, we start action. Then the system works pretty much that, in the process, you find out from the agency that one of your colleagues may be working on the same thing.

> [Also,] if we get a letter from a constituent who is in Jim O'Hara's district on the other side of the state, as a matter of protocol we write back to his constituent and say, "We suggest you talk to your own Congressman." We say, "We'll be glad to help but as a matter of propriety we think he ought to handle it." This is the way the system works and I think it works well this way. Otherwise, you will find many people will write four or five Congressmen and pretty soon the poor agency is overwhelmed. It really doesn't do any more good than if just one office made the inquiry.

Constituent correspondence

At times, because of a slack legislative schedule or other factors, the Congressman's mail may fall off sharply. Some members who can afford to do so schedule relatively extended trips to their districts or send staff employees to stimulate constituent interest during such quiet periods. Others encourage constituent mail in different ways, as indicated by the comments of one experienced member:

> In some districts perhaps it isn't necessary, because there is a super-abundance, for one reason or another, of mail which comes with-

out stimulation. Perhaps you don't have a sufficiently interested staff to handle volume, but generally speaking one of the ways in which we figure we can keep in touch is to not only reply [to] but to stimulate mail.

My office is presently engaged in developing a questionnaire— which is sure to be considered loaded by some of my constituents—and is sure to provoke additional correspondence in an airing of their views and perhaps criticism of mine, if I do get around to answering my own questionnaire at some point.

Instead of preparing a separate questionnaire containing questions on specific issues, some members simply include in their newsletter an "open-ended" request for the opinions of their constituents on any matters of concern to them. Some also include suggestions as to the form "effective" opinion letters should take; such suggestions are designed to make the responses more meaningful and easier to answer. (Examples of guidelines for correspondence appear in the Appendix, page 359.)

Stimulated or just naturally "super-abundant," the mail in a majority of congressional offices probably averages more than a hundred letters daily while Congress is in session. When important legislation is being considered, the flow of mail may become a flood of paper, with as many as five hundred letters received daily.* To escape drowning in correspondence, congressional offices have developed procedures and shortcuts for handling constituent mail in these categories: legislative or issue mail, urging the Congressman to take a particular position on a measure or expressing an opinion on matters of public concern; case mail, asking for help in dealings with federal agencies; and routine request mail, seeking information about bills, government publications, and the like.

* During the 90th Congress the House of Representatives received about two million pieces of mail per month. The total for a one-year period, from March 1968 through April 1969 was 28,820,180 pieces, according to information supplied by the House Postmaster to the Legislative Appropriations Subcommittee.

LEGISLATIVE MAIL

Experienced Congressmen advise newcomers to keep two points in mind while preparing replies to legislative mail. First, as one member puts it, such letters should be written as if their contents were for publication:

> One . . . thing that I think applies to every new member [is] to realize that you are now big news in your home district; and don't ever write anything to a constituent that you wouldn't be willing to see on Page One of the local newspaper. If you can remember that as rule number one, it will keep you out of an awful lot of trouble.

Secondly, bills are seldom enacted into law exactly as introduced. A position taken on a specific bill may be difficult—and perhaps costly—to maintain after substantial changes have been made in it in committee or on the floor. Accordingly, many Congressmen recommend taking a position on the principles of pending legislation, rather than on the bill itself.

The strong neutral position. Aside from general agreement on these points, congressional practice varies widely when it comes to responsiveness to legislative mail. For example, one member suggests that studied ambiguity is the best approach, especially where there is disagreement:

> My mother says, "I never can tell whether you are saying yes or no when I ask you a question." And I think perhaps there is some truth in that. Perhaps in many cases members of Congress respond—instead of reply—to some of the mail that they get, because in many cases it comes from some group with a very sharp axe to grind. They want to pin you down to what your view is going to be on legislation which, if it comes to the floor, may well be controversial. [It may be wise] not to take too forthright a position unless—regardless of what's in the bill—you are going to vote for or against that number when it comes up.
>
> I've seen enough happen to know that members in many cases re-

gret being too specific on issues, especially if they are controversial, when it may be that they are going to be saved by the legislative committee, or perhaps by that much maligned Rules Committee, from the necessity of taking their yes or no position on it.

If you are in agreement with the writer and you feel no hesitation about saying so, of course, it's flattering to them to have you support their views, the sensible nature of their views, and so on. But if you may disagree, or if you violently disagree, it may be just as well to say, "I have received your comments (or your views) and you may be sure that I will give [them] my thoughtful consideration should [the matter] come up to the floor for a vote." Something of that kind.

Strength through candor. Another experienced Congressman opts for candor, suggesting that those who advance their opinions strongly gain respect among their constituents:

The worst sin in the world I suppose is not to answer their letter. But if you answer them and say, "I can't agree with you for the following reasons. [Then list reasons, and close with the phrase:] Please write me again if you have another matter you want to take up," they are so complimented that you wrote them that they are apt to forgive; and generally a proportion do forgive the fact that you don't go along with them.

Old Senator Robinson who was afterward a member of the House from Kentucky used to get up and say in a speech he gave every two years on how to get re-elected (this was the most widely attended lecture given down there, by the way, how to get re-elected)—he used to say, "Gentlemen, it is better to be fur somethin' than to be agin it, but if you've got to be agin it be everlastingly agin it." In other words, don't hesitate to make your opinion known and you will be respected for it.

In similar fashion, some members are forthright in their response to abusive, threatening, or unfairly critical letters. Indeed, there are those who have become well known for pointed replies to misguided constituents. A classic example:

Dear Friend,

I want to call your attention to the fact that some crackpot in your city is writing me and signing your name.

Cordially,

Others avoid reacting hastily or sharply to such mail, believing that a considered and courteous reply setting the record straight may bring about a change of attitude on the writer's part. One member wages a two-stage telephone campaign against writers of "hot letters":

If it is a very hot letter, I have a very calm girl . . . and we put her on maybe ten of those; she takes the burn out of the calls and they just flub their lines and . . . she will say, "The Congressman wanted me to do it specially." Then I call maybe a week later. Well, by then they think maybe they are getting some attention and then we talk about other things we might agree on.

Look for points of agreement instead of points of disagreement or of putting over your own point of view to begin with. You see, you may agree on ninety-nine out of a hundred [things] and [the critical constituent] picked the thing about you that he doesn't like. I said [to an irate visitor] once, "Don't you like the weather outside?" And he looked around and said, "What's that got to do with it?" I said, "It's pretty good and I favor good weather." You see I humored him—and then he got sore at me on that, but he was off the other.

Circular file for crackpots. Persistent crackpot mail is another matter; all Congressmen receive—and ignore—it as a matter of routine. In some offices a special file is kept on "C.P.s," so that staff employees do not waste time in responding:

I have a C.P. file. We call that crackpot. They are the extremes; nobody can take care of them. I say the Twelve Disciples couldn't answer correctly on those. You had better list those in your district. You will get them repeated and you will find that there is a link among them and pretty soon you will just get a grouping of your C.P.s . . . so we avoid [answering] these. . . .

CASE MAIL

Because of the importance attached to casework, case mail gets special handling in most congressional offices. If the matter must be referred to an agency or department for action, receipt of the constituent's letter usually is acknowledged immediately and the writer is informed that the Congressman is taking the problem up with the proper officials in the Executive branch.

As has been indicated, uncomplicated requests are often conveyed by telephone or in a letter from a member. In addition, a standard referral form is available from the Stationery Room, and some Congressmen use them to send a substantial portion of their mail to the various Executive agencies for draft replies. Others limit their referral of constituent letters to the more important or complex situations, believing that service tends to diminish in quality if used indiscriminately. And some members prefer to enclose a letter of their own in all cases requiring referral, instead of simply attaching a "buck slip."

It is customary to copy all constituent letters which are referred to agencies or departments. This protects the member against loss of the original and provides a copy in the office in the event a question arises about the matter while the constituent's letter is at the agency. A suspense file may be maintained on matters referred. Then if a reply is not received by a certain date, a telephone check can be made to make sure the inquiry has not been lost or misplaced.

Executive agencies and departments generally handle congressional mail carefully, according to one experienced member, but a good check-up system is useful in case of delays or other problems:

... most liaison offices and most departments handle congressional mail rapidly. However, they—like all of us—can make errors. A letter can be lost. So we keep a very good check-up system. If we don't get a reply by a certain time we go back and find out what the trouble is. This, I have found in few instances, is very helpful and greatly appreciated by your constituents.

ROUTINE REQUEST MAIL

Letters containing routine requests often are handled by the clerk who opens the mail. In most cases, the request can be met by obtaining a publication from the House Document Room or some other source and sending it to the constituent. A simple request for factual information may require only a telephone call to the appropriate congressional committee or executive agency. Requests from students for information or material on various topics for the purpose of school debates and term papers can be referred to the Legislative Reference Service, which has packets of information already prepared on certain topics.

HANDLING THE MAIL

Responsibility for drafting answers to constituent mail is usually delegated to experienced office employees as a matter of daily routine. Only the most important or unusual items are brought to the Congressman's attention before the staff takes action.

In some offices the constituent's letter is clipped to the reply prepared for the Congressman's signature. Then he may read both the incoming letter and the reply before he signs it, at the same time keeping up to date on the flow and content of his mail. Some authorize a staff assistant to sign the Congressman's name to routine letters, in order to further reduce demands on their time. Experienced members suggest, however, that congressional newcomers read through their mail every day—skimming if necessary —to "get the feel of it" and to establish specific ways of handling correspondence of various kinds.

Replying promptly. Mail is delivered to House offices four or

five times a day. In order to impress constituents with their efficiency, some members try to answer every letter—even if only to
acknowledge its receipt—on the same day that it arrives. Others
are more flexible. Whenever possible, they try to respond promptly
in order to avoid embarrassing telephone calls and other communications from constituents. As one member, speaking in January,
said:

> . . . I still have about six letters which date back to the beginning
> of December, one of which was followed up by a phone call, today, to
> ask why I hadn't answered their invitation to speak in the middle of
> March, so I haven't gotten around to answering. But if possible, I
> think it's polite to answer promptly.

"Inspired" mail. Interest group mail usually is easy to recognize because of the similarity of language, the use of bill numbers
rather than subject titles, and the quantity in which it appears.
Persons signing these form letters may have little knowledge of or
interest in the issue involved, and many members feel that answering such mail in any depth takes time better spent on more important matters. The same considerations apply for letters which
simply express blanket opposition or support on a particular issue,
without supporting arguments.

Detailed responses. On the other hand, Congressmen generally feel that constituents who are deeply concerned and write
thoughtful, reasoned letters deserve appropriately responsive answers. In the case of complicated and highly controversial issues, it
is customary to enclose additional material—for example, a
speech, a committee report, or an article—which explains the subject or sets forth the member's position in detail. When there is a
great volume of mail on a particular issue, some members prepare
"issue packets" of such material. And when pressure mounts dan-
gerously, one experienced member finds that a weighty argument
helps:

. . . sometimes, I find at any rate, when a particular group of people . . . wants information in depth (and also a nice technique to get them off your back in case they are really pressuring you) [it is helpful] to send them a volume of committee hearings. Sometimes this will be four volumes. Say, "Please read this and then if you have any further questions I will be glad to answer them." Or you can do a little bit of editing for them to point out a particular section.

"Policy line" answers. On an uncomplicated matter that is generating a constant flow of letters, members often devise a standard answer to inquiries on the subject. A file of "policy line" letters can be kept and the staff employee who distributes the mail for draft replies only has to indicate to the typist the response that is required. If the volume of mail on a particular issue becomes extremely heavy, the standard answer may be autotyped. The letters are then individually signed by the member himself, by one of his assistants, or by an autopen device. Few offices use mimeographed form letters to reply to constituent mail.

Mail from other districts. Members frequently receive mail from persons residing in other congressional districts. Such mail is customarily forwarded to the member who represents the district in which the writer lives. There are three general exceptions to this rule: If the subject matter specifically relates to the member to whom the letter is addressed; if the reason for writing him is that he has special competence in the subject matter; or if the writer gives a sound reason for not contacting his own Representative. Otherwise, letters from outside the district are simply acknowledged with an explanation that courtesy and tradition require that they be referred to the writer's own Congressman.

Office visitors and lobbyists

With increasing frequency members of Congress are being called upon to meet, assist, guide, or entertain visitors to Washington.

The average Congressman invests almost seven hours a week in this activity and sees roughly half his office visitors personally. Some call on business matters—lobbyists and home-town delegations, for example—but the heaviest traffic generally comprises tourists and groups of constituents such as high-school graduating classes, service-club members, and the like.

ASSISTING THE SIGHT-SEER

Much of the work associated with the drop-in tourist trade is handled by staff employees. This job usually includes getting constituents into the House and Senate galleries and providing general information on sight-seeing in Washington. Also, many offices stock supplies of publications—*Our American Government, The Capitol,* and *How Our Laws Are Made*—which are helpful in answering visitors' questions about Congress and the federal government.

It is customary procedure, when visitors enter the office, to have the receptionist invite them to "sign our guest book." Insofar as such signatures are legible, they facilitate introductions, indicate hometowns, purpose of visit, etc., and provide the member with a record of his callers. This record, in turn, can be used in adding to the mailing list. Or, in the event the member was unable to meet his visitors, it can be used to direct letters to them, complete with thanks for their thoughtfulness in stopping by and a "press of legislative duty" apology for not being able to greet them personally.

Prepackaged information kits. Some offices prepackage information in kits for visitors. Such kits usually contain publications such as those noted above, plus a few items describing the member's exploits. Some also include a letter or memorandum from the Congressman giving suggestions for making the constituent's visit most meaningful and interesting.

Members using this technique find that the visitor's kit is not only well received by their constituents, but also saves a good deal of time otherwise spent in answering detailed questions about addresses, hours when various attractions are open, and times at which tours are conducted. Such information can be compiled by the staff as a matter of office routine—Washington's newspapers publish daily calendars of events in the nation's capital—or it can be provided in a wide variety of printed brochures and lists. (See Appendix, pages 325–327, for sources of items for visitors' kits.)

House gallery passes. Many Congressmen see that constituents get a brief explanation of operations on the floor of the House before they are taken or sent to the gallery. Otherwise, the constituent may come away puzzled—and perhaps irritated—by the small number of members present and their apparent inattention.

In order to watch House floor action, visitors must either secure passes from a Congressman or join a tour conducted by Capitol guides, which starts in the Rotunda. Most congressional offices keep a supply of passes to both the House and the Senate galleries, for the convenience of constituents wishing to observe both Houses.

★ Passes to the House visitors' gallery are supplied by the Doorkeeper's Office upon presentation of a letter signed by the member requesting a specific number of passes.

★ Passes to the Senate visitors' gallery must be obtained from a Senator. Generally a member of the House exchanges a supply of gallery passes with a Senator of his own state and party. When neither Senator is of his own party, the member may work out an exchange agreement with a Senator from another state; some Congressmen and Senators from the same state exchange passes despite party differences.

A member also may take individuals or groups into the House gallery personally, or he may request the House Doorkeeper's Office in writing to admit a designated group. The length of time that such groups will be allowed to observe proceedings is likely to be limited, however, depending upon the number of Capitol visitors who must be accommodated.

Special congressional tours. Members may arrange special White House tours for constituents. These tours start at 8:30 A.M. and are more relaxed and extensive than the general public tours. Reservations are required at least thirty days in advance during the peak tour season, and members generally are limited to placement of one or two families per week on the VIP tour. Congressmen may also make reservations for their constituents on tours conducted by the Executive agencies and departments.

DEALING WITH LOBBYISTS

There are two general types of lobbyists—the local delegations who come from the district or state and the professionals who are stationed permanently in Washington. Unlike the home-town lobbyist, the Washington-based professional may or may not represent a segment of a member's constituency. Experienced members make a point of determining precisely whom a particular lobbyist speaks for. Most are responsible people representing legitimate interests, but it is not unknown for a lobbying organization to front for interests other than those the member is led to think the group represents. Likewise, it may happen that a lobbyist claims he is speaking for "the folks back home" on a particular issue when in reality they are relatively unconcerned.

Home-town delegations. Congressional newcomers have contacts with both types of lobbyists. But generally, as one more senior member points out, they are likely to be most concerned with those who do represent a significant portion of their constituency or who champion a cause in which they are interested:

... the group about which care and treatment becomes most important is the group of lobbyists who will come to you from your home district. Perhaps representing a municipality, perhaps representing a hard-hit segment of agriculture or of industry or of labor, [they] will bring a problem to you, seeking your help in dealing with governmental forces or legislative forces that are most important to them and to their future. . . .

. . . it may be just . . . to get some regulation straightened out that is being construed and applied oppressively to a segment of an industry. It may just be getting a case heard before some administrative agency or board, but [your responsibility lies] in helping them prepare properly for it and being an effective representative of their interests here (not in trying to strong-arm or muscle some decision, because I don't think in the long haul that any of us in this room at this time are going to have a whole lot of muscle to influence decisions of government, for probably some time to come). But we can help in seeing that the facts are brought to the attention of the people who do make the decisions and seeing that the full story is understood and that the impact of the decisions at issue or the law at issue is fully appreciated by the folks who are dealing with it.

While Washington-based lobbyists may be content to deal with congressional office staff employees, home-town delegations usually expect to work directly with the Congressman in "preparing our case." And most members devote as much personal attention as they possibly can to the problems of local delegations and individual representatives of organizations or industries important to their districts. The relationship between service and survival in this context is spelled out by an experienced member:

I think the manner in which you deal with these folks from home and their problems here in Washington and the manner in which you are helpful to them in getting their story told will have a great deal of bearing on the way in which your representation here in Washington is reported back to the people in the district. . . .

I think this is a mission which properly is performed by a member of the House when he assists a local group in telling its story here in Washington. I think the care and treatment of groups of that kind from back home not only has beneficial national results, but it definitely has beneficial results when the next election is held so far as the Representative who is on his toes is concerned.

Washington is a convention and conference center, and local groups planning to attend such functions often invite their Congressman to speak or otherwise be a visible participant. Members customarily attempt to put in an appearance, recognizing that this raises the stock of the home folks among their colleagues. But accepting all invitations of this kind can become burdensome to the point of disrupting legislative work schedules, home life, and digestion. One speaker at the 1969 Seminar suggested that, when the banquet circuit becomes overloaded, local delegations can be invited to meet in the member's office during their stay in Washington:

Dear Friends,

I'm delighted that you'll be coming to Washington next month as a delegate to the convention of the Mousetrap Manufacturers Association. I am most anxious to see you and the other [home staters] attending sometime during your stay.

The week you'll be here is an especially busy one for me, and I regret that my commitments will prevent me from attending the banquet the night of February 7th. I will try to drop in for a few minutes at the reception preceding the banquet.

I do want you to know of my continuing interest in your problems, and I hope that you will have time to come by the office during one of the days you are here. When you arrive in town please call my secretary at ——— and I'm sure we can work out a convenient time for a quiet visit. I look forward to seeing you then.

Sincerely yours,

National lobby groups. The corps of lobbyists most visible to Congressmen comprises the permanent Washington representatives of major national trade and industry organizations, professional associations, and "cause" groups. These lobbyists appear as expert witnesses before congressional committees, call on members in their offices, and offer printed and draft materials suitable for answering constituent mail and for inclusion in speeches or testimony. Concurrently, as they endeavor to inform Congressmen fully of their group's point of view, lobbyists are informing themselves. They discover which members are likely to be for or against their position and which are least likely to be firmly committed either way— and they try to determine the appeal most likely to reach the uncommitted member.*

This sort of information guides the indirect or grass-roots lobby activities on which most national organizations rely for their major legislative campaigns. A spokesman for one such organization, the American Medical Association, emphasizes the important role of informed association members in lobbying at the community level:

. . . once an official [A.M.A.] position is reached, four other men in the Washington office, charged with the duty of informing Congress of the association's position, carry the word to Capitol Hill. . . . Additionally, physicians all over the United States, made acquainted with the provisions of the bills and the official position of the association, are every one lobbyists at the grass roots rather than in the nation's capitol. A field service of eight men (with the consent of the state medical societies) traveling about the country out of the Chicago headquarters of the association, with many duties other than legislative, are charged with the responsibility of alerting the profession regarding the seriousness and the imminence of possible action on medical proposals.

The rest of the lobby action comes from the grass roots. It is a powerful influence on the course of legislation and it is quite natural that it should be, as these men are schooled in medical matters and their opinions should be based on expertise, experience, and education. And they carry a powerful influence too, because the physicians of the United States are respected persons in their communities; they do

* For a concise and informed description of the operations of national lobbies, see Lewis Anthony Dexter, *How Organizations Are Represented in Washington* (Indianapolis and New York: The Bobbs-Merrill Company, Inc., 1969).

much charitable work, they see two and one-quarter million persons each day and are most often the best posted persons on public affairs that are to be found within a community.*

Jobs and patronage

Influential members who are of the President's party can and do assist him in identifying and recruiting talent for top-level positions in the Executive branch. Opportunities for the congressional newcomer to do likewise are few and far between, however, and in most instances job seekers are furnished information from the Civil Service Commission, are referred to the appropriate agency (perhaps with a letter of introduction), or are given the name of an official to whom they can write. Similarly, the patronage which the member does have at his disposal is severely limited, and some members find that filling the few positions available is more trouble than it is worth.

ACADEMY APPOINTMENTS

Each Congressman is allotted a quota of five positions at each of the three major service academies—the Military Academy, the Naval Academy, and the Air Force Academy. Each member may have no more than five cadets at a time at any one academy, including cadets appointed by a predecessor from his district. Thus, new members fill positions at the various academies only as cadets nominated by their predecessors graduate or drop out. New members get in touch with the academy offices in order to ascertain the current status of their quotas.

Each state is also allotted a quota for the Merchant Marine Academy. These quotas vary, depending on the population of the

* Remarks of James W. Foristel, A.M.A. legislative representative, to Congressional Fellows of the American Political Science Association. For the full text, see "How a Lobby Works," in *Congressional Record,* April 4, 1963, pp. A2028–A2029.

state. When vacancies occur, each member may nominate ten individuals for a statewide competitive examination conducted by the academy, which selects the successful candidates.

Appointment methods. When vacancies occur at one of the three service academies, the Congressman may nominate ten candidates for each opening. There are two methods of making appointments:

★ The member nominates up to ten candidates and authorizes the service academies to select the best qualified man on the basis of competitive testing and examination; or,

★ He nominates up to ten candidates and lists them in order of his preference. The person at the top of the list is the principal candidate, and the others become the first, second, third, fourth, fifth, etc., alternates. The member then submits the list to the appropriate academy and the principal candidate receives the appointment if he meets the eligibility criteria and qualifies on the entrance examination. If the principal candidate fails to qualify, then the next designated alternate candidate who qualifies is chosen.

Besides giving the member a greater voice in filling the academy appointment, the principal-alternate method also permits wide discretion in considering other factors, such as athletic ability or leadership potential.

Nomination systems. To avoid difficulties involved in making a choice and to ensure that the best qualified candidates are selected, some members base their nominations on a merit system which they describe in detail to prospective applicants and their parents. For example, some Congressmen require applicants to take the Civil Service Placement Examination or the College Entrance Board test. Then they nominate the ten with the best scores. Others set up committees of community leaders, editors, bankers, clergymen, and educators; the committee interviews all applicants and makes the final selection of nominees.

Representative Rogers C. B. Morton, of Maryland's First District, described his use of committees in the nominating process in material prepared for participants in the 1969 Seminar, as follows:

To assist me in recruiting, screening and selecting applicants for the service academies, I have appointed a Service Academy Committee in the First District. This committee is made up of people who are interested, who enjoy serving, and who turn in a first-class job. Because of the size of my district the committee is regionalized, being composed of four regional subcommittees. My district office administrative assistant serves as secretary of the committee and as such is the central contact point and coordinator.

All of the high-school principals and guidance counselors are fully aware of the existence of the committee and keep in touch with it. Through my newsletters, through news releases, through high-school appearances, and through work with civic organizations, we emphasize the importance of the service academies and the necessity for recruiting capable, dedicated applicants. In addition to the committee, I use the cadets and midshipmen themselves when they are home on leave in this recruiting effort. They can indeed be effective.

As soon as the applicant makes contact with our office, the appropriate regional subcommittee is informed, and they begin the process of investigation and interview which finally culminates in rejection or nomination. Under this system we find it more effective to nominate to the academies under the competitive system rather than principal and alternate method. Vigorous effort is made to keep all consideration of the applicants out of the political arena. On the committee are people strongly identified with both major political parties. In order to help the committee we also administer the civil service test to the applicants, the results of which are used by the committee in its evaluation but are in no way binding. We also have the applicants take physical exams as early as possible so that we don't come up to the last minute and find the applicant physically disqualified.

Under the competitive system the academies themselves examine the candidates that we finally nominate. For each vacancy we can nominate as many as ten; however, we make it a point to include only those who the committee feels are fully qualified—and, especially, career motivated.

Nominations to all four academies are made six to eight months before the vacancies are to occur. Thus, members must publicize the academy opportunities—and whatever nominating process they plan to use—well in advance. (A sample information sheet prepared for prospective applicants, a candidate's statement, and an application form appear in the Appendix, page 355.)

POSTMASTER AND RURAL CARRIER APPOINTMENTS

Until 1969 postmaster and rural carrier vacancies were filled by the Postmaster General on recommendation of Congressmen of the same party as the President. This patronage was traditionally the prerogative of members of the House, and Senators became involved only if the district in which the vacancy existed was held by a Representative of the opposition party. But the Postal Reorganization Act of 1970 (Public Law 91–375) includes provisions designed to eliminate patronage considerations in selection of local postmasters and rural carriers.

For the most part, members recommended qualified men and women for postmaster and rural carrier positions, since the member's prestige was involved in the appointment. In recent years, however, with widespread public concern over the performance of the postal system, many Congressmen and others have questioned whether *any* patronage system is appropriate for personnel selection in a major service industry.

In 1967, the Postmaster General recommended that the Post Office be removed from the cabinet and operated on a non-political basis. In the same year, the Senate passed a Congressional reorganization bill eliminating political selection of postmasters, and in 1968, the President's Commission on Postal Organization proposed, as part of a major reform of the Post Office, that postmasters and rural carriers be selected strictly on merit. In February of 1969, the new President and his Postmaster General announced that the patronage system would no longer be used and that selection of postmasters would be made instead from within the postal service by national or regional management selection boards. When qualified candidates within the service who met the residency requirements could not be found, an open competitive Civil Service examination would be given. To assure objectivity, a majority of the members of each Board were drawn from outside the postal service itself.

The long debate over postal reform included relatively little controversy on this particular question. Most Congressmen appeared to have decided that Post Office patronage added substantially to their administrative workload without corresponding benefits, either to the public as a whole, or to themselves politically.

Under the Postal Reorganization Act, postmasters and rural carriers, like other postal employees, are appointed directly by the Postal Service, without Senate confirmation. The law prohibits recommendations by anyone (and specifically mentions Members of Congress) with respect to any person under consideration for "appointment, promotion, assignment, transfer or designation" in the Postal Service, and directs that any such recommendation be returned to the sender "appropriately marked as in violation of this (prohibition)." It further orders that "necessary and proper" action, which may include removal and disqualification, be taken to enforce the prohibition. Members of Congress and others may respond to certain official inquiries from the Postal Service on personnel matters, such as requests for an evaluation of the work performance of a former employee.

The only unsolicited statement which may be made regarding an individual under consideration for a personnel action in the Postal Service is one attesting to his character or place of residence.

This change, it should be noted, has been greeted with skepticism by those who believe that traditional practices will not be readily abandoned. The performance of the new Postal Service will be closely watched, and any abuses of Congressional intent are likely to command the attention of both the "out" party and the bipartisan Board of Governors responsible for Postal Service management.

CONGRESSIONAL JOBS

Some minor patronage jobs are available in the House of Representatives itself. Included are positions as policemen, elevator operators, pages, doorkeepers, and clerical jobs in the House Post Office, Stationery Room, Disbursing Office, and Folding Room. Salaries for these jobs are relatively low, and they are customarily filled by students and older persons.

Allocation of these jobs is handled by a Patronage Committee composed of three members of the majority party. The bulk of this patronage is made available to members of that party. A few jobs are made available to senior House members of the minority party. Among majority-party members, House patronage jobs are distributed on a seniority basis as they become available because of death, defeat, and retirement of members. Thus, congressional newcomers are spared the task of dealing with this kind of patronage.

Political necessity and civic education

A NORMALLY ACTIVE congressional office not only reacts to constituency demands. In one way or another, quite apart from their overt campaigning, most House members encourage requests for information or assistance. Just answering the mail is not enough, an experienced Congressman indicated during the 1963 Seminar for Freshmen, adding:

. . . we like, I think, to encourage mail from back home. For no matter how close you live, no matter how close you keep in touch with your district, no matter whether or not you have a district office or office hours in your district—there tends to be something of a vacuum between the people that you represent and you as their legislator, their Representative in Congress.

As is the case with service work, the value placed on "keeping in touch" is an amalgam of civic virtue and political necessity.

While Congress is in session, the average member spends about six days a month in his district. He also makes about eleven radio and television appearances a month and devotes about five hours a week to press work and writing chores.* At least in part, activities such as these are self-serving. They are designed to reveal the Congressman's brilliance, effectiveness, and sense of dedication, thereby establishing or maintaining his political base. But they also have wider implications for the democratic process. In delivering speeches and engaging in other activities in the district, in writing newspaper stories, magazine articles, and books, in making radio and television broadcasts, the Congressman engages in civic education, reaching out to—and, he hopes, involving—citizens who otherwise might not take an active interest in policy issues and public affairs.

Another speaker at the 1963 Seminar stressed the importance of this aspect of the Congressman's job. Members of the House, declared Washington reporter David Broder, are in an ideal position "to convey some of the realities of this world to the people at home who are, unfortunately, dependent on newspapers and television for most of what they can grasp as to what is going on." Continuing, Broder said:

I don't know what you should tell them about the shape of the world. That is something for you to decide for yourselves, but I do think you should be as frank in defining for your constituents the problems and the prospects of this nation, both at home and abroad, as you are telling the bureaucrats downtown the facts of life about the problems and the wishes of your constituents in matters in which they are concerned.

I think you have to take the serious responsibility of telling your people as honestly and as frankly and as fully as you can what kind of shape we are in as a nation and what kind of a world we are living in. This is a responsibility that you share with those of us in the press who, Lord knows, meet our own responsibilities imperfectly on keeping the people informed. And if there were one wish which I could express to

* These figures are based on the *Interim Report on Congressional Offices*. For excerpts of this report, see Appendix, pages 303–311.

you it would be that, as you enjoy the security that your membership in this distinguished body has given you, you will recall your obligation to be a teacher to your people.

Direct personal contact

Congressmen generally agree that there is no substitute for "direct personal contact . . . in the business of getting elected and in the business of informing your people." For the member whose district is near Washington, maintaining contact is usually not difficult. He may meet with constituents on weekends and some weekdays while Congress is in session. For example, one experienced member schedules office hours in his district throughout the year:

> . . . I feel that, in many ways, just answering mail is not enough. Certainly it is true in my area, and I make a point of holding more or less regular office hours in my district where I get the problems that are really insoluble. You know, you find them pouring out their souls to you. But it does give them an opportunity to talk to their Congressman, which I think is valuable. I do also write newsletters on a regular basis, primarily to newspapers, and then I have a supplementary mailing list to individuals. [It is] an effort to close the gap between here and home.

Closing the gap presents a greater problem for members who are not able to return to their districts frequently. Travel costs mount up, and the allowance does not go far. As a result, many members must rely primarily on correspondence to develop and maintain personal relationships with constituents, to serve and to inform them, and to get some idea of their attitudes on various issues. A west coast Congressman describes his dependence on the mail:

> If you are from states that are close to Washington—and I would classify the area from Chicago to New York probably as within that general area—a member can get home fairly frequently. That is if they

want to get home on a weekend, they can. If they want to have office hours on Saturday mornings in their district, they can, sometimes Fridays. We on the west coast in most cases have found that it's impractical to try to get home on regular weekends. The airplane costs about $301 round trip for a single trip. For just a weekend that is hardly worthwhile. So most members from the west coast go home infrequently. As a result we are more dependent upon the means of communication through the mail than are members that are closer to their districts. I use the newsletter. I also endeavor to make sure that the mail is answered, and answered promptly and thoroughly. I usually issue a questionnaire each year, which is done by many members of the House. This does provide another means of communication with the people in your district. I think that the west coast members have to rely to a greater extent on means of communication of this type than is true with some of the districts close to Washington.

STIMULATING PUBLIC INTEREST

Experienced members advise their junior colleagues that no single method of establishing contact and informing constituents will be effective in all congressional districts. The following comment is representative:

> I want to bring up this other point in talking about what works for one district: No two districts are exactly alike and no two Congressmen are exactly alike, so my advice would be, instead of taking a whole lot of advice, there is not a man up here in Washington that knows your district any better than you do. After all you got elected down there, and you know what it took to get elected and you know the people that you are representing—and if you don't know them you had better get out and learn. You just do that thing that you think is the best way to inform your public, I mean your people. Certainly, get all the advice that you can, but let what you do be your decision.

"Classroom" on wheels. The same member goes on to describe what works for him—a mobile office equipped to serve individual constituents or groups such as high-school classes in government:

I have found that during the years that I have been observing members of Congress, particularly in my district, that the one big complaint most always heard was that our other Congressman comes home and he sees Bill Smith and John Jones and then drives on out of town. . . .

To counteract the same criticism being made of me (and I guess they will find some other one) I seized upon this idea of a mobile office whereby the people could know where I would be at certain times. In that office I could have all sorts of information, which I do have, and which we pass out, and we have the high-school government classes come by.

Well, it has just worked tremendously to my advantage. It may not work for you; it may not work for another Congressman; but I don't know how else I could have gotten pictures of that mobile office with me standing in front of it on the front pages of the [papers]. I couldn't have bought the publicity. The four sides of this mobile office are white with red, big boxcar letters, with dignity, of course, but with some blue also. Regardless of the direction from which they are traveling into the main part of each of eighteen counties in my district . . . they know that [I am] in town because the name is there. They can't miss it. I have had as high as two hundred people in one day to sit across my office desk asking me questions, and, of course, I have a little adjoining office and two or three helpers there. . . .

Now a lot of people tell me they couldn't possibly do all of that, but I will tell you there is not a man in my district that can tell me much about my district today because I was there last fall, even though we had a short adjournment. I was in every county in my district. I talked to any constituent who wanted to see me, and that is the beautiful part about it. How can anybody in my district say, "Well, you can't see the Congressman. He never comes around"?

It is impossible for them to say it. Newspapers carried it, the TVs are happy to carry. They come there and interview you and all that sort of thing, and everybody knows that on Monday between certain hours, the Congressman from the First District will be at this town. They name the square, the corner of the courthouse square, or what street. Then on Tuesday you may be twenty miles away at this other town. If they are not home that day they can drive twenty miles if they really want to see you.

"Grass roots Congress." Another member, Representative James A. Mackay, adapted the New England Town meeting technique in order to stimulate public interest in national and international problems. An article in *The Christian Science Monitor* described his experiment:

. . . Rep. James A. Mackay of Georgia's Fourth Congressional District, which includes part of Atlanta, says some of his colleagues in the House are interested in the effectiveness of his "Grass Roots Congress." If they deem it successful, they have told him, they will start similar "congresses" in their own districts.

After five months of study and preparation, beginning last June, 250 of Representative Mackay's constituents met Dec. 3–4 at nearby De Kalb College. They heard a report from him on legislation passed during the first session of the 89th Congress. Then chairmen of nine citizens' panels on subjects likely to come up during the next session of Congress gave Mr. Mackay their thinking and advice.

He didn't promise to base his future votes on their recommendations, but said they would influence his thinking.

Mr. Mackay, a freshman member of Congress from a newly created Georgia district, proposed the "Grass Roots Congress" to a selected group of his constituents last spring. There was need, he said, for closer communication between the people and the federal government. . . .

Some 400 people agreed to take part in the work of one or more of thirty-one panels set up to study specific problems as diverse as foreign relations and water resources. Representative Mackay sent them appropriate House bills, committee reports, and government studies on their respective subjects to digest. He assigned a member of his staff . . . to correlate the work of the panels.

Of the thirty-one panels, nine "followed through" to the extent of having reports ready for submission to the "Grass Roots Congress." . . .*

* By Joseph H. Baird, *The Christian Science Monitor,* December 10, 1965. Excerpted by permission of the publisher. Copyright 1965 The Christian Science Publishing Society. All rights reserved.

"Dial-a-Congressman." In January 1966 another member, George Grider of Tennessee, began setting aside two hours each week for long-distance telephone chats with constituents he was unable to see during visits to his district. Under his "Dial-a-Congressman" plan, constituents with problems or opinions they wished to discuss personally were invited to come to the Memphis office Monday afternoons from 3 to 5 P.M. and place a call—free of charge—to the Congressman at his Washington office.

Representative Grider reported receiving about twenty calls each Monday afternoon. "For the most part," he told *Roll Call* newspaper, "the calls are a microcosm of the mails. You might say that all of them might have been handled by my staff just as effectively. The essential value of the calls lies in the fact that Congressmen are great attention-getters. The constituents, when they talk with me personally, know that through me they have a voice in what happens, both in the district and outside. They feel that I can focus attention on their concerns—and democracy won't work unless people with problems [can] get attention."

Meeting the press

Congressional newcomers frequently confess to a sense of frustration in their dealings with the press. In a newsletter to his constituents, the late Representative Clem Miller of California described the "chasm which exists between one junior Congressman and the press":

First, there is the relationship with the home district newspapers. It is distinct and different from the Washington press. By and large, it is locally oriented, and properly so.

The key to this relationship is that it is a one-way street. The exchange almost always starts at this end, the Washington end, and flows out *to* the local newspaper. It is an arm's-length affair. It is dominated by the mimeographed press release, which, in my case, has to be mailed to every newspaper in the First District. Occasionally we will wire the germ of a news item to a specific newspaper; even more rarely, we will telephone the item. We face a constant problem of the dailies and the weeklies. The timing of a release is vital to the newspaper. It does not get run in the weekly if it does not arrive on the spot at the right time. With different press days, with the unpredictable timing of developments in Washington, and with our limited resources, this process of communication is difficult and often frustrating for all concerned.

The role of the newspaper is usually passive, and occasionally hostile. Their news staffs are overworked and understaffed, have very limited budgets, and receive a never-ending flood of materials from all sides. The congressman gets his due along with a thousand other competing interests. Anyway, why should the editor worry when he has a senator and a congressman competing to deliver the news to him on a silver platter. That's the fact. The senator wants his name in the paper, so he is in there with a wire early. The congressman wants his name in there, so he is on the phone. This is the system. Newspapers like it. They call it "competition," and in America we always like to see the other fellow engaged in competition. Whether this is good for the newspapers or their readers is another matter.

Newspapers at home usually see no need to check with their congressman on facts or on his position. The number of times that I have been contacted by *any* newspaper in my district in two years can be counted on the fingers of one hand.

Second, there is the relationship with the wire services, UPI and AP. At the opening of Congress in 1959 there was a brief flurry of contact from the wire service "regional men" handling California. Since then, there has been less contact. The reasons are the same. Overwork, understaffing, and the flood of news. The UPI regional man for California, for example, is expected to cover all the representatives and senators from ten or so western states. He is also responsible for reporting developments of possible interest to his service's clients—newspapers, and radio and TV stations—from several hundred committees and subcommittees on Capitol Hill as well as Floor activity in both houses. Harry Humphries of AP has always been most agreeable to talk to me if I call him. He will come around to the office and talk about it.

But newsworthy occasions never seem to arise. The twist or angle which would make the news does not seem to be present. The effect of this is that constituents do not generally know what their congressman is doing, nor do they have a chance to find out. What is "news"? What is newsworthy in America today? Are the views of a congressman on current legislation, his voting record, etc., "news" to his constituency? Apparently not. I feel frustrated to the extent that I make little effort to promote this sort of thing, and conversely, little effort is made to elicit it from me by newsmen.

A third category is one which might be described as the national press corps, the newsmen responsible for telling America what goes on in Washington and Congress. There is a large gallery immediately over the Speaker's chair reserved for the press. It is generally devoid of occupants. Except for crowded state occasions, there may be only one, two, or three newsmen bird-dogging the proceedings below. By and large, the reporting is quite perfunctory with little of the shading which gives political life its validity. While I believe this is unfortunate, it is understandable. The press has no time for shading today. This is the "age of the headline" and the "news capsule." Headlines come from the White House or from Senator Johnson's office, rarely from congressional debate. . . .

How the press gallery functions, I do not have the faintest idea. This is perhaps an admission of deficiency on my part. It is worth reporting only as illustrative of the chasm which exists between one junior congressman and the press.

If the press did not report Congress, Congress could hardly function. If the sound of congressional voices carried no farther than the bare walls of the Chambers, Congress could disband. We know this; it is brought home to us every day. Reporters appear very aware of their powers. From where I sit, it is a power they are not backward about using.

This suggests a basic rivalry between the press corps and congressmen. I must confess that I feel it. To the wise old birds in the press gallery, we politicians are trying to put something over on somebody. Exposure of this public show by politicians is a major portion of the routine of the newspaperman's job, and I agree it must be an important part. There is a tendency to fatuousness and fat-headedness which must be restrained. To the congressman, however, publicity is his lifeblood. It is his career, his fate, and it brings an emotion to his relationship with the press which the newsman does not comprehend, but which he can manipulate—very frequently with too much enjoyment to be bearable.

A good case in point was a recent newspaper series on nepotism which won its author a Pulitzer Prize. To my knowledge there was no news sleuthing carried on with more vigor than this investigation into the family members on congressional payrolls. It was carried on in the finest traditions of the journalistic profession. It was a joyous rousting-about of the rascally politician. Actually, it shed little light, it contributed little. It was harmful, I believe, to the public's understanding of Congress. This should not be construed as the favoring of nepotism, but there was no effort to tell the other side—the great financial difficulties which many congressmen operate under in doing their jobs. It killed for this session the addition of a staff man to each office, badly needed indeed under congressional loads presently carried by most of us.

Then, there was the famous *Life* exposé of expense accounts. What enthusiasm this engendered! There was another side to this story also that was never told. The main point I am seeking to make is that much of the press seems to regard its Washington role as it does police reporting. The broader sweep of the meaningful "why" and the "wherefore" of government is lost in the welter of what is on the police captain's blotter. . . .

Finally, there is the relationship with a host of national correspondents who are busy explaining in their signed columns and interpretative articles what the newspapers seem unable to do in the news columns. I see these men closeted with the committee chairmen in the Speaker's Lobby. I am introduced to them occasionally. I have had dinner with them and found them delightful.

I have talked to them in the Speaker's Lobby, but it is difficult for me to talk to newspapermen. I don't seem to have the hang of it. I don't like to talk in clichés and the headline phrase does not come easily. Since the press operates under terrifying time pressures, many newsmen think in clichés. They want congressmen to talk in clichés. They become uneasy if you tend toward too much "background" talk, or if your thoughts are tentative. This, of course, is due to the modern demand for slogans. Everything is compressed. People have no time to attend, to listen. We have become a nation of headline readers. It is not at all surprising that the working press has come to require the same of politicians in its day-to-day reporting. The result is distortion, the inevitable distortion that comes from oversimplification and compression.

This is not to absolve myself. The job of the congressman, in major degree, is communicating—making our political world understandable. By dealing too much in the "grey" area of political life, and not presenting sharp, didactic alternatives, I do not make the job easier. I am constantly striving to do this, but my concept of the real political world does not make for an easy fit.

There are reporters who seek background. It is hard to get the knack of talking "background," "off-the-record," "on-the-record," unless you have a firm idea of the ground rules. Reporters become frustrated by the congressman who does not know the ground rules, who switches back and forth from "off-the-record" to "on-the-record," who interlards his talk with trivia or philosophy. The reporter's standaɪ_ reaction to this sort of thing is to turn off his traveling pencil.

What all this means in terms of Congress is that the congressman who tailors his speech and remarks to the strictures of modern reporting is going to get in the news; and he who doesn't is going to have difficult sledding. It means that many capable legislators operate fairly silently, while others who might be of inferior competence are heard from quite frequently.*

Some observers may disagree with Representative Miller's over-all appraisal of press performance. A Washington reporter was, in fact, given equal time to respond in one of the Congressman's subsequent newsletters. Representative Miller's comments,

* Clem Miller, *Member of the House: Letters of a Congressman* (New York: Charles Scribner's Sons, 1962), pp. 57–62. Copyright 1962 Charles Scribner's Sons. Reprinted by permission of the publisher.

however, go to the heart of the matter for those involved in political communication from the nation's capital: The Fourth Estate
comprises many houses, and the key that will open all the doors to
one may not get the bearer through the front gate of another.

GUIDELINES FOR GIVE-AND-TAKE WITH THE PRESS

Despite the diversity of press capability and interest noted by Representative Miller, a number of general practices are considered
mutually profitable to members and the press. Those most frequently mentioned by Washington newsmen and experienced Congressmen are:

Accessibility and initiative. Reporters tend to cultivate those
Congressmen who produce news for them, if for no other reason
than that their professional status depends in part on their ability
to reach and tap a wide variety of news sources. Because in the
newsroom timeliness is next to godliness, reporters customarily
develop alternative sources, so that they can secure information
quickly in the event one source is unavailable to them. These
factors suggest that the member who is readily accessible is likely
to be asked for views on various matters more frequently than one
who is often unavailable to the press.

At the same time, there is no reason for the Congressman
to wait anxiously for his telephone to ring when he feels that he
has something to contribute. Reporters read each other's material
and the interests of leading newsmen and commentators indicate
to some extent which topics are likely to become current and choice
among the press corps in general.* Newsmen, particularly those on
regional or Washington bureau desks, look for ways in which to
give developing stories a local angle. Moreover, some observers
suggest that the press as a whole is becoming more interested in
background and interpretation—and that suggestions for topics

* See "The Influence of the Elite," in William L. Rivers, *The Opinion
Makers* (Boston: Beacon Press, 1965), pp. 41–56.

deserving this kind of treatment are welcome. A prominent newsman makes this point:

> We need you desperately in the press. In terms of trying to explain to us what are your views about these things . . . not the narrow view of what will get you elected, but the view of what you bring out of the heart of the country as to what is best for the country in the long run. . . .
>
> It is true that the press is oriented to the Senate. There is no doubt about it. But the press, I think, performs a function in this town which is a vital function. It can help you. You can greatly help us. There is a tendency, I think particularly in the Executive branch of the government, to think about the press as a problem, which it is—I would be the first to admit it. But it is also an opportunity and its role, I suggest to you, is changing all the time. It used to be primarily concerned with the "scoop," with what is happening today, with trying to wheedle out of you what went on in executive session in some particular committee. You may be sure that it is still going to try to do that, but, at the same time, in the last generation it has changed quite a bit. The radio has taken away from the newspaper the primary role of being the first purveyor of the news. The television has taken away from the press the great picture story, the great descriptive story. And in a way this has been a good thing, because it has forced the press, particularly in Washington, into the educational function. It has forced it to do what it should have been doing all along, explaining endlessly the complications of legislation.
>
> I find a singular lack on the part of Congressmen and Senators of approaching newspapermen, or when they see things in the press that are wrong merely griping about it instead of calling up and saying, "Here is an aspect of a really important bill that I think, if you don't mind my saying so, merits your taking some time to study and explain." I can't speak, of course, for all my colleagues, but we certainly on the [——— newspaper] would welcome any suggestions at any time of any sort whatsoever of that kind, because we know that once you get into your committee meeting and spend hours and days on bills you will know a whole lot more about these problems than we do and we cer-

tainly would welcome your help. This has nothing whatsoever to do
with the fact of your regional representation or the fact that you are
new men.

Expertise and judgment. Development of a specialty or of
expert knowledge in a particular area is likely to bring a member
to the attention of the press. An experienced member explains why:

Make a reputation for yourself, and my thought here is that one
way by which one advances is to develop a specialty. There is some area
of interest, some area perhaps of experience, some area where you combine your past experience with your interest, where you can by certain
application and diligence come to learn more on that subject than anybody else. I have in mind the great reputation built in the House by
[Representative ———] who has come to be accepted as so much of an
authority on China that even the Chinese consult him. And if you have
an interest or a specialty (and you get to be extremely good on it) it
isn't necessary to speak very often on the floor because there are other
outlets. . . .

It gives you an opportunity to be called upon in the television forums and radio debates, because, after all, the people who are looking
for members of Congress to appear on their programs want them to
have something to say and something to say that they know something
about. It isn't enough merely that you have a generalized knowledge or
that you were extremely active back home in the American Legion or in
some other organization. And, therefore, you are much more likely to
be called for on television, radio, and general forums, and thereby get
better known, if you have developed these specialties of your own.

Similarly, the ability to recognize the important and ignore
the trivial is regarded as an advantage, as a newsman suggests:

A great public commotion about an issue is no assurance it will become a matter of central importance to the electorate. In other words,
just because there is a lot of froth and noise and clacking around in
Washington about something doesn't mean a blessed thing. Oftentimes it doesn't, and one of the sensitivities, I think, of the great people

in Congress is that they can tell the difference. They know how to discriminate between what's just plain stuff and what's meaningful.

Candor and truthfulness. An experienced Congressman explains the value of free and frank exchanges with newsmen:

I was once in the district attorney's office for a good many years, and I worked with an assistant district attorney who would never tell the press anything. I have been a naval intelligence officer during the war when we decided to tell the press everything, and, believe me, the second system is better, because you will find that as you develop confidential relations with the press that they are for the most part to be trusted.

I believe a full, frank meeting with the press in which you tell them the background of what you are doing and make it very clear what you feel can be quoted as against what you think cannot be quoted —it will be respected. So I choose the open relationship with the press rather than the close-mouth position. It is something like Sophie Tucker, who said, "I've been rich and I've been poor, and, believe me, rich is best." So I would be a little rich in the information you give out as long as you have established a basis of confidence.

And you will find that everybody down here is talking to the newspapermen and talking more freely perhaps at cocktail parties than anywhere else (more freely than is advisable there, perhaps) but . . . there is nothing wrong in getting your ideas and getting out information which is favorable to your point of view. . . .

On some occasions, of course, comment may breach a confidence or injure a colleague. A newsman suggests that, in such cases, silence is golden:

If you can't tell the truth, the thing to do is just don't say anything. To become branded as a liar (and, believe me, quite a few public figures deservedly and perhaps not too deservedly are so branded) finishes you as far as the—I mean the network, the word gets out in this town, something awful, and you just don't mean anything any more. Your word means nothing, and people still laugh at your jokes and welcome the little tidbits you might hand out, but there has to be a very cold Monday before you mean anything.

Invective and errors. Public officials seldom win public quarrels—especially long-distance quarrels—with editors and publishers. As an experienced Congressman puts it:

Never . . . quarrel with either the press or the clergy, because the press will get you in the footnote no matter what you say. In the way in which they write your comment critical of the press, they will always get you. You write a letter to the editor and you criticize the paper; notice the headline or the footnote, the editorial note that goes on it which only doubly destroys you. And I do not believe it is, generally speaking, feasible to criticize the clergy because they can always appeal to a higher court than you can.

However, reporters are fallible. Ordinarily they do not mind being advised of their honest errors, as a newsman indicates:

I don't think that reporters generally (certainly those I know) are ever angered by a political figure calling him up and saying, if he sincerely so believes, that something that the reporter wrote was not accurate. We make mistakes almost as much as politicians, but, believe me, for all our sins very few if any reporters are venal, while all reporters, certainly the hundreds that I have known, are sensitive and have points of view. I think that basically what reporters want is the facts as they can honestly interpret them.

Whether it is *always* desirable to call errors to the reporter's attention and to ask for corrections is another matter. Some members find that, unless the error is of great importance, the record can be corrected most gracefully in another forum, without direct reference to misstatement of the case elsewhere.

NEWS RELEASE TECHNIQUES

Congressmen have at their disposal resources and facilities designed for, or adaptable to, use in dealing with news media. In

House practice, these are employed in a wide variety of ways to make it easier for the newsman to get the facts and report them accurately.

Use of press assistants. Whereas some members prefer to handle their own press relations, working directly with district editors and publishers whom they know personally, a substantial number of Congressmen delegate this responsibility to a staff employee who has had newspaper or related media experience. The 1969 *Congressional Staff Directory* lists only seventy-seven individuals with the title of press assistant, press secretary, or public relations aide, but this figure is misleading; in many offices, the administrative assistant is a former newsman, and a major portion of his time is devoted to work with reporters and editors in the district and elsewhere.

Statements and releases. Some congressional offices produce highly polished press releases for distribution on a regular schedule. Others do not attempt to write releases at all, preferring to make the raw materials—copies of speeches backed up by personal interviews, for example—available to those reporters who can be enticed in a casual telephone conversation to drop by. On occasion, of course, these techniques are combined. A release containing excerpts from a speech or statement may be accompanied by the full text; and newsmen, particularly those representing media with outlets in the district, may be notified by phone that the material is both available and significant.

In any event, newsmen and experienced members alike recommend that texts of speeches be made available to the press, in advance of their public presentation whenever possible. Thus, reporters are given an opportunity to familiarize themselves with their contents, and the possibility of misquotation or error is reduced. Accompanying press releases containing excerpts give the members an opportunity to emphasize those portions of their remarks which they think are most important, at the same time reducing the possibility that reporters will overlook significant statements in their haste to meet a deadline.

Reporters maintain that they do not want the story to be written for them, that the press release need only contain basic information about the occasion for the speech and pertinent quotations from it. However strong this preference may be, it is not unusual for well-written releases to turn up substantially verbatim in newspapers and broadcasts. Releases are most frequently published in weekly or smaller daily newspapers, which have limited editorial staffs; but even the larger dailies and the wire services occasionally use them as they have been written.

Generally, members who prepare releases for publication as written attempt to follow standard newspaper format: One to three pages, double-spaced, in clear and concise language, with editorial comments about the author's brilliance and effectiveness either implied or attributed to someone else.

Distribution of materials. Copies of speech texts and press releases are customarily made available in the House Press, Radio-Television, and Periodical galleries, which provide facilities for correspondents employed by the major newspapers, wire services, news broadcasters, and magazines. These galleries are situated adjacent to the House Chamber in the Capitol. Between twenty-five and fifty copies of releases and texts are usually sent to the Press Gallery, with perhaps ten each to the Radio-Television and Periodical galleries.

Many congressional offices maintain an up-to-date list of all district newspapers and broadcasting stations, complete with press and news broadcast deadlines for each. On important news breaks —establishment of a federal facility in the district, or the award of an important government contract, for instance—the information is often telephoned or wired to the news outlets most likely to be interested. Less timely releases, and other materials, are customarily mailed well in advance of local outlets' deadlines, with a release date prominently displayed as part of the heading.

Photo services. The House Republican and Democratic campaign committees employ photographers who are on call to record meetings between members and their constituents, individually or in groups. Usually this service must be requested well in advance, for these photographers are seldom available on a moment's notice. Many members keep a camera handy in their offices and take their own pictures of constituents. These can be mailed, or if the camera develops the picture immediately, passed out at the time. Extra prints of photographs are useful for publicity or filing purposes.

Radio and television. Radio and television station licensees are required to devote time to public-service programming. Perhaps as a result of this requirement, local outlets have been found by Congressmen to be relatively receptive to tape, film, or telephone reports from the nation's capital. Among techniques developed to exploit this opportunity are:

★ The one-minute television report. Usually such a report comments on major news events of general significance or on items of special interest in a particular district. Because of the time needed to make the film and ship it to local stations, reports of this kind usually have to be planned somewhat in advance.

★ The radio-television "beeper" report. Used for commenting on news events as they occur or reporting on legislative activity of particular local concern, this report can be produced with little advance planning, for the physical arrangements involve only a call to local radio stations. In agreement with local stations, some members are prepared to make such reports whenever an event occurs that lends itself to this technique. The Capitol switchboard can also set up a conference call so that the report can be given to several stations at once, thereby minimizing telephone costs.

★ Regular radio or television programs. These can be sent to local stations on a weekly, biweekly, or monthly basis. They usually are three- to five-minute presentations that require considerable advance planning in order to present effective discussion of a topic at some length.

★ The interview. This format is recommended by experienced members for five- to fifteen-minute programs. It is customary to invite other federal officials (a cabinet member, an Assistant Secretary, or a prominent Senator, for example), or state or local dignitaries visiting in Washington, to participate in these programs, which usually focus on topical issues of direct concern to the district.

An experienced Congressman suggests that it usually is better to keep radio and television tapes short:

It is easier to fit the shorter tapes into a regular news program on a TV station than if you send out a longer length tape. This is also true with radio time. Five minutes or less tends to be more usable on news programs in the radio stations in your district. The recording facility has suggested if you do pick a longer period, such as fifteen minutes, that an interview type of program usually seems to go over better than just a straight discussion on your part alone. These are just suggestions. They have suggested that you try to make arrangements for your local stations, either TV or radio, to carry your programs on a specific set time each week. People will become accustomed to the time, know the time and can turn on their sets at that particular time if they are interested in hearing you each week. That way you usually get the best reception.

If you send out one- or two-minute tapes, either radio or TV, you have a chance of having them put right into a news broadcast they might have on that day, and be picked up as current news, which of course gives you wide coverage.

Although production requirements delay television reports somewhat, a film may sometimes be produced on the day of an event and transmitted to local stations in time for evening news broadcasts. Delivery of a filmstrip may be speeded by sending the negative, rather than having the film fully processed. Technical details of this method of meeting airline shipping schedules, as well as other aspects of television and radio reporting, are available in the House Television and Recording Studios.

Publication by mail

Competition for the attention of the Washington press corps is intense—and distasteful to some. Moreover, items about "those fellows back in Washington" must compete with local news for space and time in newspapers and broadcasts in the district. To supplement information available to their constituents through commercial outlets, most members rely heavily on direct mail and the use of the frank to distribute, in quantity, various publications and government documents.

CONGRESSIONAL NEWSLETTERS

Because they have encountered difficulties in gaining access to the news media, many members have gone into the publishing business themselves, informing their constituents of their activities through a "Letter from Washington" or "Congressional Newsletter." The use of this technique has increased steadily in the past several years:

I think when I first came down in 1950 it was the exceptional Congressman who wrote a newsletter. I would say today that it is pretty much the exceptional Congressman who doesn't write a newsletter. Somehow or other we have found, I guess by experience, that we don't really get through to our people through the media. And each one in our own way is coming around to the point that we have to develop other techniques to get through to them.

Not all members agree, however, that publication of a newsletter is a good idea or a technique to be adopted without consideration of the production problems involved. One experienced Congressman points out that, while a newsletter is easy to start, continuing publication may be a different matter:

I am an old newspaperman from way back, but I never have written a newsletter because I know what a problem it is to keep something going after you have one time started it. Now with some members it has worked beautifully, and I intend to start a newsletter maybe this term, I'm not sure just yet. I have done my informing in other ways, and there are plenty [of] other ways whereby you can inform your constituents about what is going on here and that which you want them to know.

Variations in format and content. Newsletters come in many different shapes and sizes. Some are handsomely printed and include a picture of the Congressman; others are everyday mimeographed sheets. Some contain in-depth treatment of a single topic; others are composed of several items, giving the Congressman an opportunity to set forth his position on various issues, to explain how certain events or legislation will affect the people of the district, and to comment on significant developments in related areas of government and foreign affairs. Some members give their newsletters a lighter, more personal touch, adding chatty comments about visitors to their office and the doings of their children and grandchildren. This approach is described by one experienced member:

. . . I do believe that it helped me more in vote-getting than any single thing I did that I kept them advised. They don't ask for weighty information. They don't ask that you agree with them, I may say. What they do want is to know that you care enough about them to write home and that makes the big hit, that you are still aware of the fact that they sent you here. . . . Try it out if you like the idea and you will be surprised how many people have read [the newsletter]. . . . Include in it some little homely news, at the bottom maybe a list of the visitors who came in. Keep a visitors' guest book. People are honored to be asked to sign it. Keep the guest book and then write in that newsletter that "Mr. and Mrs. So-and-So came in this week to see me. They were on their way through to Florida . . . and I was so happy to see them," and mention all these people. They love to see their names in print even if your newsletter has a small circulation.

Some newsletters are published on a weekly or biweekly basis, while others appear only once a month or at irregular intervals. Some go to only a few hundred people, but most are distributed far more widely. As a general rule, most newsletters are sent to all news media in the district; and some newspapers, especially weeklies, reserve a regular space for those which appear regularly. Most members also send their newsletters to party officials throughout the district.

Newsletters may be mailed under the franking privilege as long as they adhere to the franking regulations. Even so, however, a newsletter can become an expensive item, especially if it is published on a weekly or biweekly basis and distributed to a large mailing list. (See Appendix, page 309, for circulation ranges and other statistics on newsletter preparation and mailing.)

USE OF QUESTIONNAIRES

Although little agreement exists as to their merits, apparently the trend is toward more general use of questionnaires. Some Congressmen feel that questionnaires stimulate constituent mail unnecessarily and overburden the staff with requests for assistance of one kind or another. Others feel that they may possibly become committed, against their better judgment, to supporting a legislative proposal *only* because of the published results of a questionnaire. Those who use them, however, are willing to take on any extra work involved, arguing that questionnaires provide a valuable check on constituent attitudes and create good will by giving those who respond a sense of participation in the operation of the national government.

Distribution and design. Questionnaires can be sent either to everyone in the district, using simplified address forms, or to all registered voters. If a list of voters is not available, a fairly representative sample can be obtained by taking names at random from telephone books—for example, every fifth or every tenth name.

Some newspapers, especially weeklies, will publish a blank questionnaire so that readers may clip it out and send it in. If this cannot be arranged, a member can announce in the press that he is conducting a poll and that he will send a questionnaire to any constituent who requests one.

To make the results more meaningful, besides questions relating to issues, respondents may be asked to indicate their political affiliation, the area in which they reside, and perhaps their occupation. Some members make a practice of sending a tabulation of the results to everyone who was sent a questionnaire, whether or not they answered it. This procedure is rather costly, and the more general practice is to send results only to those who request them and to all newspapers and radio and television stations. Some Congressmen also insert the results in the *Congressional Record* and then have reprints made for mailing purposes. (For statistics on distribution, constituent response, and other details of questionnaire preparation and tabulation, see Appendix, page 310.)

THE CONGRESSIONAL RECORD

Reprints of speeches and other materials from the *Record* are the bread-and-butter items of congressional mailing practice. They are relatively inexpensive and can be produced quickly in response to requests from constituents for detailed information. Depending on the subject matter, reprints may be sent either to selected constituents—if the member's mailing list is divided into categories—or to everyone on the list. In addition, when members testify on behalf of a bill they are sponsoring, they often send constituents copies of the committee hearing transcript containing their remarks.

The Congressional Record Clerk, whose office is on the ground floor of the House Wing of the Capitol, takes orders for subscriptions to the *Record* and for reprints of members' speeches. Additional copies of the *Record,* including back issues, may be purchased at this office. A limited number of extra copies sometimes may be obtained free of charge from the House Document Room. The subscription price of the *Record*—which had been $1.50 per month since 1883—was increased in 1970 to $3.75. The price of individual copies was set at 25¢.

Members' record allotment. A member of the House is entitled to seventy-one subscriptions to the *Congressional Record*. Three subscriptions are for his personal use; one is delivered to him at his office, one at home, and the third is made available to him on the House floor. The remaining sixty-eight subscriptions are credited to the member and will be sent to persons he designates. A list of those who are to receive the *Record* must be prepared for the Congressional Record Clerk, and if a member wishes to receive more than one copy in his office each day, he must place his own name on the list. Some keep copies on hand in their offices in order that they may respond quickly to individual requests for particular issues.

Any portion of the allotment that is not used each day is lost to the member unless he has put his own name on the mailing list to receive the unused balance. Failure to supply a complete list of names at the beginning of the session does not, however, mean the member loses the unused portion of his quota permanently; the unused portion is lost on a day-to-day basis, and *Record* mailing lists may be changed at any time.

Bound copies. Members also receive one subscription to the *Record* bound in temporary form—the "Greenbound Record"— and one bound in permanent form. Twice each month members receive the Greenbound Record, which comprises copies of the daily *Record* stitched together, with an index added, and bound in a green paper cover. The permanent set, printed on book paper and bound in a permanent cloth binding, is deposited to the member's credit in the Folding Room some months after the close of each session.

Ordering reprints. A member may have reprints made of his

own speeches and statements appearing in the *Record*, but only at his personal expense. This may not be charged against his stationery account. Charges for this service—payable to the Public Printer—are relatively low, making it attractive to most members. Referring to the cost of various kinds of reprints, an experienced member says:

> You will find that printing through the means of reprints of remarks in the *Congressional Record* is about as inexpensive a printing job as you can have done.

Written permission is required if a member wishes to reprint a speech or excerpt from another's statement. This authorization from the member whose remarks are being quoted must be included in the order submitted to the Congressional Record Clerk. Anything a member himself has inserted in the *Record* may be reprinted, for distribution to constituents and other interested persons, without additional authorization. Such reprints may be produced in a number of ways—on *Record*-sized paper, or as a 5" × 9" booklet, for example. The phrase, "Not Printed at Government Expense," appears on all reprints, and prices vary depending upon the style and form. If reprints are not ordered within thirty days after the speech or statement appears, an additional charge is made. Orders must be at least one thousand copies, and the bill for reprints is due within thirty days after the order is placed. If payment is made by check drawn by someone other than a Congressman, the check must be endorsed by the member placing the order.

DOCUMENTS AND REPORTS

Each session public documents on a variety of subjects are printed by Congress and made available to members for distribution to constituents. The member, his wife, and one staff employee who is listed in the *Directory* receive free copies of the *Congressional Directory,* with their names engraved on the cover. In addition, each member receives eight indexed copies for staff use, plus twenty-five plain copies for constituent or other use.

Bills and public laws. Copies of pending bills and public laws may be obtained from the House Document Room for use in answering constituent inquiries. Similarly, transcripts of committee hearings may be obtained from the respective committees; committee reports on legislative proposals are available from the House Document Room. Although only a limited number of committee hearing transcripts is available for distribution, both these and the committee reports are useful as sources of detailed information for constituents whose questions would otherwise have to be answered with a lengthy and complex statement. Some members find committee reports particularly useful when they include minority as well as majority views:

I do want to emphasize the importance of committee reports. A good committee report, in my judgment, will usually contain the majority views and minority views . . . usually most of the issues that people write about are in dispute in some manner . . . if a committee report does contain the majority views and minority views, you will then have one of the best documents you can send to your constituency to let them know what the real issues are, not what might have been printed in the newspapers or elsewhere or what your opponent has stated the issues to be. This will be the considered view of the members of the committee, the majority and the minority on those particular issues.

Supreme Court opinions. The office of the Clerk of the Supreme Court routinely distributes single copies of court opinions to each Congressman. The Clerk also will make available one or two additional copies for mailing to constituents. If copies of opinions are required in quantity, however, they must be ordered directly from the Superintendent of the Government Printing Office, and the cost will be charged to the member's GPO account.

Government publications. As was indicated in Chapter Two, selected government publications are made available to Congressmen in quantity. Often one congressional staff employee, either in the Washington or in the district office, is given the task of clipping wedding and birth announcements from local papers. The appropriate publications—packets for brides, or *Infant Care*, as the case may be—are then sent to the couple.

The Department of Agriculture publishes a wide variety of materials of interest to both farm- and city-dwellers. The department prepares separate lists of bulletins for members who represent rural districts and those who represent urban areas. Members may obtain copies of the bulletin lists in quantity and allow constituents to make their own selection of publications. It may be necessary, however, to limit the number of bulletins a constituent may receive. The department will mail its publications directly, at the Congressman's request; or, if he prefers, they will be sent to his office first so that he may stamp his name on them.

Additional instructions on obtaining government publications of various kinds are contained in departmental listings, such as the Department of Agriculture's *Congressional Guide to Information Services,* and from the Legislative Reference Service of the Library of Congress. The latter, beginning in 1967, began maintaining a current listing entitled *Where To Get Publications from Executive Agencies,* which contains detailed instructions for acquiring publications of most federal departments and agencies.

Depository libraries. At least two libraries in each congressional district may be designated as depositories for government documents. These libraries are selected by the member who represents the district. If the depositories have already been designated by a former member, they may not be moved unless the library ceases to exist or voluntarily requests that its role as a depository be discontinued.

In addition to the district depositories chosen by Congressmen, each U.S. Senator may designate two, and all land-grant colleges and state libraries are automatically designated as depositories. The librarian at each depository library may choose either to receive all journals, books, and public documents issued by the

Government Printing Office, or he may select items from a list furnished by the GPO. Members may request a list of depository libraries in their state from the Public Printer, and constituents requesting public documents and other government publications can then be referred to the depository library nearest them.

U.S. Capitol flags. Schools and other groups frequently ask for an American flag that has flown over the Capitol, and a procedure has been established to fulfill such requests. The flag itself may be purchased from the House Stationery Room. It is then sent to the Architect of the Capitol with a letter requesting that the flag be flown over the Capitol. Then the flag is returned with a letter, addressed to the member, certifying that it has been flown over the Capitol for the group or individual specified in the request.

BUILDING MAILING LISTS

A substantial mailing list is considered to be a valuable asset, and many types of lists are used in congressional offices. Some are broken down into categories, for selective mailings. Others are on a single set of plates or cards, so that a mailing reaches all of the individuals or groups on the list. One experienced member attributes his ability to survive politically in part to the use of a list including a broad cross section of his constituents:

> It is . . . my personal reaction that one of the things that helped me most often to get re-elected in a Democratic district as a Republican was the fact that I sent so large a newsletter list out and carefully selected it so as to spray it across the district (and some of them were shotgun; in other words some of them went to every fifth family), there being no better way to reach certain areas, and some went to people who had written me and some went to all those lists, those mailing lists you collect every time you appear on a banquet program. You get the Lions and the Kiwanis and the Rotary, and you get the Grange and the Farm Bureau and the rest of it.

Using a single list can be costly, however, and some members prefer to maintain several lists, each of which includes those individuals and groups likely to be most concerned with a particular subject or category of issues. For example, separate lists may be kept for labor union members, businessmen, party officials, contributors, precinct workers, urban and rural residents, and personal friends.

Sources of names. Telephone directories are especially valuable for mailings to selected areas, such as certain towns or counties. And most cities have special directories that list telephone subscribers by street address rather than by name, making it possible to prepare mailing lists by wards and precincts, or by neighborhood characteristics. Other name sources include voter registration lists, property tax rolls, automobile registration records, business and city directories, and membership rosters of local clubs, business groups, and labor unions. Once started, a mailing list grows as people on the list suggest other names and as constituents ask to be placed on the list. Congressmen themselves can augment the list with the names of people in the news, especially leaders of various groups, as an experienced member indicates:

> . . . a mailing list more or less grows. When you come to Congress you may have a very restricted list; whatever list you might have had during your campaign may be confined to those who were helpful and maybe were precinct captains or something of that kind. After you begin to send out a newsletter you will have requests from others who want to be put on the list or letters from those that are on the list giving you the name of somebody else they feel should be on the list. I have also followed the practice of, if I notice that somebody is elected president of some specific group in my district, I automatically put him on the list. If I notice that somebody is appointed legislative chairman of some organization in my district, I automatically put that person on the list. I put the principals of all schools on the list because I figure that there might be classes within that school that would be interested and therefore if I put the principal on the list . . . he can make the news-

letter available to whatever class might be interested in the newsletter. And therefore it gradually grows year by year because of this process.

Because putting all constituents on mailing lists would be virtually impossible, as well as prohibitively expensive, Congressmen often concentrate their efforts on the kinds of people who, they feel, can mold opinion in a community—businessmen, union leaders, the clergy, educators, and newsmen and other news media representatives, for example. Many members list such places as doctors' offices, barber shops, and beauty parlors. In addition, it is customary to set up a special press release mailing list containing the addresses of all news outlets in the district.

Keeping lists current. To reduce waste and ensure maximum effectiveness, mailing lists must be kept up to date. Local post offices are authorized to correct mailing lists used by members of Congress free of charge and as frequently as requested. (Details of U.S. Post Office Department regulations pertaining to this service appear in the Appendix, page 336.) Because this requires either preparation of a duplicate set of mailing-list cards or doing without the lists while they are being corrected, many members prefer to correct their lists themselves, a task that may be accomplished easily on a periodic or continuing basis. For example, after each mailing the post office returns a number of letters that could not be delivered. Usually, only a few minutes of staff time are needed to correct the addresses or remove these names from the list.

USE OF THE FRANK

The franking privilege, under which Congressmen are entitled to mail official correspondence free, is governed by laws administered by the Post Office Department—which defines the term "official" quite broadly.* As a department spokesman advised congressional newcomers in 1963:

---

* The Postal Reorganization Act of 1970 (Public Law 91–375) leaves existing law on use of the franking privilege unchanged.

Inasmuch as Congress has in no way attempted to define official business, the Post Office Department construes the term in its broadest and most liberal sense, with all doubts being resolved in the favor of the Congressman. The standard applied by the department is that frankable material must involve matters or issues which may reasonably be construed as arising from the member's work in Congress. Official correspondence has been defined by the department as that in which the member deals with the addressee as a citizen of the United States or as a constituent, as opposed to the relationship of a personal friend or the relationship of candidates or prospective candidates in voting.

Thus, for example, under this concept a member's newsletter—in which he discusses his position on foreign policy—even though it is opposed to that of the particular administration in office, regardless of his political affiliation, is frankable. The fact that no legislation upon the subject has been introduced is immaterial so far as frankability is concerned. On the other hand, a member's discussion in his newsletter of matters or issues of purely local concern or interest to his state or congressional district, such as his attendance at a local Boy Scout camp exercise, is held to be nonfrankable material.

As has been noted, official correspondence may—and frequently does—take the form of printed or mimeographed newsletters or special reports to constituents. The standard used in defining official business is that it must involve matters or issues which may be reasonably construed as either arising from or dealing with a member's work in Congress. Members who have any doubt about the frankability of a proposed mailing piece may submit it to the Post Office Department's general counsel for an advance *advisory* ruling before having it duplicated.

In addition to official correspondence, the franking privilege may be used to mail the *Congressional Record,* public documents printed by order of Congress, and seeds and agricultural reports from the Department of Agriculture. Reprints or copies of speeches published in the *Congressional Record* may be mailed under frank regardless of subject matter. The public-documents provision includes bills, committee hearing transcripts, and committee reports.

Errors and violations. Inclusion of nonfrankable material, such as personal comments or a political appeal, in official correspondence at one time subjected it to postage, even though the majority of the communication dealt with official business. Some of the problems involved in interpreting and applying these regulations were pointed out in the 1963 Seminar for Freshman Congressmen:

Q. You mentioned where you had a picture and material that was going out in a newsletter, some question as to citing the local interest of the Boy Scout picnic in the newsletter would be out. Could you include the Boy Scout picture along with a number of other items that are currently before the Congress? Are you saying it is nonfrankable?
A. That has been the ruling of the department.
Q. This is really standard procedure?
A. Yes, if it's brought to our attention. Of course, the postal department has very little means of policing of congressional mail. However, that is the position of the department.
Q. How about—he raised something really interesting here—if I make a speech out in [the district] telling the voters what a great job I've done and how I deserve to be re-elected? I get [a colleague in the House] to put this in the *Congressional Record* with a tribute to me as one of the leading statesmen in this or perhaps any other nation. This is a blatant plea for votes, but it's in the *Congressional Record*, so I can frank it all over the state. My colleagues would not recommend that procedure, I am sure, [but could I do it?] I raise this hypothetically.
A. Right. If it is in the *Congressional Record* it makes no matter what the subject matter. That is one thing that's done quite frequently.

Prior to the 91st Congress, when a possible violation of the franking laws was reported, the Post Office Department investigated and, if the charges were substantiated, could seek reimbursement for the postage involved from the member responsible. However, on December 27, 1968, the department's General Counsel announced that, although his office would continue to give *advisory* opinions as to frankability, the department would no longer be responsible for "determining" the use of the franking privilege. Said the Counsel in a department press release:

The use of the franking privilege for correspondence on official business is a matter strictly between the member of Congress and his conscience.

In each of these cases there is no way—and should be no way—in which the Post Office can assess a payment. Congress has not ordered the department to police the behavior of the members in the use of franking privilege, nor is there any regulation under which the Post Office Department can collect payment if such abuse occurs.

Therefore, it is obvious that Congress never intended that the Post Office should be a collection agency regulating the Congress.

Further, we receive full payment through Congressional appropriations for franking mailing.

Under these circumstances, we therefore feel that we can provide advisory guidelines to the officials possessing a franking privilege, but that they themselves should have the responsibility for policing themselves.

Of course, other interested citizens not connected with the Post Office may remain quite willing to help the member "police" himself. And should the member find his conscience an inadequate guide—at least in the sense that his use of the frank for a mailing has been skillfully misrepresented by an unscrupulous potential opponent—he may wish to avoid harassment by acting promptly along lines indicated in this comment by a department spokesman during the 1963 Seminar:

Q. What if you made a mistake and sent out something that should not be under the frank. Can we come down to the Post Office [Department] and buy postage for it and get a statement?

A. The best thing to do in a case like that would be to either come down or call us—put the situation to us or make a clear estimation of what happened—and buy the postage stamps. . . . Then we will be able to say that it had already been taken care of to any one [who complains].

Limitation on use. The franking privilege covers only ordinary surface mail. Airmail postage, registration, and special delivery fee must be paid by stamps or the equivalent. Some members find that the cost of extra postage mounts up rapidly. This is particularly true for those whose districts are relatively far away from Washington. As one member from the west coast put it:

> I come from California. A great many of my constituents write me by airmail. I attempt to extend the same courtesy in matters of urgent concern to them. I respond by air, and I probably use more of that in correspondence than I do the frank itself.

The franking privilege is for use of the members of Congress only. It may not be loaned to other persons or organizations, or be used for the benefit of other persons or organizations. Hence franked envelopes may not be supplied to nonofficial organizations so that they may mail *Congressional Record* excerpts or similar items for their own purposes. Likewise, franked envelopes may not be sent to constituents, or other persons with whom a member is corresponding, for the purpose of replying to the Congressman. A Congressman may, however, supply his district office with franked envelopes for use by his employees there. (A summary of laws on the franking privilege and regulations pertaining to the handling of franked mail—weight restrictions, simplified addresses, preparation requirements, and the like—appears in the Appendix, pages 331–337.)

★ 5 ★

Information for the lawmaker

DURING THE 89TH Congress, the chairman of a House committee had occasion to request a specific item of information from an Executive department. Attached to the reply he received was a memorandum from one departmental employee to another. Said the memo—which the Congressman obviously was not supposed to see—"You'll note we have purposely not answered the question except in a very indirect way."

This inadvertent admission says a great deal about the information-gathering problems of the individual Congressman. In order to make decisions on increasingly complex and constantly changing issues, to respond to a mélange of requests from constituents, to keep abreast of the activities of the Congress itself—all require constant acquiring and sifting of information. And while many are eager to *supply* the Congressman with information, not all are willing or able to *answer* questions promptly, fully, and in a form ready for his use.

Congress has its own research and investigatory agencies, including the Legislative Reference Service of the Library of Congress and the General Accounting Office. Both provide information and conduct studies at the request of individual members.* In addition, committee staff employees generally are highly competent and responsive to requests for assistance. But in addition to using these resources, most members find they must rely heavily on their own reading and staff research, on conversations with their colleagues, and on such sources of information outside Congress as staff specialists of the Executive branch, lobbyists, and consultants from the academic community.

Congressional research

General legislative research is largely an individual effort, conducted by the Congressman and his staff. Most also call on committee staff employees for assistance, especially on work done in preparation for committee meetings and hearings. And, in connection with floor debate and voting, members look to specialists among their colleagues and their party leadership for information and advice on legislation with which they are unfamiliar.

In handling constituent requests for information, aside from those concerning legislation or current issues, most Congressmen use the Legislative Reference Service and various Executive departments and agencies.

In a typical week, the average Congressman devotes about seven hours to legislative research and reading. Most pay close attention to the *Congressional Record,* published daily when either

* Since 1965 numerous proposals have been made for broadening and strengthening the research functions and capabilities of both the Legislative Reference Service and the General Accounting Office. The Legislative Reorganization Act of 1970 redesignates LRS as the Congressional Research Service, gives it new and expanded duties—particularly in the area of policy and program review—and makes it somewhat more independent of the Library of Congress. See Appendix, pages 401–418 for a summary of H.R. 17654, the Legislative Reorganization Act of 1970.

or both Houses are in session, not only as a means of keeping up with congressional activity but also as a source of ideas for legislation and for other information as well. Many other publications of Congress are generally regarded as valuable sources of information. Committee calendars, reports, and hearing transcripts are examples. In addition, many members subscribe to specialized commercial publications or reporting services dealing with congressional activities. Best known among these is the weekly *Congressional Quarterly,* which in 1969 reported 272 House subscribers.

CONSULTING COLLEAGUES

In discussing sources of information, experienced Congressmen stress the value of consultation with those colleagues who are recognized as experts in their legislative fields and in their knowledge of House rules and procedures. These are the "old hands" who, "whenever they get up to address the subject before the House, receive the attention of those on the floor," and who "know more about their subject than you would ever guess." Moreover, as one member said in recalling his early career, these senior Congressmen are disposed to help the newcomer:

When I came back here I just threw myself on the mercy of the old hands and said, "Boys, you've got to help me. I am as green as a gourd and if you don't do something to help me out I don't know where I'll land." And [in] every instance those old hands got in and helped every way they could. I wouldn't be backward if I were you either about participating in committee discussion or in urging legislation beneficial to your own area. And I would lay it right on these older members to . . . help me out. And I would say that's true on both sides of the aisle; the older hands try to help the newer members, to help them get a grip on what they are doing, to help them be successful in their legislation.

House floor conferences. The late George B. Galloway has pointed out that Congressmen customarily use the House floor as a clearing house of information on pending legislation and other matters. Talking things over with trusted, expert colleagues, he adds, is regarded as a "valuable shortcut to knowledge." Such conversations are particularly helpful, according to one experienced Congressman, when a member is uncertain about his vote:

> . . . you'll see them [colleagues who are recognized as experts], and go over and ask them, "Why did you do that? That isn't what I'd expect you to do. Why are you doing this?" Or, "Why are you so strongly against it?" Go on over and sit beside them, Republican or Democrat. Say who you are and they will talk to you. I've done that with [a senior colleague of the other party] here. On veterans' affairs I'd go [to] one of the Veterans' Affairs Committee [members] and say, "Now what is it? Why is [a ranking member of my party] so upset about this thing on our side?"

Informal House groups. Numerous informal congressional groups help to indoctrinate newcomers, provide a social outlet, give members an opportunity to exchange ideas, serve as a rallying point for those with interests in common, or otherwise function as sources of information. In both parties members elected in the same year maintain loose organizations (class groups); and groups of staff employees meet periodically for discussions with ranking Executive branch officials or with experts in various fields. Included are such party-based groups as the Burros and the Bull Elephants, and such bipartisan organizations as the Congressional Secretaries Club.

Largest and most active among the informal organizations of members is the Democratic Study Group, which is composed of younger, more liberal Democrats. This group elects a slate of officers and employs a full-time staff. The DSG prepares position papers and conducts briefing sessions in advance of action on major legislation, gives advice (as well as more substantial assistance) on campaigning, and occasionally operates a whip system to get like-minded members to the floor for an important vote.

Smaller, less well-organized study or social groups operate

among Republicans in the House. Examples are the Chowder and Marching Society, the SOS Club, and the Wednesday Group.* A member describes his participation in such a group:

. . . a number of us have set up thoroughly informal associations, which meet at least twice a week. In the case of the group to which I belong, we meet Tuesday afternoon to discuss what has been going on in the various committees of which we are members. We talk about what action or position we are going to take on legislation which is coming up in the next week or two, and to discuss other matters of public interest that we have in common with one another. As another example of what that kind of group does, this morning we had Admiral Rickover to breakfast. Breakfast seems to be an easier time than evening for a group of people to get together. We meet at 8:00 and we get through about 9:15 or 9:30. It may be Secretary McElroy, it may be Mr. Dulles of C.I.A. or Mr. Dulles of the State Department, or any of a number of others. We may also get together as Republicans to talk about what we can do to strengthen the party. More often, though, we make an effort to know more about the other man's problems. The basic question is how we can get a greater perspective than we do.

READING THE RECORD

For most Congressmen, paging through the *Congressional Record* is one of the first tasks of the working day. Each issue is composed of four sections: the House and Senate sections, referred to as the "body" or "record" proper, contain a substantially verbatim account of debate; the Extensions of Remarks (customarily called "the Appendix," as it was formally designated until the 90th Congress) contains items inserted by members, such as articles, speeches, and editorials believed to be of general interest or import; and the Daily Digest contains a summary of legislative activity.

* Staff personnel were assigned to the Wednesday Group during the 89th Congress, and the House Republican Conference also maintains a research staff that works with members in the preparation of Task Force reports on policy issues.

Although reading the entire *Record* each day may be too time-consuming, experienced members maintain that there is no effective substitute for personal perusal and selective reading as a means of keeping up with congressional activity. To save time, some senior members assign a staff employee to go through the *Record,* marking or clipping sections for their attention. But they advise congressional newcomers not to do this:

> Your first term, or at least this first year, you read it and read every issue and read it all the way through. And back where the bill section is, read the descriptions of all the bills and if one looks like it is interesting to you get a copy of it and read it. You might follow from that into an idea of your own and introduce some original legislation or you might want to cosponsor that particular bill. So, above all, read the *Congressional Record.*

Eventually, as work loads increase, members find detailed daily reading of the bulky *Record* impossible. Accordingly, some develop short-cuts or skimming techniques:

> . . . let's take an example, the debate in the Senate on their rules change. Now, unless you are interested in this, or think you might want to run for the Senate, that sort of thing could be skipped. You will get into, oh, we will have within a month or so a big housing bill. There will be extended debate both in the House and Senate on it. If you are keenly interested in this, I would suggest you read the whole thing. If you really want to understand all about it.

> But you are going to have to do some skimming. For instance, you will find that if some Senator has come up with a new bill—Senators ———— and ————, for instance, will introduce a labor reform bill within a few days. They will put a speech, each of them, the same day in the *Record* where they explain the bill, its purposes, what they have in mind, how it differs from the one last Congress and so on. If you read that (I believe that's the type of thing that is very vital) you will understand a lot about that issue immediately. Other than a lot of the debate which may cover subjects you are not interested in, I am suggesting

that you read the speeches. This is both in terms of understanding legislation and understanding the institution. You will understand what
Senators and what Congressmen are spokesmen on particular issues, and
what their point of view is.

In the Appendix, do skimming. But you will run onto things
there that are excellent. It may be editorials from somebody's home-
town paper. It may be a scholarly article. It may illuminate a whole
field that you don't know anything about.

So I am not saying read every word. You can't. But don't just skim
lightly through it and don't give your office people the job of doing
that. I would suggest that you check the bills; there are a lot of them
in these first issues. I took a *Congressional Record* home last night
and read the descriptions of each of the bills. This is the way that you
will get onto legislation that you want to introduce yourself.

Daily Digest section. Careful reading of the *Record's* Daily
Digest section is considered essential on Capitol Hill. Occupying
the last several pages, this section includes a summary of all action, in both House and Senate, for the previous day. Each item
lists the pages on which a full account of the action may be found;
thus, the Digest serves as a table of contents for each day's
Record. It summarizes committee activity for the previous day and
provides schedules of committee meetings for the day the *Record* is
published. It lists all bills introduced on the previous day. Referring
to the problem of keeping up with committee activities in both
House and Senate, a member describes how he uses this section to
alert himself to matters in which he is interested:

I try to look at the *Record* every day but I can't do it. . . . If I can't
do it every day I do get the summary that is in the *Record* every day in
the back and I read what happened in the House, what happened in
the Senate, and what is scheduled in each of these committees and what
they did. If you do that and then when something attracts your interest
you can follow up (and I would think that unless you would have a
legislative aide who did nothing but run the trap lines, so to speak,
on these committees, that is the fastest way you can do it). And for

your own satisfaction it doesn't take very long. Very often when you go
to sit on the floor [for] a roll call, while they are getting to your name,
you [can] pick up that Record and run through it. Your day gets divided awful thin but it will keep you abreast as well as anything. Then
when something alerts you, you can hop over there and find out what
they are up to.

FOLLOWING COMMITTEE ACTIVITY

Some Congressmen make it a practice to attend meetings personally
when committees other than their own are considering matters of
interest to them, even though they do not plan to testify. As the
following exchange between a senior member and a newcomer indicates, this method of getting information about legislative issues
may, however, be overly time-consuming:

Q. Do you attend those committee meetings though you are not on
the committee itself?
A. Well, if hearings are open there is no reason [not to attend]. If they
are in executive session it's confined to members of the committee.
That's a good way of acquainting yourself with a major problem if you
have nothing better to do with your time, but you will find that time
usually comes pretty fully occupied.

Instead of attending the sessions, members more frequently
rely on committee reports and transcripts of hearings, available in
printed form. Reports, which are obtained from the House Document Room, contain a concise summary of the legislative proposal
involved as well as arguments pro and con. Hearing transcripts,
which may be obtained only from the committee, contain testimony
of other Congressmen, experts from the universities or the scientific
community, and witnesses whose organizations the legislation could
affect, and provide detail on the probable consequences of proposed legislation.

Committee calendars. Most committees maintain and publish
a calendar of all bills referred to them. These are published, or

"printed," as needed, generally every few weeks, but an up-to-date calendar is maintained in the committee office. (During 1969, seventeen of the twenty-one House standing committees were publishing calendars; included among exceptions to this practice were the Committees on Rules and on Appropriations.) In addition to the current status of House and Senate bills, committee calendars list special reports, documents, hearings that have been held, and Presidential messages and Executive communications related to the committee's operations. At the close of each session of Congress, the committees print their "final" calendars, each of which includes an index. The final calendars for previous sessions are a convenient source of information on the disposition and legislative history of various measures.*

Committee staff personnel. Staffs of House committees and subcommittees vary greatly in size, organization, expertness, and partisanship. Members, of course, generally work most closely with the staffs of the committees on which they serve, relying on them for information and assistance in their fields of activity. Experienced members indicate that it also is desirable to become acquainted with professional staff employees of other committees:

. . . the committee staff people are not only there to serve [members of] the committees. They are to serve all members of Congress and you have some of the most knowledgeable people on the Hill at the committee staff level. Use them. They will help you oftentimes in drafting legislation. They will let you know at any time what is going on in the committee, what they expect will happen with regard to particular legislation. They are servants of the whole Congress as well as of the committee.

---

* For a detailed description of the contents of calendars, which vary widely from committee to committee, see Walter Kravitz' *The Legislative Calendars of Committees in the House of Representatives as of 1968: A Comparative Analysis* (Legislative Reference Service multilith report, November 7, 1968).

USE OF THE LIBRARY OF CONGRESS

The Library of Congress has more than fifty-nine million items in its collections and employs a staff of about 3,700 in its six departments, one of which—the Legislative Reference Service—is the major information and research arm of the Congress. The other five departments are used by members, but the bulk of congressional work is done by LRS, which handles more than 150,000 inquiries annually.

Legislative Reference Service. LRS has *research* divisions specializing in American law, education and public welfare, economics, environmental policy, foreign affairs, government, and science policy. (Planning for establishment of research divisions in national security-defense policy and urban affairs was under way in 1970.) A section of senior specialists includes experts in a variety of fields, and these, along with specialists in the research divisions, conduct studies on request and are available for consultation in members' offices, at the library, or by telephone.

LRS also has a congressional reference division, staffed largely with librarians trained to handle a large volume of information requests promptly. Through a "hot line" facility, this division provides quick telephone response to requests for isolated facts, such as the date of an event or the source of a quotation. Moreover, the reference division identifies materials required to deal adequately with questions generated by constituents and responds to the bulk of these requests received by the Service.

In addition to research and reference, LRS furnishes a number of research-related services, including publication of the *Digest of Public General Bills and Resolutions* and *The Legislative Status Report,* preparation of charts and graphs, and translations of foreign-language materials for members and committees. In recent years LRS also has maintained a small staff of systems analysts to assist in the application of modern data-processing technology to the legislative workload.

Requests for LRS assistance may be made by telephone, by letter, or personally. In the case of complicated inquiries, it is customary to make a written request or to relate the general nature of the inquiry by telephone and ask to be called back by the appropriate division chief or specialist. Experienced members suggest that extensive or complex research projects be discussed directly with the LRS researcher who will be doing the work.

LRS also asks users to indicate how soon they require the information requested and—to ensure that the report is suited to its intended purpose—how the information is to be used. All work is done on a confidential basis; LRS researchers do not "kiss and tell," and users can be certain that the nature of their requests or even the fact that they have asked for a given item will not be made known to any other member.

The Service makes every effort to meet deadlines imposed by the congressional schedule. "Rush" requests are sent electronically to the various research divisions and ordinarily are filled before the end of the day on which they are received. On occasion, however, because of the heavy volume of demand or the complexity of the work involved, the researcher must negotiate the deadline with the congressional office, perhaps sending along a partial report initially with the completed study following later.

The research product is reviewed carefully to ensure that it does not reflect partisan, institutional, or professional bias. Exceptions are made to a policy of "objective and nonpartisan" analysis where material is to be used in preparing factual arguments for or against a bill or in drafting a speech to reflect the views of an individual member. (See Appendix, page 340, for specific research and information services performed by LRS.) Describing this policy, a LRS official advised House newcomers in 1963:

. . . the one thing I do want to emphasize is that all of the questions will be answered in an objective and nonpartisan manner. I think we would lose our usefulness to you if we ever took sides. Objectivity is a rigid policy requirement. There are two exceptions. The first is when you ask us to prepare, as you can, a brief in support of or against some bill in which you are interested. In that event, we will gather together all of the logical, factual arguments in favor of or against the bill, not the partisan arguments. A second exception is when you ask us to draft a speech or a statement for you. This is another service which we will perform. There we will attempt to tailor your speech to your own views.

Constituent requests. In recent years Congressmen have become a favorite target of students and others who seek assistance in the preparation of term papers and the like. Some members turn aside requests for this kind of assistance with a tart reminder that research is the function of the individual student, not of the Congressman, who has other duties to perform. One member, Representative Charles E. Bennett of Florida, requires students to secure the approval of their principal or teacher before he will provide such assistance. In a form letter, he writes:

Dear Student Friend,

Thank you for your request for information. The Library of Congress is the only source of information I have for such material, as I do not have this knowledge, or possess it in my office.

The Library officials have told me they are not heavily enough staffed to handle inquiries like this any longer and they therefore require a letter or an endorsement by your principal to make this material available. So, I am returning your letter to have it endorsed by your principal to allow me to present it to the Library of Congress for the information you seek.

With kind regards, I am

Sincerely,

Endorsements, he reports, have been few and far between.

Some members argue that LRS should not handle any information requests originated by constituents, suggesting that the time spent by the service on this work might be better used for studies more directly related to legislative matters.* But others point out that many constituents—including, of course, state and local officials and civic leaders—have a legitimate need for information relating to governmental matters. Moreover, questions tend to recur in the general run of constituent information requests, and these can be handled more efficiently in LRS' congressional reference division than by the individual members' staff. Many individual requests are triggered by various national debates and scholarship competitions, for example, and these can be answered with multiple copies of a single report. And, as one member suggests, these requests usually pertain to areas in which LRS already has done the necessary research:

I would like to say that one particular thing that you will find you get frequently will be letters from chairmen of legislative committees for various organizations in your district. They are frequently desirous of getting the arguments for and against some particular subject. This is a service where the library provides great assistance. All of us have college students who are preparing term papers on various subjects and desire assistance for and against aid to Latin America or something like that. They think the Congressman should write their term papers for them, apparently, from the number of questions they ask. Once again the Library of Congress many times has been able to bail members of Congress out of a very difficult set of requests, because the library does have material available for and against the various topics that might be listed on these queries. This will make it possible for you to give constituents a reply without burdening your own office staff with subjects that they really don't have background on just off-hand, whereas

* However, in a survey of Congressional offices conducted by LRS in 1969, "provision of materials to assist you in responding to general questions originated by your constituents" received the highest "useful" rating (89.8%) among all research and information services listed. Constituent originated requests loom large as a statistic in LRS' annual reports (about forty percent of the total in recent years). But processing these probably accounts for less than ten per cent of the funds available to the service each year. LRS had an authorized staff of 323 in fiscal 1970.

the library has already done the research on it and the information is available.

In short, whereas the service is not equipped to undertake extensive research for constituents, it attempts to assist congressional offices in answering constituent mail by supplying readily available information or by furnishing references to sources from which relevant information may be obtained. All such information is sent to the congressional office requesting it; LRS does not communicate with constituents unless specifically directed by a member to do so.

Digest of Bills. To help members keep track of the thousands of bills introduced in each session, LRS publishes a *Digest of Public General Bills and Selected Resolutions.* The *Digest* contains a brief summary of the essential features of all public bills and joint resolutions introduced, the name of the member who sponsored the measure, the date of introduction, the committee to which it was sent, and status information. Five to eight consolidated issues of the *Digest* are published each session, and supplements are published every two weeks between the consolidated issues. Each issue has a subject and sponsor index. Copies of the *Digest* are distributed directly to all members by the Government Printing Office; extra copies may be obtained from LRS.

Legislative Status Report. LRS also publishes a monthly *Legislative Status Report* summarizing selected major legislation pending or passed during the current session of Congress. The summaries, arranged according to general subject categories, are succinct, intended only to identify and note the basic content of the bills included. Status information is updated between the monthly *Report* in a "checklist," issued weekly. The *Report* also includes citations to Presidential messages to Congress and to congressional documents, reports, and published hearings. Like the *Bill Digest,* the *Report* and weekly checklists are distributed to all members' offices.

The Green Sheets. LRS produces multilith reports of various kinds on a wide variety of subjects. Some are analytic and relate to current policy issues; others are designed to assist members in responding to questions originated by their constituents. Titles of these reports are listed in *LRS Multilithed Reports,* familiarly known as the "Green Sheet," which is distributed to all congressional offices monthly; users order the reports they wish from the service. To some extent the multilith reports also indicate the nature of research under way in LRS—they are in effect the tip of an information iceberg—and experienced members often use the "Green Sheets" as a guide to experts within the Service whose listed work is of interest and who may be useful in a consultant capacity or as a source of additional information in a given area.

Legislative tracking and information systems. As a by-product of computer applications in support of its own research and reference functions, LRS was developing (in 1970) a number of new information services to be offered directly to congressional users. For example, a legislative tracking system—using the *Bill Digest* and *Status Report* files, both of which are processed by computer—was scheduled to be in operation in its pilot phase during 1970. This system, containing up-to-date status information as well as basic elements of the legislative history of all public bills, will provide for great flexibility in "searching" for the specific information sought by the user. For instance, the system may be asked to display (on a television-like console) or print out digests of all bills introduced by a particular member. Or it may be asked to search the file and report the status of all bills dealing with a given subject, such as "water pollution from industrial wastes." Another LRS system, operating in its pilot phase in 1969, directs citations to selected publications to the researcher working in the field to which they relate. Each individual researcher's "interest profile" is stored in the computer, and he receives a weekly listing of relevant new books and articles. This selective dissemination of information system also was scheduled to be extended to members and congressional committees.

Congressional Reading Rooms. A Congressional Reading Room is maintained in the Library of Congress especially for use by members, their families, and staff employees. Desks may be reserved, and assistance is available to fill emergency requests for information and requests for loan of books or other materials. Members may withdraw books and other materials for their personal and official use, and these borrowing privileges extend to their families. They may also authorize their staff employees to borrow books, which are ordered directly by telephoning the library's Loan Division. The library maintains book rooms in the House office buildings and in the Capitol itself, and all deliveries and collections are carried out through these facilities. Encyclopedias, dictionaries, yearbooks, and other reference materials are provided for congressional office use in each book room.

GENERAL ACCOUNTING OFFICE

Established in 1921 as a nonpartisan agency in the Legislative branch, the General Accounting Office assists Congress in controlling the receipt, disbursement, and application of public funds. In carrying out its functions, GAO makes special audits, surveys, and investigations at the request of congressional committees and individual members.* According to a report prepared in 1962 for the Senate Committee on Government Operations, GAO's Office of Legislative Liaison handles special congressional requests on a "very high priority" basis, and the performance of such work— particularly for committees—is an important part of the work of

* The Comptroller General, in testimony before a Legislative Appropriations Subcommittee, estimated that almost 500 professional GAO staff members would be involved during fiscal 1970 in assignments resulting from specific congressional requests or in work for congressional committees. GAO's total staff in 1969 was 4,544, of which 2,793 were professionals.

the office. "A great number of requests are received from individual members," the report continues, "for information that can be supplied as the result of work already performed or for information relating to specific transactions that can be obtained readily." (See Appendix, page 347, for assistance available from GAO and excerpts from testimony by the Comptroller General relating to the work of GAO.)

HOUSE INFORMATION SERVICES

The House itself operates several specialized information services, including a legislative library and a document room.

House Document Room. Copies of bills, committee reports (but not hearing transcripts), public laws, and all House and Senate documents may be obtained from the House Document Room, in the Capitol. A similar service is maintained for the Senate. Any House or Senate bill or resolution is available in the Document Room the day after its introduction. Requests for bills and other documents usually are made by telephone, unless a large number of different items is required. In this case, a typed list is often sent to the Document Room via "inside" mail. Documents are delivered to member's offices by House pages.

Compilations of laws on nearly forty different subjects are available from the Document Room. As has been noted, printed transcripts of committee hearings are not available through the Document Room but must be obtained from the committee that held the hearing. Nor does the Document Room stock Executive orders and proclamations. These are obtained through the Federal Register or the National Archives.

Legislative Library. The House operates a Legislative Library on the first floor of the Cannon Office Building. This library has a small staff and specializes in conducting quick research on bills, public laws, and Supreme Court reports. The library is not able to conduct detailed studies of legislative proposals. Its collection includes most of the Federal Reporting System: Federal Reporter, first and second series; Federal Supplements; General Digest; Shephards; complete file of U.S. Reports; the Federal Code, completely annotated; most of the statutes; bills introduced; *Congressional Record;* House and Senate *Journals;* House Documents from the First Congress on; and bound hearings from the 62nd Congress on. The library permits withdrawal of most volumes in the collection, with the exception of the bills and those volumes published prior to 1843.

Sources outside Congress

National headquarters of both parties maintain research staffs, and they supply information of one kind or another at the request of individual Congressmen. Also, as Dr. Galloway indicated in comments to congressional newcomers in 1963, private and governmental specialists are available in or near Washington, and most are eager to consult with members of Congress:

In addition to the professional staff people here on the Hill there are subject-matter specialists outside in the city and in the country, who will be happy to assist you and who have long rendered assistance to members and committees of Congress. I have in mind the staff of the Brookings Institution, for example, here in Washington; the National Planning Association, the professional staffs in the Executive agencies of the federal government, and various other private research institutions.

To take a single example, the Chamber of Commerce of the United States maintains a professional staff of some thirty-three subject-matter specialists, in as many different subject-matter fields, who will be happy to help you in the analysis of legislative proposals. . . .

In addition, there are panels of experts who from time to time are retained by particular committees of the Congress to brief them on technical subjects. Thus, for example, the House Committee on Science and Astronautics has had the benefit of a panel on science and technology for the past year or two, which has been highly valued.

THE EXECUTIVE BRANCH

Members of Congress can and do initiate requests for information and other assistance directly with staff specialists and ranking officials in the Executive branch. However, the major departments and agencies maintain special liaison offices, which are equipped and staffed especially to deal with congressional requests. And some senior members recommend the establishment of close working relationships with these offices. The comments of one experienced Congressman, who served in an Executive branch liaison capacity for a period of time, are illustrative:

> . . . every major agency and department has a section of some kind that is set up to deal with the Congress . . . and the guy that is in charge of that is close to the boss; he is close to the Secretary or the head of the agency as the case might be. They are anxious to help. Some of them are more efficient than others, but you will get further in handling your cases downtown if you work through that person, whoever he is, or through his representative on the Hill, whoever that is.
>
> If the head of your office gets to know the legman or whatever you call him for the various Departments . . . so that he drops in when you've got a problem, you will be able to give faster, quicker, and better service. . . . You won't get bogged down in all the red tape in these departments and it is staggering when you first get here. I know the ramifications of some of these major departments. But you get to know the bird that's got the responsibility of dealing with the Congress and he will be anxious—he doesn't want to push himself on you—but he will be anxious to be of service and be of help, and you will find your task much easier in getting . . . the right service, the right information to your constituents. . . .

THE WASHINGTON LOBBY

Because of practices of a bygone era—when the votes of legislators were sometimes traded openly on the floor—the presumption of corruption remains attached to the term "lobbying." All too often, as Representative Thomas B. Curtis of Missouri points out, "those on the outside of the Congress, those who do not understand the important informational function which the lobbyists play in the legislative process, consider lobbying a mean and underhanded process of wining and dining legislators, playing on their personal weaknesses and vices to gain unfair advantage and undermine the national interest."* And the negative impression persists, although flagrant cases today are few and far between.

Professional lobbies now emphasize their service function. Perhaps most importantly, they provide expert witnesses and detailed information on policy questions of interest to the groups they represent. In this as well as in other service capacities, they can be extremely helpful to members of Congress, as a 1950 Report of the House Select Committee on Lobbying Activities suggests:

> The service function in lobbying takes many different forms. When representatives of organized groups appear before committees of Congress, for example, they are not only presenting their own case but they are also providing members of Congress with one of the essential raw materials of legislative action. By the same token, the drafting of bills and amendments to bills, the preparation of speeches and other materials for members, the submission to members of detailed memoranda on bill-handling tactics—all of these are means by which lobby groups service the legislative process and at the same time further their own ends.

In addition to these general services rendered to Congressmen in their official capacities, the Select Committee report adds, lobby groups perform services of a more personal nature. But, once again, these are a far cry from the crude pressure tactics of the past:

> Three generations ago, when standards of congressional morality were less exacting than they are today, the lobbyist could favor the

---

* *Congressional Record,* April 4, 1963, p. A2028.

member in ways which strike the modern mind as crude. The lobbyist
of the 1880's was a bountiful host, a social guide, a financial confidant,
and a freehanded companion at the gaming table. But times change,
and while the theme of personal attentiveness still runs through modern
pressure tactics, the forms which it takes have changed. Formal dinners
for members of Congress and, in addition to these, more casual and inti-
mate gatherings, remain part of the lobby group's stock in trade. But
apart from these vestiges of the old "social lobby," the personal service
aspects of lobbying have been considerably revamped. Today, the re-
sourceful pressure groups may seek to serve themselves as well as
members of Congress by arranging remunerative speaking or writing
engagements for them, or by such friendly acts as helping the new
member to secure housing in Washington.

Because lobbyists are in business to advance their own causes,
few experienced members rely on a single lobby for information on
a given matter. Furthermore, members and their staff employees
soon become sensitive to the fact that some lobbyists are highly
professional and capable—and trustworthy—and others are not. It
is generally accepted that the untrustworthy lobbyist does not remain long in Washington. He can misinform a member only once.
For the professional, the most important tools are an established
reputation for integrity, factual information and logic, assistance
and good will. Word of an individual lobbyist's veracity—or, particularly, lack of it—travels fast in the House office building complex. Members and staff employees often exchange references on
Washington-based lobbyists.

Service to members. Lobbyists representing national organizations ordinarily attempt to establish direct contact with as many
members as possible by offering to perform various services for
them. For the most part, however, direct and continuing contacts
occur between lobbyists and Congressmen who are on the same
side of the fence. Washington professionals recognize that the best

lobbyist is a well-informed member of Congress. Thus, they concentrate on trying to help their friends rather than attempting personally to persuade their foes. Nevertheless, some members encourage and maintain contacts with lobbyists regardless of viewpoint because they can provide detailed information on questions of public policy:

You know that there are some lobbyists who approach a problem in one way and there are lobbyists who approach it another way, but I think we have on the whole here in Washington a group of very constructively minded and helpful lobbyists in terms of informing the members of Congress and of being helpful to them in an understanding of the problems of an industry or a group or a profession.

The source of information which they constitute is one that has to be recognized right from the outset as having a bias or prejudice on a question and yet, I think, you will find that the most helpful information that you receive in detail on questions that you are considering— either as an individual legislator or a member of a committee passing on legislation—will come to you from the spokesmen of organizations who are seriously concerned about the importance of the legislation being considered.

They will be calling on you in your office. They will be getting a good deal of mail to you and printed material to you. They will be endeavoring in every way in their power to see that you understand their point of view, and are sympathetic to it. I think a general rule that probably ought to be followed with regard to them in Washington is to hear them out and to be openminded with regard to the information that they pass along to you, and to try to get a maximum personal benefit in terms of understanding and information from the people who do come to you representing industries and organizations.

The Washington-based lobbyist often is satisfied to talk with a top assistant; if he wants to talk to the member, he can make himself available at the member's convenience. Indeed, one basic function of a Washington lobby is to act as a service agency whose facilities are available to the member at his convenience. The major Washington lobbies are backed up by research staffs, specialists in various fields, speech writers, and public relations experts. Most are eager to provide drafts of speeches and information for Congressmen whose legislative interests are similar to theirs, in effect serving as an extension of a member's staff.

THE ACADEMIC COMMUNITY

Congressmen often work closely with colleges and universities in their district or state, consulting informally with faculty specialists on pending legislation or general problems of public policy. In some cases, a faculty member may be brought to Washington for a short period of time to work on a particular matter in his field of specialization. In testimony before the Joint Committee on the Organization of the Congress, Representative John Brademas of Indiana described the benefits of such an arrangement:

I sit on the Education Committee. From time to time, I want staff assistance on educational problems, if I am working on a speech or on education legislation. Yet I cannot afford to keep somebody on my staff full time who is an expert on education. At the same time, I am hesitant to call on the education experts on the staff of my committee because they are already overburdened. And I do not like to call on the Office of Education because I may want to criticize what they are up to. Where do I turn for advice and help?

A couple of years ago, when I was working on the technical education bill, I felt it important to have somebody on my staff at least part time who understood the subject matter and I arranged with Purdue University to have one of Purdue's outstanding young engineering deans work in my office part time for a period of about six months. It was very helpful to me to have him there and I think it was also helpful to him and to Purdue University to have one of its top university administrators get acquainted with the legislative process here in Washington. Although I think this would not require a law or a change in law, I think that more and more members of Congress might consider working with the universities in their own districts and their own states to arrange such sabbatical leaves in Washington for university administrators or experts in given subject matters.

★ 6 ★

Committee assignment and service

IN A SENSE, the House chamber operates as a court of appeal. Original jurisdiction over legislation lies elsewhere, for immediately after a bill is introduced in the House it is referred to committee. There—subject to the pushing and hauling of congressional politics—its fate is largely determined. More than ninety per cent of all legislation introduced never gets out of committee.

If the committee does not act or acts adversely, an appeal may be taken to the floor. Procedures exist under which a bill that is being allowed to languish and die may be taken from committee and brought directly before the House for action. Then it is possible that supporters of a bill may get the votes necessary to overturn an adverse committee report. But cases in which these appeals have been successful are few and far between. If, on the other hand, proper procedure is followed; if public hearings are held; if the prolonged rub of opposites in committee is followed by compromise and a measure of consensus in executive session; if the committee reports the bill out with a strong recommendation that it "do pass"; and if, when appropriate, the Rules Committee also acts favorably—then the chances of passage are good. Occasionally, after debate on the floor, the bill is voted down or substantially modified. But, more often than not, the committee's judgment prevails. (The stages through which a bill goes, from introduction to enactment, are outlined in the Appendix, page 380.)

In short, the committees occupy a central position in the business of lawmaking. And it is in his committee room that the individual Congressman is most likely to make his legislative mark, as an experienced member suggests:

> You will find here that most of the work that you do legislatively is going to be in your committee room. I think for that reason you are wise in attempting to get the best possible committee assignment that you can and one that's in line with the interests of your constituents and of your district.

Assignment and jurisdiction

There are twenty-one *standing* committees of the House. Although House rules provide guidelines for referral of measures in some two hundred subject-matter areas, committee jurisdictions do overlap. Occasionally, this leads to jurisdictional disputes, which are resolved by the majority party leadership, as the following comment indicates:

> . . . there is a certain amount of jealousy between committees as to who should get and who did get jurisdiction. As a case in point, the Education and Labor Committee—in the past at least—has felt somewhat sensitive that the college dormitory program did not come to the Education Committee, even though it involved improving the educational system. But we did get the academic facilities program, which is a broadening of the college housing program, and logically one should be an extension of the other. But they belong in the jurisdiction of different committees, which is, from our point of view, regrettable, because it prevents an over-all look at perhaps the same

approach used for all aspects of the building programs in colleges. There are limitless possibilities for trouble, but there is a pretty good definition of the jurisdiction, which prevents too much scrambling.

There also are formal mechanisms and guidelines for the assignment of individual members to committees. Categories generally followed in making assignments, and the broad outlines of committee jurisdiction, are:

Exclusive committees	*Jurisdiction*
Appropriations	Appropriation of all revenue for support of federal programs; the federal budget
Rules	Scheduling of legislation; rules establishing conditions of debate— time allowed, amendments permitted, etc.
Ways and Means	Revenue measures generally; the national debt; tariff and reciprocal trade agreements; social security measures
Semi-exclusive committees	
Agriculture	Agriculture generally; price supports, research, and soil conservation; rural electrification; forestry in general
Armed Services	Common defense generally; the military departments and armed services; selective service; military reservations and establishments
Banking and Currency	Banking and currency generally; financial aid to commerce and industry; public and private housing;

the Federal Reserve system; urban renewal

Education and Labor

Education and labor generally; wages, hours, and labor standards; federal aid to elementary and secondary education; higher education; teacher training and scholarships

Foreign Affairs

Relations with foreign nations generally; mutual security; protection of Americans abroad; the United Nations

Interstate and Foreign Commerce

Interstate and foreign commerce, transportation, and communications generally; civil aeronautics; Weather Bureau; interstate oil compacts; securities and exchanges; interstate transmission of power; public health

Judiciary

Judicial proceedings, civil and criminal, generally; constitutional amendments; federal courts and judges; civil liberties; patents, copyrights, and trademarks; immigration and naturalization

Post Office and Civil Service

Federal civil service generally, including pay, classification, and retirement; postal service generally; census and the National Archives

Public Works

Flood control and improvement of rivers and harbors; navigational benefits, including bridges and dams; water power and pollution; public buildings and grounds; highways

Science and Astronautics

Astronautical research and development; outer space, including exploration and control; scientific research and development; standardization of weights and measures

Nonexclusive committees
District of Columbia

All measures relating to the municipal administration of the District of Columbia, except appropriations

Government Operations

Budget and accounting measures; reorganization of the Executive branch; general oversight of Executive branch; study of intergovernmental relations between U.S. and states and cities, and between U.S. and international organizations

House Administration

Measures related to House funds generally; employment of persons by the House, including clerks for members and committees; travel by members; measures relating to assignment of office space and House services to members

Interior and Insular Affairs

Public lands generally including entry, easements, and grazing; mineral resources of public lands; irrigation and reclamation; mining interests generally; Indian affairs; measures relating to Puerto Rico, Guam, Virgin Islands, and U.S. possessions

Merchant Marine and Fisheries

Merchant marine generally; measures relating to regulation of common carrier by water; U.S.

	Coast Guard, and Coast and Geodetic Survey; administration and operation of the Panama Canal; fisheries and wildlife, including research, restoration and conservation
Internal Security	Communist and other subversive activities affecting the internal security of the U.S.
Veterans' Affairs	Veterans' measures generally, including pensions, life insurance, and education; veterans' hospitals and medical care

The twenty-first standing committee, Standards of Official Conduct, does not fall within any of the three categories of exclusivity. Established during the 90th Congress, it is composed of an equal number of Democrats and Republicans and is empowered to deal with measures relating to the code of official conduct, and financial disclosures by members, officers and employees of the House. (For details of this committee's operation, see Chapter 8, "Decorum and Congressional ethics," pages 237–244.)

NUMBER OF ASSIGNMENTS

During the 89th Congress well over half the members held only one standing committee assignment.* In allocating places, both parties generally follow the categories noted above: Members serv-

---

* In addition to *standing* committees, there are *select* committees (e.g., the Select Committee to Conduct a Study and Investigation of the Problems of Small Business); and *joint* committees (e.g., the Joint Committee on Internal Revenue Taxation) composed of members of the House and Senate. These are generally study or supervisory committees rather than legislative committees, and—particularly for the joint committees—assignments to them usually go to senior members. Finally, there are *conference* committees set up to iron out differences between bills passed by the House and by the Senate. For the background, rules, and procedures of the *conference,* see Appendix, pages 389–395.

ing on one of the *exclusive* committees—Appropriations, Rules, or Ways and Means—usually are not assigned to another standing committee. Members may serve on one *semi-exclusive* and one *nonexclusive* committee, or they may serve on two *nonexclusive* committees. But there are exceptions. During the 89th Congress, for example, eight Democratic and eleven Republican members held two committee assignments in the *semi-exclusive* category. Six members serving on *exclusive* committees also held positions on a second standing committee. Opinion varies among members as to the desirability of dual committee assignments.* One experienced member, who serves on an important committee, suggests that service on any one of the House committees is a full-time job:

I think if more members could hold one assignment—and do a major job on that committee—the better and more effectively this Congress would work. Over on the other side, on the Senate side, they hold down many committees. It is my feeling that they can't do a good job on any of them. Over here, it's a full-time job on any of the committees that we have in the House.

Another member—who is on two committees—disagrees:

I might just comment, as a member of two committees. I can't resist the opportunity to say I disagree violently with ——— about the advisability of only being on one. It does keep you somewhat busier, but I feel that the load isn't that strenuous that you don't have time for more than one major interest.

The total number of members on each committee is fixed by the Legislative Reorganization Act of 1946 but may be changed

* The number of members serving on two standing committees has, however, increased steadily since the 81st Congress, as this table indicates:

81st Cong.	48	87th	147	
82nd	65	88th	157	
83rd	89	89th	170	
84th	107	90th	180	
85th	116	91st	202	(includes Standards
86th	138			of Official Conduct)

from time to time by House resolution. At the beginning of each Congress, the majority party establishes the ratio of Democrats to Republicans on each committee; generally, except for the Committee on Standards of Official Conduct, this apportionment follows the division of the House itself.

Allocation of assignments. In making committee assignments, both parties attempt to help their members politically. But there are not enough "good" places to go around, and newly elected members often get their second or third choices, as a strategically placed member indicates:

> I want to say that we do consider it a serious and a heavy responsibility. Part of the problem is the fact that there never are enough good assignments to go around for all of the members and we can't possibly fill all the first requests, at least, for committee membership. That's why we must go to the second and third requests. We have many things to consider. I think it's true of the Republicans as well as the Democrats . . . we want the members from our side re-elected. Committee assignments have an important bearing on that problem, because how you function in Congress, the effectiveness of your work here, depends in no small measure on the committee assignment that you are given.

The same member also points out that those who do not get their first choice initially can and do transfer to other committees later:

> You will find that you new members will not get the committee assignments that you choose in at least half or more of the instances, I would say more than half of the instances. I don't think you should be too disappointed. Remember this: With seniority you can move along to the committee assignment of your choice. . . . One advantage of gaining a lesser committee assignment is the fact that while you are sitting in Congress you [can] observe the committees and find out for sure which committees you want to serve on. Then move along a year or two or three later and get the committee of your choice. . . .

"Ranking" committees. Service on some committees is considered more important, demanding, or desirable than on others. The three *exclusive* committees are generally regarded as being of special importance. As the following chart indicates, members rarely transfer *from* these three to other committees, congressional newcomers are rarely assigned to them, and the average seniority of nonfreshman members who transfer *to* them is relatively high.

Transfers of committee assignments*
80th to 89th Congresses

Standing committee	Transfers to:	Transfers from:	Average years of seniority of nonfreshman new members	Percentage of freshman among new members
Agriculture	22	18	3.2	53.4
Appropriations	85	2	3.6	26.3
Armed Services	26	6	4.5	44.8
Banking & Currency	15	33	2.8	65.9
Dist. of Columbia	2	13	5.7	31.8
Education & Labor	18	15	3.4	80.8
Foreign Affairs	34	5	4.2	30.9
Government Ops.	8	33	5.6	50.5
House Admin.	5	29	4.7	40.8
Interior	4	31	3.3	70.2
Int. & For. Commerce	32	17	3.1	45.8
Judiciary	19	12	3.4	59.5
Merchant Marine	4	35	5.9	61.2
Post Office	2	40	3.9	72.3
Public Works	13	28	4.9	65.3
Rules	33	1	6.1	6.4
Science & Astronautics	6	7	9.2	54.4
Veterans' Affairs	2	46	4.5	78.9
Ways & Means	47	0	6.4	8.2

* This table is based on a study of committee assignments conducted by Warren E. Miller of the Survey Research Center, University of Michigan.

Since 1946, no newly elected member has been assigned to Rules, only three have been assigned to Ways and Means, and eighteen have been assigned to Appropriations. Aside from these committees and several others—Armed Services, for example— which are considered to be of major importance, committee rankings change over time and vary from region to region. Science and Astronautics for instance, is often mentioned as an increasingly important committee. Service on Merchant Marine and Fisheries, and Interior and Insular Affairs, is considered desirable by seaboard members and westerners, respectively.

PARTY COMMITTEES ON COMMITTEES

Each party has a Committee on Committees that is responsible for assignment of newly elected members and for reassignment of members who wish to transfer from one committee to another. These committees meet during the beginning weeks of a new Congress, although "lobbying" for assignments on choice standing committees may begin much earlier. While their deliberations are private, procedures of the Committees on Committees are widely known in the House. Experienced members generally agree that the first person the congressional newcomer should contact about his own choice of committee assignments is the dean, or most senior member, of his own party's state delegation.*

For the Democrats. The Committee on Committees comprises the Democratic members of the House Ways and Means Committee. Each member of the Committee on Committees represents a zone composed of one or more states, and he is responsible for members of his party from that zone. When the Democratic Com-

---

* In this and subsequent sections, the description of committee-on-committee operation and other aspects of the assignment process follows closely and relies heavily on material from Nicholas A. Masters, "Committee Assignments in the House of Representatives," *American Political Science Review* (June 1961), pages 345–357. Selections reprinted by permission of the author and publisher.

mittee on Committees meets in executive session to make committee assignments, the various standing committees are called up in alphabetical order. As a rule they are disposed of one at a time, but in practice flexibility is maintained throughout the process. Otherwise, a member who preferred but failed to get Ways and Means, for example, might also be denied a chance to compete for vacancies on his second choice or even third choice among the committees, which had been called up earlier. Generally, however, as each committee is called up, members of the Committee on Committees proceed in order of seniority to nominate candidates from their zones who are interested in assignment to the vacancies on that committee. When a candidate is nominated, his qualifications for the committee under consideration are discussed. As soon as nominations for a particular committee's vacancies are completed, a secret ballot is taken to determine who will receive the assignments, and the Committee on Committees moves on to consideration of vacancies on the next standing committee.

For the Republicans. The Committee on Committees is composed of one member from each state that has Republican representation in the House. Ordinarily the senior member among the state's Representatives serves on the committee. Each member of the Republican Committee on Committees casts a vote equal to the number of Republican Representatives from his state. Thus, a member from one state might cast ten votes while a member from another state casts only one vote. Because of the size of the Republican Committee on Committees, however, an executive committee is designated to work out the committee assignments subject to approval of both the full committee and the party policy committee. In recent years, this executive committee has comprised members representing the seven or eight largest state delegations, plus a representative from a small state and spokesmen for recently elected classes. The floor leader serves as ex officio chairman. Executive committee sessions are informal; each member may speak for or against any proposed assignment. And members of the full Committee on Committees who are not on the executive committee may participate, making nominations and speaking for particular assignments. Otherwise, the Republicans follow procedures similar to those employed by the Democrats, calling up the standing committees one at a time, nominating members for the various vacancies, and voting by secret ballot in the event two or more members are nominated for the same committee seat.

CRITERIA FOR ASSIGNMENTS

The making of committee assignments involves much more than these formal procedures. Indeed, for the congressional newcomer, the placement process is not unlike "rushing" for a fraternity. Neither of the Committees on Committees employs *explicit* standards in determining who gets which committee vacancy. However, on the basis of a study of House committee assignment practices in the 86th Congress, political scientist Nicholas A. Masters concluded that, "with minor differences, both parties apply the same criteria for making committee assignments."

"Exclusive" committees. Masters suggests that the following considerations are particularly relevant in making assignments to the Rules, Appropriations, and Ways and Means committees:

LEGISLATIVE RESPONSIBILITY. "According to the party leaders and the members of the committees-on-committees, a responsible legislator is one whose ability, attitudes, and relationships with his colleagues serve to enhance the prestige and importance of the House of Representatives. He has a basic and fundamental respect for the legislative process and understands and appreciates its formal and informal rules. He has the respect of his fellow legislators, and particularly the respect of the party leaders. He does not attempt to manipulate every situation for his own personal advantage. In the consideration of issues, he is careful to protect the rights of others; he is careful to clear matters that require clearance; and he is especially careful about details. He understands the pressures on the members with whom he cannot always agree and avoids pushing an issue to the point where his opponents may suffer personal embarrassment. On specific issues, no matter how firm his convictions and no matter how great the pressures upon him, he demonstrates a willingness to compromise. He is moderate, not so much in the sense of his voting record and his personal ideology, but rather in the sense of a moderate approach; he is not to be found on the uncompromising extremes of the political spectrum. . . . In short, a responsible legislator is politically pliant, but not without conviction.

A legislator can demonstrate his responsibility in many ways: How he manages a major bill; what he contributes in committee work; the sort of testimony he presents before other committees; the nature of his remarks on the floor—all these are tests of his responsibility. If he behaves properly in these settings and refrains from criticizing the party leadership—and gets reelected at home—his chances of being selected for a major committee post are very good."

DISTRICT REPRESENTED. "It would be rare indeed for a member to earn regard as 'responsible' in only one or two terms. . . . So the concept of responsibility is connected with an element beyond the member's personality, an element that takes into account the nature of his district. The members of the committees-on-committees have something more in mind here than simply a particular member's ability to be reelected. Long tenure by itself is an obvious objective fact, and common sense proof that a district is 'safe'; but this is not enough. It is not necessarily to the point either that the member's district may be safe for the incumbent but not for any one else. The essence of the criterion lies in the terms on which the member is returned rather than in the fact of his return alone. The committee-on-committees wants to feel that his district will not only reelect him but also allow him to operate as a free agent, enabling him to make controversial decisions on major policy questions without constant fear of reprisals at the polls. His district must not be one that forces him to take definite, uncompromising positions, for this would jeopardize his usefulness in committee work."

GEOGRAPHICAL BALANCE. "A legislator who is responsible and who comes from a district that allows him considerable independence on issues still has no guarantee that he will be selected to fill a major committee vacancy. He simply has a better chance than others. A third factor serves to narrow the range of choice. For both party committees tend to follow the practice of selecting a member from the same party delegation as the member who vacated the seat, in order not to disturb the existing geographical balance. . . .

"Along this line, each party attempts to have every section of the nation represented on the Appropriations and Ways and Means committees. These are the only two committees, however, on which geographical balance is regarded as especially important. . . ."

Other committees. Masters concludes that in distributing assignments to all other committees political survival of individual members is the most important single factor:

"Although a number of factors enter into committee assignments

. . . the most important single consideration—unless it can be taken for granted—is to provide each member with an assignment that will help to insure his re-election. Stated differently, the most impressive argument in any applicant's favor is that the assignment he seeks will give him an opportunity to provide the kind of service to his constituents that will sustain and attract voter interest and support. In distributing assignments the party acts as a mutual benefit and improvement society, and this for the obvious reason that control of the House depends on the re-election of party members."

Other factors which have a bearing on committee assignments are described by Masters:

SENIORITY. "When two or more members stake a claim to the same assignment, on the ground that it is essential to their electoral success, both party committees usually, if not invariably, will give preference to the member with longer service. Members have often maneuvered for a position on a particular committee long before a vacancy existed, and sometimes even long before other applicants were first elected. But open importunity may be self-defeating, for no one likes a pest."

GEOGRAPHICAL BALANCE. "The proposition is sometimes advanced that geographical balance is a deliberate objective in distributing assignments to all committees. If so, it has a low priority. There is no evidence of systematic effort to provide each section with representation on the various committees proportional to its representation in the House. The Appropriations and Ways and Means committees may be considered as exceptions, but even here a much more pressing consideration is representation for the large tax-paying states."

PROFESSIONAL BACKGROUND. "The professional background of an individual legislator is seldom in and of itself the controlling factor in his assignment. However, some general rules relating to the professional backgrounds of legislators are followed by both parties. Almost without exception, lawyers only are appointed to the Judiciary Committee. Members with outstanding experience in international relations or with extensive military service are regarded as excellent choices for the Foreign Affairs and Armed Services committees respectively. Other things being equal, former bankers and financiers may be given a slight edge over competing applicants for such committees as Appropriations, Ways and Means, and Banking and Currency. The same holds true for farmers who apply for the Agriculture Committee and for members closely identified with the labor movement who apply for the Education and Labor Committee. But all agreed that holding elective office, particularly a state legislative office, outweighed any other type of professional experience as a qualification for any committee assignment. Holding elective office is regarded as a profession by members of the committees, and they feel that the rewards of the system should go to the professionals. Although the patterns of committee assignments tend to document the importance of professional background, it would be a mistake to assume that the committees-on-committees seek out applicants on this ground. Normally, the reverse is true. Applicants tend to apply for assignments where they think their professional skills can be used to best advantage."

"OUTSIDE" SUPPORT. "All members of the committees-on-committees recognized that organized groups outside Congress take a hand in the assignment process from time to time. . . . Nevertheless, organized groups, with occasional exceptions, appear to refrain from direct intervention in committee assignments; overt intrusion is apt to be resented and so be self-defeating. Rather, they have certain 'expectations' about the type of person who should be selected for the vacancies on committees which affect their interests. Each group usually counts several members 'friendly' or responsive to their needs. Organized interests do not often concern themselves too much with the selection of a particular member of the 'friendly' group so long as one of them is eventually chosen."

PARTY LEADERSHIP. "The role of the party leaders in making committee assignments is difficult to define; no simple definition fits all the realities. Generally speaking, the leadership of each party in the House is formidable and independent to a great degree, though the leaders' power varies with their personal relations with the other members. . . . The Democratic and Republican leaders not only play the principal role in the selection of the members on their respective committees-on-committees, but their personal judgments also tend to become the norm for major committee assignments. In practice, the leadership of both parties is directly involved in assignments to all the major committees, though the leaders do not usually concern themselves with applicants to lesser ones."

CAMPAIGNING FOR COMMITTEES

Despite differences in the composition and operation of their respective committees on committees, newly elected Democratic and Republican members follow much the same general practices in securing assignments, relying heavily on their senior colleagues in deciding which committees to apply for and how to go about campaigning for them.

Application for assignment. The newly elected member who does not make his preferences known is likely to be assigned to the less coveted committee places left after the Committee on Committees completes action on the applications it receives. Experienced members generally advise their juniors, as a minimum effort, to convey committee preferences to the dean of their state delegations. It is also customary for newcomers to write directly to their respective party leaders, setting out with all due modesty their qualifications or other appropriate reasons for assignments to the committee of their choice. Democrats ordinarily include their zone's member on the Committee on Committees, as well as its chairman, on their mailing lists.

Support for applications. As indicated earlier, the GOP Committee on Committees is composed for the most part of the deans of state Republican delegations. In the case of the Democrats, the dean of the state delegation customarily negotiates for assignments with the Committee-on-Committees member for his zone. Small state Democratic delegations sometimes combine forces, appointing a single dean to give them more "clout" with their zone's member. Thus, while newly elected members may seek assistance elsewhere, the active support of their dean is extremely important, as Masters suggests:

. . . Members seeking assignments, and particularly freshmen, channel their requests through the "dean" or senior member of their state party delegation. In negotiations between the Committee-on-committees and the applicants he plays a crucially important role in securing assignments. It is his special responsibility to see that his members receive adequate representation on the various committees. In performing this task, he tries to protect or maintain the delegation's place on a major committee when a vacancy occurs and the seat has previously been held by a member of the delegation; he consults with, and advises, the members of his delegation seeking assignments as to what their chances are, and which committee assignments he will support for them. The dean's decision must be made in consideration of the needs of his state, the qualifications of his own members, and the necessity for adjusting the requests among his members to prevent duplication on committees. It falls to his lot also to discourage and dissuade members who have unrealistic designs on the major committees—Appropriations, Rules, and Ways and Means.

"Fair" campaign practices. Although impressive qualifications or political needs and the active support of senior members are important considerations in determining assignments, the manner in

which the newcomer campaigns also may affect his chances of success. Masters makes this point:

The manner in which a congressman campaigns for a committee is an important factor in the outcome. For example, a member seeking an assignment often solicits the support of members already on the committee. Another technique is to obtain the support of influential political leaders, such as endorsements from the governor, senators, or members of the state legislature. If an individual is comparatively unknown in national politics, he may attempt to familiarize the members of the Committee-on-committees with his background and training as it relates to the type of service he can give on the committee he desires. All these tactics, properly employed, can go a long way toward helping a member get favorable consideration by his party. He must be careful, however, to avoid giving the impression of exerting undue political pressure on the members of the Committee-on-committees. For example, if the committee tells him that a vacancy has already been promised to another, he is *expected* to accept this decision. Attempts to challenge either committee's decisions are generally regarded as serious departures from the norms of conduct in the House.

It also is considered bad form for a newcomer to *reject* an assignment—and the cost of such insurgency can be high, as a former rebel, speaking to congressional newcomers, suggests:

I am the only member of my party who acted contrary to what I would advise anyone else to do at this time: That was to resign from a committee as soon as appointed on it. . . . I am the only one in fifty-some years who did it (so perhaps I am not a good one to give advice since I started off by making what appeared to be a rather large-sized mistake) and I paid for it by three years' standing in line before I got on any committee of any responsibility at all.

Organization and operation

The committee system is characterized by autonomy and diversity of organization and operation. Each standing committee establishes its own rules, operating procedures, and staff bureaucracy. The committees can also prepare their own agendas and work at their own pace—depending, of course, on their ability to withstand pressures from outside the committee room.

SENIORITY AND THE CHAIRMAN

Since 1910, committee members have been ranked on the basis of seniority.* The chairmanship usually goes to the member who has served longest on the majority side of the committee. Similarly, all members of a committee are ranked according to length of service and advanced up their party's side of the committee ladder only as vacancies occur. And seniority is not transferable, a fact that affects members who wish to move from one committee to another:

Now this presents a problem if, after you have been here a couple of terms, you decide you want to switch from one committee to another. If you switch from one committee to another you go on at the bottom of the new committee and start the seniority process all over again. . . . Some time in the future you may find the problem of transferring is that although you like another committee a little bit better, you will lose the seniority you have built up in the meantime on the committee to which you were first assigned.

"Ranking" of new members. If a member loses his seat in Congress and then returns several years later, he too starts at the bottom of the list again, except that he outranks those who are beginning their first terms. There are a variety of precedents for ranking new members when several of the same party are assigned to the same committee (e.g., by alphabetical order, by seniority of their zone's member on the Committee on Committees, by date of

* Early in 1970 studies of the seniority system were initiated within both parties in the wake of criticism—most of it from younger members—that the "generation gap" was yawning ever wider in the House. Significantly, these studies were officially sanctioned by the Democratic and Republican leaders.

their state's entry into the Union, and so on). But these customs are not necessarily followed. Sometimes seniority is established by the flip of a coin:

> I might say I was fifth of five [assigned to] the committee of which I am now ranking member, as the result of the flip of the coin. So it can make quite a difference.

Powers of the chairman. How a particular committee operates depends to a great extent on the temperament and ability of its chairman, whose powers—established by rule and by custom—are impressive:

★ He can decide when or whether hearings should be held on various matters, which bills should be taken up first, and how much time, if any, should be devoted to them in hearings or otherwise.

★ He can schedule committee meetings, preside over them, and recognize members wishing to question witnesses or make statements for the record.

★ He can control committee organization, the establishment of subcommittees, their jurisdiction, membership, and who shall chair them.

★ He can initiate or approve requests for special projects and committee travel.

★ He can hire and supervise activities of the committee's professional staff.

Unless he delegates his responsibility, the chairman also serves as floor manager for bills voted out of his committee, deciding which members will share the limited time for debate. Furthermore, particularly in the case of important legislation, the bill frequently bears the chairman's name. A senior member describes how a bill becomes "the chairman's bill":

Most bills do come to the floor as a bill of the chairman's committee, particularly those of some magnitude and scope. Those bills have been considerably amended in the legislative committee from the form in which they were originally submitted. After the committee holds rather lengthy hearings on general bills at which people are invited to testify, then the committee will usually have closed executive sessions at which they mark up the bill, taking it up point by point and section by section, giving members of that committee an opportunity to offer amendments to the bill in committee. . . . After you have completed this procedure and the committee is satisfied, in general, with the bill and the form in which it finally appears, you could present the bill under the number and the authorship of its original introducer. Then all these amendments offered later would have to be adopted separately by the House after they debate the bill. Or the second thing to do is to instruct the chairman to introduce a clean bill, embodying all the changes the committee has written into the bill. This is what frequently occurs and it is a simple matter of clarity to present to the floor one package of legislation the committee wants. It becomes the chairman's bill; that is, the committee's bill in reality, the chairman speaking for the committee when he introduces that bill under his name.

However, the powers of the chairman, although impressive, are by no means unlimited, nor are they ordinarily exercised without reference to the interests of his colleagues on the committee and in the House generally. For example, chairmen customarily consult with ranking minority members on a wide range of committee activities and housekeeping operations, as an experienced member indicates:

The fact of the matter is that usually there is a very close working relationship between the chairman and the ranking minority member; and the longer they serve together the closer they usually work together. . . . (I stress this for the Democratic members because I would suggest to you that a bold attempt to clobber the minority may get difficulties up at the top of your committee if it isn't checked very carefully both with your chairman and either with the author of the bill or with the fellow who manages the legislation.)

In the matter, for instance, of the designation of subcommittees . . . when I was chairman I would select the Democratic members and then ask [the ranking minority member] to select the members on the subcommittee for the minority and that was a standing rule. [He] was chairman before I was [and] he, with absolute perfect circumspection, followed every line of protocol set down for the recognition of the ranking minority member; when I [became] chairman I followed exactly the same rules, so when it came to establishing subcommittees, for instance, I consulted with him about how many members would be on that subcommittee and what the [party] ratio would be. . . . I gave him the prerogative of selecting . . . the members of his party who would serve on it. That goes also with reference to travel, and that can get rather important you know. . . .

And finally there is the ultimate check on the power of the chairman: A majority of the members of a committee can—and sometimes do—circumscribe their leader's activities, perhaps by adopting formal rules or establishing subcommittees against his wishes. Such tactics were used in the Education and Labor Committee in 1959 and 1966, for example, and in the Post Office and Civil Service Committee in 1965.

RULES AND PROCEDURES

Basically, the rules of the House are, wherever applicable, the rules of the committees. But committees can and do supplement them with rules of their own. Some have detailed, written rules. Others have no formal rules but adhere to what one member calls "unwritten codes":

I have served on two committees, first on the Interior and Insular Affairs Committee for four years, and then on the Ways and Means Committee. I want to say that they operate quite differently, and I am sure that every other single committee of the House would operate differently from the other. They depend a great deal, in great part at least, on the personality of the chairman. They depend in part upon the subject matter that the committee has to take up, the association with the leadership, and many other factors. But most of them have rules. Some of them are adopted formally and some are unwritten rules.

Generally the rules of the House are applicable in the absence of other rules, but again the final authority rests with the chairman. In the case of the Interior and Insular Affairs Committee we very meticulously adopted . . . each year a set of rules patterned after the rules of the House but modified to suit the needs of the committee. And we meticulously followed those rules in consideration of every single bill that came before the committee.

On the Ways and Means Committee, while we generally follow the rules of the House, there is a pretty much unwritten code of procedure in the committee and an *esprit de corps* that allows the committee to function without formal rules. . . . But it works very effectively. . . . I am amazed at what we do get done without a formal set of rules, and the caliber of legislation that comes out of that committee, meticulously done, thoroughly considered. I am sure that [another Ways and Means Committee member present] will also tell you the minority has its full time in the committee and is allowed to modify the bills as they come up and improve them. I have never heard of any complaint against the chairman of that committee in that regard, despite the fact that they don't have any formal rules of procedure.

Learning and applying the rules. In order to learn the rules and how to apply them in their particular committees, newcomers are advised by senior colleagues to sit back and watch for a while —and to avoid being too technical:

Now there is a problem, I would say, with reference to the use of rules in committee. Let's assume you get to be rather expert in the rules. You look them over and you know them. It is a little like

Churchill said: "The difference between number one and number two is . . . that number one has to decide what's right. Number two not only has to decide what's right but whether it's appropriate to say what's right." . . . By that I mean that maybe you will find that somebody isn't proceeding according to the rules [but] the attitude you take toward your colleagues with reference to a strict compliance . . . could be very detrimental [to the member who] got a point of order and exercised it immediately and all that sort of thing. There ought to be an effort not to be super-technical with reference, I would say, to the operation of these committees by new members. Sit back and watch it for awhile. . . .

Basic operating procedures. Basic procedures for committee operation are described in House Rule XI, which also sets forth the responsibilities and jurisdiction of the standing committees.

Committees may meet wherever they choose, but most usually meet in their committee rooms. Committees may also designate when they will meet. However, with the exception of Rules, Government Operations, Internal Security, and Standards of Official Conduct, committees may not meet while the House is in session unless the House gives them special permission to do so. By a special resolution customarily adopted at the beginning of each Congress, the Ways and Means and Appropriations committees are also permitted to meet while the House is in session. Committees usually meet from about 10 A.M. until noon, and sometimes in the afternoon and evening when the House is not in session.

House rules require that at least two members of a committee be present to transact such business as taking testimony and receiving evidence. Otherwise, committees may determine for themselves how many members shall constitute a quorum. The rules do require that a majority of the full committee be physically present in order to vote approval or report a measure. All committee and subcommittee hearings—except executive sessions for marking up a bill or for voting—are open to the public unless a majority of committee members vote to hold a closed session for some special reason. And each committee is required to keep a complete record of all action, including any record votes taken. Committee records are the property of the House, and all members are entitled to access to them.

SUBCOMMITTEES

All but four of the House standing committees—Rules, Internal Security, Standards of Official Conduct, and Ways and Means— have standing subcommittees.* However, the significance of these subcommittees varies greatly over time and from committee to committee. In some, even though subcommittees have specified jurisdictions, the important work is reserved for the full committee. In others, all the most important deliberations and decisions occur in the subcommittee rather than in the full committee, which generally meets only to give routine approval to the subcommittee's work:

In the case of the Appropriations Committee, the subcommittees are all important. The subcommittees, for all practical purposes, write the legislation and it is very seldom that it is ever changed by the full committee. It's more or less just a formal procedure of adopting the work of the subcommittee. In the case of the Ways and Means Committee [there are] no subcommittees. All of the complex legislation handled goes before the full membership of the Ways and Means Committee. And all the other committees vary from one extreme to the other.

Organization and operation. Some subcommittees have descriptive titles and established subject-matter jurisdiction (for ex-

* There were 124 *standing* subcommittees and 99 *ad hoc* subcommittees during the 88th Congress. The Post Office and Civil Service Committee accounted for 41 of the *ad hoc* subcommittees, which were set up to handle individual bills.

ample, Interior and Insular Affairs), whereas others are designated by number or by general titles (for example, District of Columbia), and the committee chairman distributes bills among them on a case-by-case basis. During the first session of the 89th Congress, the number of subcommittees ranged from five—in the District of Columbia, Interstate and Foreign Commerce, Merchant Marine and Fisheries, and Veterans' Affairs committees—to Agriculture's fifteen. (See Appendix, pages 384–388, for a complete list of subcommittees.) The subcommittees of some committees (e.g., Government Operations) have staffs, meeting rooms, and telephone extensions separate from the parent committee's suite. Other committees do not provide these symbols of autonomy, pooling the staff in a single suite of rooms and assigning personnel to the various subcommittees as the need arises. And still others combine these two organizational schemes, keeping "regular" subcommittees close at hand and establishing a "special" subcommittee with a staff and separate quarters of its own.

· As a rule, the committee chairman, in consultation with the ranking minority member, determines the number of members who will serve on each subcommittee and the party ratio. Similarly, he designates the chairmen and members of subcommittees. Occasionally chairmanships are given to junior members, but the rules of at least one committee—Interior and Insular Affairs—specify seniority as the basis for appointment of subcommittee chairmen, and this practice is prevalent in roughly half of the remaining committees.

COMMITTEE STAFFS

The professional committee staff member is an important source of information and assistance, as a senior member indicates:

> I would like to emphasize at this point the importance of the committee staff, the professional staff, many of whom, such as on Ways and Means, have been with us for years. A good bit of the staffs on most of the committees are not on a partisan basis. They are pro-

fessional people, there to serve all members of the committee, and you frequently find in dealing with another committee, as well as your own committee, that the best source of information will be from the staff members, as well as the assistance that they can give you in following a piece of legislation that you are interested in before another committee or even following it before your own committee.

Each standing committee is authorized to employ a basic staff of at least four professional and six clerical workers.* Most, however, have more, and some subcommittees (for example, the Subcommittee on Military Operations of the Government Operations Committee) have staffs of their own.

Staffing arrangements vary. As is the case with individual members' office staffing arrangements, no standard method of committee staff organization and operation is used. Many different titles are applied to professional staff positions, and the responsibilities that go with them vary widely from committee to committee. Some staff members are expected to maintain the base of their operations in the committee rooms. Others serve as a link between the committee room and an individual member—perhaps the chairman of the full committee or of a subcommittee. And still others spend most of their time in an individual member's office.

Some committees (Interstate and Foreign Commerce, for example) designate a professional minority staff assistant and several minority clerical assistants. Others do not designate minority staff as such (for example, Agriculture), but the staff's apparent second-in-command, the assistant clerk, or assistant counsel may in fact operate as a minority staff member. According to a Republican Task Force report issued during the 89th Congress, staff size and distribution between the parties on eighteen of the standing committees were as follows:

* The Legislative Reorganization Act of 1970 authorizes up to six professional staff, with provision for selection of two of these by the minority party.

Committee	Democratic	Republican
Agriculture	11	2
Appropriations	36	13
Banking and Currency	55	4
District of Columbia	11	1
Education and Labor	32	7
Foreign Affairs	17	1
Government Operations	53	3
House Administration	5	0
Interior and Insular Affairs	10	2
Judiciary	37	2
Merchant Marine and Fisheries	9	1
Post Office and Civil Service	15	2
Public Works	36	8
Rules	2	1
Science and Astronautics	19	0
Un-American Activities	47	0
Veterans' Affairs	11	2
Ways and Means	17	4

Recruitment and hiring. Professional staff positions are eagerly sought. They tend to be regarded as a promotion from a position on an individual member's staff. Committee staff personnel often have worked with several members, with several different committees, and in both Houses of Congress. The careers of a substantial number indicate movement in and out of the Executive and Legislative branches, and many professional staff employees have had experience with the Executive agency over which their committee has jurisdiction.

As in other aspects of committee operation, the degree of specialized knowledge that the professional staff brings to the committee and the use that is made of it depend in large part upon the chairman. Not all committees have highly professional and capable staffs. On a few of them, staff positions are primarily patronage positions. On the other extreme are committees that hire only people with specialized knowledge and demonstrated professional competence. In some cases (for example, Foreign Affairs), the views of the entire committee are solicited before a new employee is added to the staff. Committee staff directors frequently are asked to participate in recruitment and interviewing and to make recommendations on hiring. More often than not, however, the chairman, with the advice and consent of the ranking minority member, actually hires, promotes—and fires—staff personnel.

WORKING IN COMMITTEE

Committee work is time consuming.* In the opinion of some mem-

* Probable demands on the time of members are indicated to some extent by the number of meetings held by the various committees and their subcommittees. The following information was prepared by the Joint Committee on the Organization of the Congress, and appears—along with other valuable information on and analysis of the legislative work load—in Appendix A of the Joint Committee's *Final Report* (Washington, D.C.: Government Printing Office, 1966), pp. 59–74:

Committee (88th Congress)	Total meetings	Full committee meetings	Sub-committee meetings
Appropriations	614	24	590
Interior	456	82	374
Education & Labor	403	40	363
Judiciary	334	58	276
Foreign Affairs	321	135	186
Armed Services	296	107	189
Int. & For. Commerce	274	90	184
Agriculture	251	62	189
Science & Astronautics	235	37	198
Banking & Currency	229	125	104
Government Op.	207	10	197
Ways & Means	180	180	—
Post Office	163	44	119
Public Works	141	53	88
Rules	134	134	—
Dist. of Columbia	132	25	107
Merchant Marine	127	47	80
Un-American Activities	81	12	69
Veterans' Affairs	66	19	47
House Admin.	27	19	8

bers it can be "grubby" or "dull" as well. And while it is axiomatic that effective legislators are made not on the floor of the House but in committee, not all Congressmen act accordingly. Some find it more profitable to apply the better part of their energies and talents elsewhere than in the committee room, perhaps in informing public opinion nationally or, on the other extreme, in serving their constituents.

Most members, however, place great emphasis on the *value* of committee service. The committee room is considered not only the best place in which to develop expert competence in a given field, but also the place where members learn how to get along with their colleagues. Both these attributes of committee service are mentioned frequently when one Congressman expresses his respect for another: A good Representative is one who "does his homework," or "pays attention to the details of legislation," or "works constructively with his colleagues in committee."

Attendance and specialization. In their advice to congressional newcomers, experienced members cite attendance and specialization as the essential ingredients of productive committee service and, eventually, influence. Regular attendance is deemed a prerequisite for constructive participation in reading a bill for amendments in committee and debating its merits on the floor. The development of special competence in a field relevant to the committee's work is considered the pathway to both respect and influence relatively early in a member's career, as experienced Congressmen indicate:

ON ATTENDANCE. "The committees are the phase of House procedure where the real drudgery is done, the day-after-day hearings. Your committee may have a bill upon which literally hundreds of people may want to be heard as witnesses for and against that bill. It is a great temptation to skip a lot of those meetings because a lot of the witnesses will be repetitive and you have a lot of work piled up in your office and, as I say, it is a great temptation to skip some of those meetings; but yet the place that you will earn on your committee over a period of time will depend on how regularly you attend that committee. So if you have an important bill that has about thirty days of hearings and you are there only on two days of the hearings, when you finish those hearings and start reading the bill for amendment in committee you are probably not going to be in a very good position to take too active a part. . . . So, over a period of time you are going to attain a position of greater significance among your committee members if you are in regular attendance in that committee than if you skip most of the committee meetings."

ON SPECIALIZATION. "The committee is the place where your own understanding, if you will specialize and know your lessons on the subject matter (and the more complicated it is the more opportunity to specialize and know your lesson) you will find before you know it that they will be listening to you on the committee. I don't mean [that you should] talk all the time. But when an issue comes up and in the discussion—particularly in the executive sessions—if you can speak with authority and you know both sides, you remember the testimony, you can summarize it in a few words (and believe me my service in the House taught me the value of brevity which I am not displaying here) but if you can focus in that five minute rule you've got it made on the floor of the House, and if you can focus in two or three minutes on something to say in the committee, you've got it made there."

Recognition and speaking. Experienced members advise their junior colleagues to avoid wasting committee time with repetitive questions or irrelevant comments and to observe other proprieties in making statements in the committee room:

ON RECOGNITION. "In your committee work, when you have something particular in mind other than just informal discussion, the thing to do is to talk to the Chair. Arrange for recognition so that you can present your particular argument and your particular viewpoint and then the power of recognition in the Chair will operate in your favor. Otherwise you are competing with everybody and it gets rather rough."

ON BLUFFING. "Don't get up and talk unless you know what you are talking about, because this House of Representatives is the fastest judge of people of any group of men I ever saw in my life. It is important to know what you are talking about when you get up and speak either before the House . . . or on your committees. In other words, take dead aim because many of these fellows are experts in their particular fields. It is very easy early in the session to get an adverse impression. . . . So when you get up to speak in the early stages be sure you know what you are doing. Be sure you know it is well calculated."

ON QUESTIONS. "There is a great tendency sometimes to take an awful lot of time in committee; and one member out of a committee of thirty can take two hours questioning some witness, if he wants to do it. It is quite important from the standpoint of good judgment to try to limit your questions to those that are actually constructive; to see that you can cover much ground in that committee; and to see that you don't repeat what somebody else says. . . . Now the reason I say that this is important is that [there is no situation] that makes a committee member feel more unhappy [than when] you get to 12 o'clock noon on Friday and . . . one of the witnesses still sitting before your committee (and not yet heard) is from your own congressional district—and he has to be back [home] by Monday so he can't stay over the weekend. Yet, because a few members of your committee have taken an awful lot of time of a few preceding witnesses, he is sitting there at noon not yet heard. So, even though on a particular day you may not have any constituents that are witnesses, it is well to observe the proprieties. If you are going to question the witnesses, make the questions constructive, don't be repetitive, and don't take up unnecessary time with the witnesses. Because if you are doing that and you are causing other witnesses to be barred from the opportunity to testify, sometime the shoe is going to be on your foot. And you are going to have the witness down there who didn't get a chance to be heard and he is not going to be happy if he flies back three thousand miles without a chance to participate in that hearing."

★ 7 ★

Entering the legislative arena

WHERE LEGISLATIVE PROPOSALS are concerned, many are called, but few are chosen. During the 186 days of the first session of the 91st Congress, for example, the House was presented with 17,728 bills, resolutions, and other measures requiring consideration and action. The Senate was presented with 3,825, some of which eventually came to the House. After committee consideration, 521 bills* were reported back to the House for action. Of these, 484 were approved. And of those approved in the House only 265 were passed by the Senate and signed into law by the President.

Congressional newcomers seldom overcome these odds, nor are they often given an opportunity to shepherd a major bill through Congress. An exception still noted by senior members occurred in 1913, when in his first term Mr. Sam Rayburn managed an important railroad securities bill and secured its passage in the House. Ordinarily, however, the first years of service as a legislator consti-

---

* This total includes only House of Representatives bills and joint resolutions; it does not include concurrent and simple resolutions.

tute an apprenticeship, a time which experienced Congressmen feel is most usefully devoted to the development of workable legislative proposals, to learning the rules under which the House operates, and to getting a "feel" for debate and speaking for the record.

Drafting and introducing bills

Ideas that can be translated into legislation are not easily come by; most members find they must actively seek—and develop—them. There is the Administration or party program, of course, which must be introduced in bill form by members of the House or Senate. And there are proposals that originate in the various departments and agencies of the federal government but which are not part of the Administration's program. An idea may come from a simple constituent request, or it may be the result of extensive planning by well-organized interest groups.

IDEAS FOR LEGISLATION

An experienced Congressman lists sources of ideas to be developed into legislative proposals:

The first source of ideas is your campaign. If you came to Congress on the basis of a campaign in which you said you were going to try to do certain things, you certainly want to bear in mind these objectives and try to do something in each field. Now it may be that you promised to save the family farm. At least you ought to consider some minor amendment which might improve the operation of the Soil Bank. If you agreed to restore prosperity, you at least ought to take an interest in some aspect, say, of the bill to aid depressed areas. . . .

The second source of ideas is letters from constituents. Occasionally, you will get a letter from a constituent who has a very workable idea. It may be well worth following through with the Library of Congress or the staff of a particular committee.

A third source of ideas is consultation with state officials and some of your specialists in your universities back home. Some of these people in education, in agriculture, in economics, have ideas that may well recommend themselves to some sustained action on your part to obtain legislation.

Finally, of course, your own reading, reading from the *Congressional Record* or from the newspapers. I have found it helpful to keep some sort of a file of ideas, a notebook broken down into various areas. Many of these are probably castles in the air. But sometimes you can see a way to transmit some idea into an amendment to a particular bill or change of a governmental regulation.

Additional sources of ideas. Others identify committee work and their colleagues, in the House and in the Senate, as important sources of legislative ideas. Many bills are introduced in the early days of a session, and all are listed in the *Record*. A member may wish to support some of them by introducing an identical bill. In other instances a colleague's bill may contain the germ of an idea for an entirely different proposal. One member describes his experience in this regard:

A colleague and I and the committee we are on were holding hearings on this big education bill that passed last year. As part of the process we made a field trip one day up to an educational television experiment the Ford Foundation is underwriting at Hagerstown, Maryland. I became convinced through some other reading that I did that this was a very worth-while idea, a very challenging idea, in education.

I noticed one day in the *Congressional Record*, by a speech that was put in, that Senator ——— had introduced a bill for each of the forty-eight states to get educational television networks started. These networks not only step up adult education but might actually save a lot of money in this whole educational process. So I talked to his people. I talked to the staff on his committee, the committee chairman, and nobody in the House was interested in this legislation, it appeared. So last year I introduced it. I not only introduced it, I talked with Senator ——— and said, "When you have hearings, I would like to testify."

It turned out that I was, I think, the kick-off witness on it, and this was a very useful experience again in getting behind a piece of legislation and working with people on the Senate side. Ultimately, the bill passed the Senate. We got it out of the House committee and it got lost in the log jam, so there is nothing to report except that I got a lot of experience out of it. But this is the way a new member can get right in the thick of the process.

ASSISTANCE IN DRAFTING

Members may obtain assistance in drafting bills, resolutions, and amendments from the Office of the Legislative Counsel. The first responsibility of this office is to the various committees of the House, but it also assists individual members who request help. The office is staffed by career personnel, is completely nonpartisan, and maintains an impartial attitude with respect to the policies that are to be incorporated in legislative proposals.

To request a draft bill, the member simply furnishes the office with precise ideas of what he wants the bill to do:

. . . all you have to do is either phone down there and say, "Would one of you, whoever handles this particular subject, can we set a time for him to come up and discuss what I want to have drawn up?" Or if you have an outline of what you want drawn up you can send down a little memorandum of what you want and say, "This is the kind of bill I would like drawn up. Would you be kind enough to draw it up and submit a draft to me?" They will do that. That's their job. Sometimes . . . you may want to consult with your committee staff, if it is a bill that would come to your committee, and have them help you with the drawing-up. But the Legislative Counsel primarily is here for that purpose and if you have something in mind you can either phone them or send them a memorandum and get it cooking.

The office does not provide legal research services, but it does give advice and counsel on the legal problems that may be involved in drafting proposed legislation. Any work the office does for a committee or individual member is held in strict confidence.

POLITICAL CONSIDERATIONS

Dropping a bill in the hopper can serve several purposes, experienced members of the House indicate:

The reasons, of course, why you introduce legislation are varied. I would say that primarily you would introduce legislation in areas where you have a particular interest, where you feel it is something that needs to be done and has not been done, or where you want a positive expression of how you would have things done if you only could get your way. To answer constituents' mail or pressure from some group at home you may put a bill in to show that your heart is in the right place. They may write and ask how you feel about providing medical care for those under twenty-five or whatever the problem is and you have a bill all ready to send them, and that is the last word.

Of course, Congressmen—because we are conscious of the press and its great power—introduce bills for two reasons. One of them . . . is to get publicity for ourselves and to appear to be taking a stand for something. The other is that we actually hope to see the legislation enacted. . . .

Another approach that I have used a term or two, not always, [is to introduce bills setting] out my basic position on general legislation in the various fields so that if someone writes me on banking and currency, I say, "Boy, here's my bill." Or on housing or on education, so that you have something to shoot along with your correspondence and that thing gradually gets the community to know just about your general slant.

Law of the next campaign. Any member may introduce a bill at any time while the House is in session. It is not necessary to get anyone's permission. Nor is there any formal limitation on the number of bills he may introduce. However, among other considerations, the unwritten law of the next campaign is cited by senior members who advise against introducing too many bills:

If you've got a bill for your own state for public works or something like that, I wouldn't hesitate at all to be sure to do that. You are going to be asked to introduce claim bills. You are going to have a certain number of local bills that I would not hesitate at all to introduce. Or if you have thought out other things that you wish to achieve, I would go ahead and do that. But I have never felt that the number of bills a man introduces is necessarily the measure of his success. In fact, I have seen it run to the reverse—that a man running for election that introduced some three or four hundred bills, but [his opponent] says, "How many did he pass?" He only passed two. That is kind of a blow to your prestige in the House and sometimes your batting average on the number of bills you passed is more important than on the number you introduced.

I remember one of my colleagues here who the first time, I think, introduced twenty-six bills. None of them passed. His opponent's slogan was, "Went to bat twenty-six times, struck out twenty-six times," and there you have it. And then we remember the new Senator last year, I think, in his enthusiasm introduced and co-sponsored a lot of bills and someone sat down and added up the total [cost] and it made a pretty good thing to talk about.

——— got beat out in California and one reason he got beat is because the only bill he had passed was one relating to the care and culture of jack rabbits and his opponent used that on him . . . and ——— had put in some bills but he hadn't gotten them through. In other words, they take your batting average and I have seen that done time and time again. . . .

Scrutiny of "by request" drafts. All bills and resolutions must be introduced by a member of the House, even though the bill is an Administration proposal or one supported by a private organization or constituent group. And senior members advise careful scrutiny of drafts of legislation to be introduced "by request" of various groups:

I never let anybody hand me a bill that I introduce. I mean it may be your best friend; it may be a person in whom you have extreme confidence. Rewrite that bill yourself because there are a few gimmicks in the language, a reference to amendatory legislation. You may miss it in the reading of the bill and it may be something that you wouldn't personally want to see done so give it to the Legislative Drafting Service. Get the explanation of what the bill seeks to do if you are in favor of it, but have the language be the language of the Legislative Drafting Service and not a lobbyist or even a friend that has some interest that he wants to legislate.

In similar fashion, members advise extreme caution in introducing private bills, particularly in immigration cases:

I had some people not so long ago ask about putting in a bill to keep a fellow in the country. They were just about to deport him. He came in on a visitor's visa and got into difficulties because he took a little work and they were going to throw him out so a great clamor [started] to put in a bill to hold him. I checked with the Immigration Service and he was one hundred per cent solid, so I just took up that bill. [However] I recall that one time when ———— was here somebody handed him a hot spud and he got a bill in for somebody who was described by the Attorney General on a good many of these lists for all sorts of associations with Communist organizations and they really put him in the cooker over that one. . . . He didn't check it and if he had called the Immigration Service or . . . the F.B.I., he would have ducked that one.

Others suggest that it is good government—and good politics— to ensure that the fees charged by lawyers in handling cases of aliens are reasonable. A comment by one experienced member during the 1969 Seminar is illustrative:

I just want to remind you that there is a lawyer out there who's working on that poor devil's case, and he comes around (to his client) for his fee as soon as you drop in a bill. I know of cases where that bill has come pretty high for very little work on the part of counsel. . . . So I make it a rule to require the correspondence to show how much the lawyer is going to get and if it is unreasonable I don't introduce any bill.

To assist members in handling this kind of legislation, Subcommittee No. 1 of the Committee on the Judiciary issues rules of procedure that set out conditions under which consideration will be given private bills. These rules may be obtained by calling the Committee.

Introducing identical bills. Until recently House rules did not permit cosponsoring bills, as could be done in the Senate. However, the same end was—and still is—accomplished by introducing identical bills. This may be done simply by taking a copy of the bill and pasting a piece of paper with the cosponsor's name over the top portion of the original bill, where the bill number and the name of the original sponsor appear.When this device is used, several strategic considerations should be kept in mind:

You can either make your statement, insert it into the *Record*, and file the bill and make a release to your home papers and then solicit colleagues to follow suit with similar bills—sending them, perhaps, an explanation of it. Or you can decide to do everything at once and allow your colleagues the honor of introducing it the same day you do. I think as far as people from different states and districts are concerned that most members don't mind if the initiating member takes the lead and gets back into his state with the news. The other member is still first in his area. There isn't that sort of competition usually.

Now, still a third means [is interesting] an older member, and in that case if you can find a show of interest by an older member and he is willing to introduce the bill either on the same day that you do or a day ahead of you to get the lower number, then, I think, the disadvantage you get by not being first on the field is more than outweighed by getting a senior man with more authority on the committee to help you carry the ball.

In 1967 a rules change—hailed as an economy move—provided that up to twenty-five members could put their names on the same bill, resolution, or memorial.* Cosponsorship has been used

* The new rule does not apply to private bills; these can be sponsored by only one member.

for the most part by members from the same state who want to launch a measure benefitting them all and by members of one party (or persuasion) who want to display a sense of common purpose. But many members continue to follow the earlier practice of attaining maximum visibility by introducing separate, identical bills.

Finding the friendly committee. For the newcomer who is concerned about his legislative batting average, the judicious use of joint introduction of bills may be the answer—if the proposal involved goes to a friendly committee. Otherwise, it may be tabled in committee; the political consequences of this fate are essentially the same as if a bill was introduced and simply disappeared in the legislative labyrinth. One experienced member describes this problem:

> . . . let's say our friend from Alabama has the housing bill in and let's say you are interested in housing so you put in the same bill. Now, his bill will go through; there isn't any doubt about it. That bill is going to move and it would be nice to be on the housing bill [but] when they print the record it will say that your bill is tabled and your opponent next time will pick that up and say, "Look, here this Congressman introduced fifteen bills and all it said in the record was tabled, tabled, tabled," and they will get a piece of literature out on you.
>
> Now, in our committee . . . I tried to block that. Whenever there was authorship of bills in the committee report I referred to all bills by number and by author. In other words we would take one bill and say, "This bill is reported and this measure was cosponsored by identical or similar bills or bills for a similar purpose by ———— of Utah, ———— of California," and so on right down the line so that these fellows actually had a political document they could take home to protect them. But it can get extremely dangerous . . . so you ought to take dead aim and get the bills that you think you can pass, or if you get them in a committee that you think will give you credit for co-authoring, it is beneficial.

Similarly, because of overlapping committee jurisdiction, the way in which a bill is written determines to some extent the committee to which it will be referred. An experienced Congressman explains the implications of this situation for the legislative batting average:

Now, you might think there is a very clear line in the jurisdiction of committees but there is not—and that is something to which you ought to give some close attention if you are introducing legislation. Because you will find out that in some instances where you think you are going to land in a particular committee with your bill, it isn't going to be there at all.

Well, as an illustration, last session we put through the bill that controlled the power of the Defense Department to set up military installations on the public lands of the United States. We corraled and inhibited their action. . . . People would think that that would land in Armed Services, but it didn't; it landed in the Committee on Interior. . . . I call that to your attention and say that you should give some consideration to just where these committees operate, especially when you are introducing legislation, because very often you can write the bill in such a way that it will land in the committee where you want it.

Sometimes it is very important to get a bill in a committee that you know will be friendly. Let me give you an illustration. If you are on Interior for instance . . . you can write legislation in such a way that it will land either in Public Works if it deals with power and flood control, or if it deals with power and flood control, and irrigation and reclamation matters, so that it lands in Interior. Now, very often I would sit down and draft a bill in such a way that it would land in my own committee with the firm intention . . . of amending the bill at a later time to include other matters that I wanted in it. And that's a matter that ought to be taken up with the Parliamentarian if you have no one in your office who knows how to draft legislation.

But very often the controlling factor is the title of the bill and the first paragraph. And if you design those in such a way that they land where you want them to, sometimes the matters in the later sections of the bill are not particularly important. So with respect to the jurisdiction of committees I say that you ought to understand those fairly carefully. You ought to make a careful study of the [1946 Legislative] Reorganization Act with reference to that subject matter and you ought to have in mind that the jurisdiction of committees is not clear; that is, there are fuzzy lines and there is overlapping and conflict between the committees themselves. And often bills will have subject matters in them that would go to any one of three committees, so draftsmanship becomes important when you put in your legislation.

Hearings and legislative clearance. Once a bill has been referred to committee, it is customary for the sponsor to write to the committee chairman, requesting (1) clearance by the Executive department or agency affected by the proposal, and (2) hearings by the committee "at the earliest possible date." The following exchange indicates the significance of these two steps:

Q. Mr. Chairman, after a bill is introduced, what steps would you recommend be taken by the sponsor to get the maximum assurance that the bill will receive some consideration?

A. Well, of course, the committee to which the bill is referred is the prime mover if the bill is going to move. I think it also is wise to get the department's point of view with respect to it. If the Bureau of the Budget or the department is opposed to it it's not likely to move very far. And the more friends you can win in committee the more likely it is that the committee will take it up either for hearings or for consideration in executive session, depending on the character of the bill. There's not much specifically that a nonmember of the committee can do to encourage interest *except in an unofficial way*. . . . Two steps that are pretty good ideas are to write to the chairman of the committee and ask him to secure departmental reports if they haven't already been secured and also to write to him and ask him to set up for hearings at the earliest possible date, and to get those requests in in writing as soon as you feel you are ready to move. It may be quite a while after you write him, but you at least lay the groundwork with the formal request for it from the staff standpoint inside the committee.

Q. You pose another question here. You said write to the chairman and ask him to get departmental reports. By inference this means that

the departmental reports would not normally be provided to the individual member.

A. No, they would come to the committee on the request of the committee [chairman] for departmental reports.

Q. Well . . . assume now that I have a bill that I am considering introducing. I want to make certain that it is going to have the effect I want
it to have. Will the departments respond to my submitting the proposal
to them? What effect will this have, what loss of revenue, what increase
in revenue, etc.? Can I get a report from them? Does it have to come
through committee?

A. I think the department's information to you would be on an informal
basis, if it was going to be of maximum use to you. I think they would
probably make available someone to discuss what you have in mind and
to give you more or less informal judgments as to what the position
would be. But I don't think they would be inclined to give you an actual
report of what their position would be on the legislation until it was requested by committee. If you had serious doubts about the effect of your
proposal it might be wise not to introduce the bill until you've explored
it with the department that knows something about the subject. In other
words, you might well try to get their advice as to the advisability of this
course of action. There might be some policy reason that would suggest
to you that you might pursue a different avenue.

Craftsmanship on the periphery. Another key to legislative
effectiveness for newcomers, in the view of some members, is
emphasis on improvement of existing legislation rather than the
introduction of bills proposing major new programs or major revisions of existing programs. Bills introduced by new members have
a slim enough chance of passage as it is, they argue, and it is possible to be more creative in the early years of a congressional career
by thinking small:

Ordinarily . . . our chance of being creative or craftsmen must
occur on the fringes of legislation. I call this peripheral creativity. What
I mean is a desire and willingness to add something to legislation to
[solve] the problem you may face in your own district without upsetting

the whole pattern of the legislation. It is within the realm of possibility; it improves that bill . . . and it is an achievement. It is something to be proud of. The role is not that of manufacturing a complete suit of cloth but rather that of minor tailoring. This is possible even for the new member. . . .

One way you implement this is not to introduce a major bill overhauling the financial system of the United States or even your own school construction proposal, which is radically different from every other proposal which has been approached. You rather try to file bills which are in effect amendments to other bills which are the major ones, or amendments to existing legislation. For example, you might have an interest in rural areas and want to improve medical facilities in rural areas. You might, therefore, address your attention to a very small amendment in the Hill-Burton Act—but one which is significant if it ever is passed. You might have an amendment to the Small Business Act broadening the type of loan that can be made beyond existing categories. It is not a massive new program but it is a helpful thing in the area in which you are interested.

Another Congressman describes the experience he gained on the periphery by pursuing a legislative hobby:

. . . a particular subject . . . might have nothing to do with your district but it is good experience to get one substantive thing that you will devote attention to, that you will attend all the hearings on, that you will suggest witnesses. Get into the thing so that you learn right away how best to present a case to the Congress; become an expert in one thing and maybe after the first year you will forget that you are going to make it your hobby. If it . . . has an affinity with your district, fine. But [even if it doesn't, it still will be valuable for the] experience that you can get. And if you don't do it the first year you are never going to get around to it.

I remember when I first came here I happened to come as a member of the majority party in the Congress. (I have never been in the majority party in the Congress since the first session.) I was put on a committee—it happened to be the Post Office Committee—and in the spring in my first year here an opportunity came to go into a subject and I talked the chairman into letting me have a subcommittee to go into a subject of the organization of the Post Office Department. . . . Well, I got into the subject; it didn't make much difference to the people of my district . . . what I was doing. I doubt if many of them understood what I was trying to get at. . . . You may have to take a subject that is not "alive" to your district—but you do have the time in your first year or two to do that—and I think the experience is invaluable.

Learning the House rules

In the advice senior members offer their junior colleagues there is a constant refrain: If you want to become an effective legislator, master the rules. Study the rule book, watch procedure on the House floor—and be sure that you understand all you know about the operation of the rules before attempting to apply them. The rewards of knowledgeable performance are described by Speaker John W. McCormack:

If I might make a suggestion to new members, going back myself thirty-five years when I came here as a new member, study the rules of the House of Representatives. That's the legislator's Bible. Study the interpretations of the rules as made by the various Speakers. Watch and study older members participating and putting into execution the rules. Learn from them through their experiences. It will be very, very helpful to you. . . .

I served in the Constitutional Convention in Massachusetts and in the Massachusetts Legislature. Dry work, hard work, digging in, but those of you who do will find that it won't be long—maybe a couple of years—but it won't be long before you will make far more rapid progress than if you ignore them. A decent, profound study of the rules of the House of Representatives. Some day a question will arise and you can participate in the debate. A point of order or some other parliamentary question might arise. And even if you are not on the right side but make the correct arguments on your side and address yourself to the question that is before the Chair, members will then realize that you know what you are talking about, that you know your rules and immediately and automatically respect for such a member will be created in the minds of the other members.

So if there is one direct, straight observation that I could make based on experience—dry work, laborious work, perhaps uninteresting, but those who devote themselves to it and become conversant with the rules of the House and the interpretation of the rules will . . . become model members of the House.

Skill in applying the rules also can make the difference between success and failure in a major legislative effort. Speaking of a colleague with little influence in the House, an experienced member illustrates this point:

——— couldn't control a single other vote in the House of Representatives, but because of his knowledge of parliamentary procedure [he] has changed the progress of legislation merely with his . . . ability to make a point of order. . . . Remember, that's the way we defeated the ———law when they were trying to take out some of the tough parts. . . . It was a point of order that . . . caused it to go over twenty-four hours—and by that time we had picked up the three votes we needed to kill the bill.

THE CONGRESSIONAL SCHEDULE

In the First Session of the 91st Congress—in response to requests by many members who wished to plan in advance for trips to their districts and summer vacations with their families—the House leadership initiated a new practice of announcing in the *Record* the full schedule of recesses early in the Session. The practice had been to announce dates of each recess some weeks or days in advance "as the work schedule permits," giving the leadership on occasion a method of encouraging action of one kind or another on the part of recalcitrant colleagues. Whether the new policy of advance scheduling becomes a permanent fixture remains to be seen. Past attempts in this direction have succumbed to the pressures, among others, of foreign and domestic affairs.* An "August recess," for example, was in the schedule for the First Session of the 91st Congress but was not included in the early announcement for the Second Session. Otherwise, the schedule for the First Session was fairly typical:

Schedule of Recess for 1969

Lincoln Day Recess, from the close of business on Friday, February 7, to the morning of February 17;

Easter Recess, from the close of business on Thursday, April 3, to the morning of April 14;

Memorial Day Recess, from the close of business Wednesday, May 28, to the morning of June 2;

Independence Day Recess, from the close of business Wednesday, July 2, to the morning of July 7;

August Recess, from the close of business Wednesday, August 13, to the morning of September 3, assuming there is no sine die adjournment before this recess takes place.

The legislative program. It is customary for the majority leader, usually in a Thursday floor statement, to announce the legislative program for the following week. This announcement, printed in the *Record*, gives members time to order and review various bills and reports prior to debate and voting. A typical program announcement follows:

Legislative Program for Week of January 26

(Mr. GERALD R. FORD asked and was given permission to address the House for 1 minute).

---

* Although the Legislative Reorganization Act of 1946 requires adjournment "except in time of war or during a national emergency" by July 31, this has occurred only twice since 1946. Not since 1958 has Congress adjourned earlier than September 1st, and not since 1961 has it adjourned earlier than October 1st. The Legislative Reorganization Act of 1970 also contains provision for an August recess; see summary, Appendix pages 401–418.

Mr. ALBERT. Mr. Speaker, will the distinguished gentleman yield?

Mr. GERALD R. FORD. I yield to the distinguished gentleman from Oklahoma.

Mr. ALBERT. Mr. Speaker, we have no further program for this week, but the program for next week is as follows:

Monday is District Day, but there are no district bills.

On Monday we expect to have consideration of the so-called Nelson amendment to H.R. 13111, the Department of Labor and Department of Health, Education, and Welfare appropriation bill, fiscal year 1970.

On Tuesday we will consider H.R. 860, to provide employer contributions for joint industry promotion of products, under an open rule with 1 hour of debate.

On Wednesday we will have H.R. 13111, the Department of Labor and Department of Health, Education, and Welfare appropriation bill, fiscal year 1970, for consideration of a possible veto message. Of course, this is subject to change, but I have been advised this morning that will probably be back for action by the House on Wednesday.

For Thursday and the balance of the week, we will have H.R. 14864, the Defense Facilities and Industrial Security Act of 1970, under an open rule with 2 hours of debate.

This announcement is made subject to the usual reservations that conference reports may be brought up at any time and any further program may be announced later.

STUDY AND OBSERVATION

Members are not required to be on the floor whenever the House is in session, but they are expected to answer quorum and roll-call bells. Regular attendance on the floor is, however, an important part of the learning process for newcomers. Floor attendance gives them a chance to meet and to observe their more experienced colleagues. One member describes how, early in his career, he took advantage of this opportunity to learn by watching:

I noticed that my colleague from ———— was in the House when I first came . . . and he was one of the members . . . who whenever he got up to address the subject before the House received the attention of those on the floor whether there were two hundred on the floor or whether there were fifty on the floor. There were many others, not many but there was a group who always got attention. I didn't say much my first few months here but I watched that phenomenon at work and stayed on the floor probably more in that first year than I have been on in my combined service in the Congress since to try to find out how. I mean I said, "I'm going to be getting up here and talking and I would like to have at least the attention of my colleagues while I am talking. How is it that this group of ten, twelve, or fourteen get attention and everything else is just pandemonium here?"

. . . Well, I found that those who got attention in the first place weren't always on their feet. Maybe they would go for two or three weeks without ever getting the floor for anything more than insertions in the *Record,* but when they did say something it was a matter of importance. It was well prepared. They knew what they were talking about. It was temperate regardless of how strongly they might feel, the position which they were advocating, the side of the question which they were taking; they were not intemperate. They were not making all kinds of wild claims. They were not going into a great emotional speech and attacking those who were taking the opposite side. And I also found that they were the effective ones. They were the ones when the chips were down that could swing votes.

Education on the floor. Observing the House in action is considered to be essential to a working knowledge of parliamentary procedure. And experienced members advise against attempting to digest the rule book in absentia or all at once, recommending instead that it be studied rule by rule in conjunction with observation of floor action:

When I was a new member of the House, one afternoon there were not very many of us there. The great Speaker of the House, Sam Rayburn, was in the Chair and he very seldom ever addressed himself to the House from the Chair. But this was a rather informal session and he said, "I'm disappointed there are not more members of the House on the floor this afternoon. You can read the rule book, you can read every precedent that has ever been written about procedure on the floor of the House, but the only way you can really learn is to be here and observe the House proceedings."

Certainly the best way to learn all of the usual procedures and commonly used motions of the House is to be there on the floor when legislative business is under consideration. Watch and you will see some of the old-timers work and this is probably the best way to learn.

The only way to learn them is to study the rules, to observe the operation of the rules and where you have a chance, to use the rules. If you take [the rule book all at once] you will get thoroughly confused and it just gets so big that you can't digest it all. But if you will take it piece by piece and watch the operation of the rules eventually you will get the idea.

Consulting the Parliamentarian. Particular attention to the operation of the rules—including consultation with the Parliamentarian—is recommended when a member's own bill is coming up for consideration:

. . . you are going to run into occasions when you have a bill of your own that's coming up and you want to explore whether or not it would be possible to bring it up under suspension of the rules or some other procedure. . . . Then you might want to dig in the rule book for that, but for the commonly accepted procedures the best way to learn is by watching and then when you see something you don't understand, ask an older member or ask [the Parliamentarian]. . . . If you are in doubt about something, you should try to work it out yourself; I think that is true. But if after trying to determine just what the proper procedure is, you are still a little bit dubious or have any doubts at all, you ought to consult with [the Parliamentarian].

He is available on the phone most of the day, and he is available on the floor of the House when the House is in session. . . . Rather than end up making what may appear to others to be a foolish point of order, it might perhaps be best to talk to [the Parliamentarian] ahead of time and find out or get some notion. He won't make a ruling for you, but he will certainly give you a few notions of just what you are getting into.

The penalty for speaking out without knowing "just what you are getting into" can be more than acute embarrassment, as a bit of inspired congressional doggerel suggests:

> The Clerk's reading a bill
> when an eager young pill
> bounces up and moves to amend,
> which all comes to naught,
> he didn't move when he ought,
> and all that he did was offend.

PROCEDURE AND HOUSE ACTION*

Introduction of a bill is accomplished by dropping it into the hopper at the Clerk's Desk on the House floor at any time while the House is in session. The attention of the House is not usually called to the introduction of a bill, at the time, in a floor statement by its sponsor. After being deposited in the hopper, the bill goes to the Parliamentarian, who, under the supervision of the Speaker, designates the committee to which it will be referred. It is then given a number and sent to the Government Printing Office for printing.

Printed copies are placed in the House and Senate Document Rooms and sent to the committee that has jurisdiction over the measure. The printed bill carries only the name of the member who introduced it. Sometimes the words "by request" follow the member's name, indicating that he introduced the bill in behalf of someone else. If "by request" is to be included on the bill, these words must appear on the heading of the bill when it is placed in

* This section follows closely Charles J. Zinn, *How Our Laws Are Made* (Washington, D.C.: Government Printing Office, 1965), pp. 4–6.

the hopper. The designation cannot be added or removed after the bill is introduced.

There are four means by which action in the House of Representatives may be initiated:

Bills. The bill is by far the most frequently used means of initiating action. It is used for most legislation and may be either public or private. A public bill is one that affects the public in general, or a segment of it, while a private bill affects only a particular individual or a particular class. A bill that originates in the House is designated by the letters "H.R.," for "House of Representatives" —not "House Resolution," as is commonly assumed—preceding the bill number (H.R. 8362). A bill originating in the Senate is designated by the letter "S" (S. 3162).

Joint resolutions. Practically speaking, there is little difference between a bill and a joint resolution. Both are used to propose legislation, although the joint resolution is most commonly used for extending the life of existing laws. A joint resolution may originate in either House of Congress and receives the same treatment as a bill. If it originates in the House, it is designated "H.J. Res.," for House Joint Resolution, followed by the number. If it originates in the Senate, it is designated "S.J. Res.," for Senate Joint Resolution. Like bills, joint resolutions become law when passed by both Houses of Congress and signed by the President, or when repassed by a two-thirds majority of each house in the event of a veto. One exception, however, is that a joint resolution proposing a constitutional amendment—which requires a two-thirds majority in each House— does not require the signature of the President.

Concurrent resolutions. Concurrent resolutions are used for matters that affect both the House and the Senate. They are not generally used to enact legislation and are not binding or of legal effect. They are commonly used to correct errors in enrolled bills and as a means of expressing the intent, purpose, or sense of Congress as it relates to a particular matter. A concurrent resolution that originates in the House is designated "H. Con. Res."; one that originates in the Senate is designated "S. Con. Res." A concurrent resolution takes effect when passed by both Houses and signed by the Clerk of the House and the Secretary of the Senate. It need not be signed by the President unless it makes law.

Simple resolutions. Simple resolutions are used for matters that affect only the operations of the House or of the Senate. They are commonly used to create special House or Senate investigating committees, to authorize printing of a report or some other material, or to express the will of the House or Senate on a particular matter. Those originating in the House are designated "H. Res."; those originating in the Senate are designated "S. Res." Special orders or "rules" controlling the time and manner of debate, which emanate from the House Committee on Rules, are also designated "H. Res." Simple resolutions are considered only by the body they affect. They take effect as soon as they are passed and signed by the Clerk of the House or, in the Senate, the Secretary of the Senate.

GAINING SPEAKING EXPERIENCE

A Congressman's maiden speech on the House floor during debate is an important event in his career. As likely as not, his family, his staff, and his friends in the Congress will be alerted and on hand for it. Afterward, his close associates will commonly gather in his office for a post mortem and critical evaluation of his speaking mannerisms. To get a feeling for the techniques of debating, many newcomers practice under special orders on the floor at a time when the House is not considering legislation. More experienced members urge even those with considerable state legislative experience to do this:

I would suggest that even for those of you who have had extensive legislative experience, that before you participate in general debate on a bill that you get some practice. Get a special order and have a few of your friends participate with you. Get the feel of being in the well of the House, how the lectern can move up and down, how the microphones work. Practice in the somewhat stilted language of yielding to other colleagues and so forth, so that when you do get into the real legislative fight it isn't all new; you have a little bit of the feel of debating in the House.

Testifying in committee. Committee hearings in the House and Senate offer another opportunity for newcomers to practice their debate techniques:

One thought ran through my mind during the presentations here, when it was suggested by a couple of the speakers that a good way to get your feet wet is to testify before a committee. I would even go beyond that and say that when you get a subject that you feel competent on, or that you are interested in, go over and testify before a Senate committee.

To demonstrate one man's experience on that, because it will give you a little confidence and you will learn a lot about the whole process, the first year I came here I happened to be a little bit of a reformer at odd times and I have always had the view that our laws governing elections—I am sure a lot of you agree with me—are outmoded. . . .

I noticed that the Senator from my state, Senator ———, and Senator Hennings of Missouri and others had introduced a bill to do something about this as they have been doing for years on end. So I took up the same bill and threw it in the hopper, expressing my approval of this idea. Later on I noticed that the Senate committee was going to hold hearings on the subject, so I got hold of the hearings from the two previous Congresses where this subject had been taken up. I delved into them. I asked the Library of Congress to prepare for me a bibliography; this is always a good starting point on any particular subject. I read until I thought I had a pretty good grasp of it; then I asked the Senate committee if I could testify.

They, of course, not only let you testify, but schedule you first and give special treatment. I prepared a statement and put a couple of phrases in that I hoped newspaper reporters would pick up, and I walked over and testified before the committee.

I had a very interesting time. A couple of Senators didn't like some of the things I said. They took me on and I at least thought I held my own with them. I knew as much about it as they did and I came away out of that experience not only understanding a great deal more about the legislative process but I understood more about the Senate.

I made a couple of friends on the Senate side. As a matter of fact, Senator Hennings and I later drafted additional proposals carrying out other ideas and the strange thing was—and this is one of the wonderful things that can happen to a Congressman—that in odd places like St. Louis and Keokuk, Iowa, and West Hoboken, New Jersey, some editors even took account of some of the things that we had said and the content of some of our bills. And then, you see, some of your friends back home say, "Why, he is becoming a national figure." This helps a new Congressman.

Special orders. Special orders are designed primarily to authorize the House to disregard the regular rules of procedure so that a particular matter can be handled with dispatch. They also are used to authorize individual members to address the House for a specific length of time. These speeches usually are made at the end of the day, after all legislative business has been completed, when not many other members are on the floor. As has been indicated, a member making a special order speech can gain additional experience by arranging for a few friends to be on hand to ask questions after he finishes his formal presentation.

Special orders may be obtained for any length of time the member desires—fifteen minutes, a half-hour, or an hour or longer if necessary. Sometimes the member reads only a few lines of his statement, then gives it to one of the official reporters for insertion in the *Record*. Or he may read until his time has expired, then insert the remainder in the *Record*. Special orders may be used to discuss any subject. If a member intends to mention another Congressman or discuss a subject with which the latter is identified, however, tradition and propriety require that he be notified in advance so that he may be on the floor to defend himself or his side of the case if he wishes.

Requesting time. A member may request a special order at any time he can gain recognition without disrupting House proceedings. The proper form for the request is, "Mr. Speaker, I ask unanimous consent that I be given permission to address the House for fifteen minutes at the conclusion of legislative business on Monday, April 15." It is convenient to request special orders during the so-called one-minute period following reading of the *Journal* at the beginning of each day's session. Any member will be recognized during this period for up to one minute for the purpose of making a request or to make a brief statement on some topic and for various other purposes. Technically, a member may not request permission to extend remarks in the *Record* during the one-minute period, but a "one-minute" speech which is simply read in part or handed to the Record Clerk may be of any length.

PARTICIPATION IN DEBATE

Under House procedures, a bill's majority and minority floor managers control allocation of the limited time available for general debate. Although congressional newcomers can and do participate, their senior colleagues advise restraint in asking for time, particularly when the bill being considered is not from their own committee. But even in this case exceptional circumstances may make it advisable for a member to speak out or take a stand. One experienced Congressman, referring to the way in which time for debate is parceled out, offers the following guidelines:

> Well, the time for general debate is doled out by the chairman of the committee to the majority members and by the ranking minority member to the minority members. And when I say doled out, I mean

doled out—in two or three minute bites at most, particularly when you
are down at the bottom of the ladder. . . . Now, unless you are a member
of the legislative committee that is reporting the bill, my practical suggestion to you would be to be reluctant to ask for time in general debate unless (a) your background or experience or studies in this particular field equip you to bring a new angle to the bill that would be
helpful to the members at large or (b) if the legislation is of such importance to you for your re-election, of such local interest that you
pretty well have to make a speech or take a stand in order to get re-
elected.

Clarifying legislative intent. To protect a purely local interest
covered by a bill of wider import, a member may either offer an
amendment or attempt to clarify legislative intent, an action that is
taken into account by the Executive branch in carrying out programs authorized by Congress. A member indicates how this is done,
citing his own experience:

Under an open rule, the floor manager—and that is usually the
chairman (or a subcommittee chairman) of the committee—is very
reluctant to see his bill amended, because one amendment encourages
other people to propose amendments, and he fears that the bill might
be gutted by a number of amendments. Now, suppose you have a situation where you would like to have a clarifying amendment that might
clear up some local interest that you are concerned about. But this
situation is not so complex that it could not be cleared up by legislative
history. In this situation, I think you will find that the floor manager
will be quite willing to yield you some time where you can ask a question which clarifies the legislative intent of the Congress to cover the
situation you are interested in. An example happened to me, just last
year.

We were debating the Public Works Acceleration bill. This bill
talked about the erection or construction of public works. Back home
the people were interested in a public improvement which involved
tearing down or demolishing a bridge which was no longer in use. I
was able to have the chairman of the committee yield to me for a

question of whether this destruction of a bridge would be within the intent of Congress in passing this legislation. He answered affirmatively, and I don't think that an amendment was necessary in that instance.

Considering an amendment. The same member outlines procedures—and strategic considerations—for preparing and offering an amendment:

I would get the office of the Legislative Counsel to draft the amendment for you so that you know that it is technically correct. Then I would suggest that you go to [the Parliamentarian or his assistant]. Show them the amendment, tell them what you intend to do. They will give you good advice. Then I would suggest you talk to either the floor manager or the ranking minority member, depending on your party. Show him the amendment so that he is ready for it and he is not caught off guard. He will probably be willing to help you. Having done that I would go back to [the Parliamentarian], tell him what has developed thus far, and find out who the chairman of the Committee of the Whole House is likely to be. When you find that out, tell the chairman of the Committee of the Whole House that you are going to propose this amendment. Finally, I would suggest that you sit right in the front row so that you can be recognized at the time that is proper for you to propose your amendment.

Now, let's face it . . . if you don't have your floor manager with you on an amendment, prepare to be defeated. In analyzing your own situation, consider . . . whether you are better off to have been defeated on an amendment or whether it is the better part of valor not to propose it at all.

Now, if you go ahead and propose your amendment and if the chairman of the Committee of the Whole House rules that your amendment has been defeated [by voice vote], then you have the right by yourself to demand a division vote where the members who favor the amendment stand and then the members who oppose it also stand. [And you should think] about the tactics of whether you should possibly embarrass your friends by asking for [such] a division. . . .

Comments by other experienced members point up the possibilities for embarrassment in voting on amendments—and it is considered sound practice to line up sympathetic colleagues in advance:

It can be pretty embarrassing to offer an amendment in the Committee of the Whole and then when the vote is taken by voice vote, to find yourself the only one shouting "aye." So I think it's a pretty good practice if you are going to offer an amendment, even if you don't think it has a chance, if you would speak to a few of your friends ahead of time and say, "Now the chairman is against this thing, I know it hasn't got a chance, but I feel I have to offer it. I believe deeply in it and besides my constituents would defeat me if I didn't, so when I offer it and the vote is taken would you shout with me and then we'll forget the whole thing."

Now you've seen members, particularly new members, making [this] mistake when they feel very strongly about an amendment they've offered: They've lost on a voice vote [and are] demanding a division [and] everybody in the committee rises with the exception of two or three—you and your brother-in-law perhaps—and then the two of you rise in favor of an amendment. It's even more embarrassing than a weak voice vote. So I think that one bit of advice on amendments is that if you are going to offer an amendment you had better circulate around a little bit before you offer it. Let a few people who you think might support the thing know you are going to offer it and ask them for their support. . . .

Speaking for the Record

The *Congressional Record* is the message center of the Congress. Members use it to communicate not only with their constituents but also with their colleagues, and it is here that the congressional newcomer begins to establish an identity for himself. Accordingly, in the view of more senior members, the new congressman is well advised to use its pages judiciously.

CORRECTION OF ERRORS

The body of the *Record* contains a substantially verbatim account of Senate and House debate; prior to publication members are granted permission by unanimous consent to revise and extend statements made during debate. Thus they have an opportunity to correct grammatical errors and unintentional misstatements, to clarify remarks that might be misinterpreted when read rather than spoken— and to eliminate impolitic comments made during the heat of debate.

A member may strike out any portion of his speech or omit it entirely. Or he may add comments not included when the speech was delivered, perhaps changing the meaning or intent of what he has said. However, substantial changes of this kind raise questions of individual ethics:

At the conclusion of your remarks the official reporter will supply you with (if you are still on the floor) a copy of the remarks. You can correct them there or back in your office. If you have returned to your office, the copy of your remarks from the official reporter will be sent to your office. Then you revise and add as much material as you may want to add. I don't comment on the ethical correctness of this, but this is the way it works: You can add a lot of things you didn't say, if you wish. Or you can even go to the extent of changing the meaning or the intent of what you did say, if you wish. Although, I say, I won't comment on the ethical question involved. . . .

No criticism of members. As was indicated in Chapter Five, each day's issue of the *Record* contains four sections: House floor proceedings, Senate floor proceedings, the Extensions of Remarks, and the Daily Digest. The House and Senate sections are referred to as the "body," or "record" proper. Under revise-and-extend procedures, members may have material printed in either the Extensions of Remarks or the body. Since 1968 there has been somewhat greater use of the Extensions of Remarks section because of the introduction of an index (on the last page of the *Record*) listing the member's name. Also, remarks and other materials in the Extensions section now form a part of the permanent *Record*, which was not formerly the case. Generally, members may insert anything they wish except direct, personal criticism of another member of Congress:

> I think the principal prohibition that you have to concern yourself with is that neither in debate nor in the *Record* should you or can you direct personal criticism toward another member, his motives, his character, his honesty, and such. Likewise, you cannot direct such criticism toward a member of the Senate, nor can you technically mention Senators by name. You can call them the senior Senator from Arizona, or you can describe the Senate as having taken some action or other. I would suggest you check into the rules of the House of Representatives [on this].

Content of material important. Anything that appears in the *Record* automatically becomes official business and may be mailed under the franking privilege. No formal limitations are placed on the number of insertions in the body or the Extensions of Remarks that a member may make during a session. Too frequent use of this device may lead to difficulties, however, if adequate attention is not paid to the content of material inserted. As one more senior member delicately put it for the benefit of his junior colleagues:

> Finally, just let me conclude by saying that while you can—and many do—make hundreds of insertions in the *Record* in the course of a session of Congress, I would suggest at least that you be judicious about just what you insert. . . . I have never heard of a member of Congress who was defeated for re-election on account of something that he didn't say. And sometimes you can put too much in the *Record.*

Changes for the permanent Record. Most members check the *Record* daily for errors in their remarks, in material they have inserted in the Extensions of Remarks or body, or in the way they are recorded as having voted. After obtaining authorization from the House, a member has thirty days from the day of publication to correct any errors in the permanent *Record.* Authorization for correction of errors is usually requested and granted under unanimous-consent procedures.

REVISING AND EXTENDING

The opportunity to extend remarks beyond what was actually said in the House chamber is a time-saving device. It permits members who might otherwise be unheard to state their position for inclusion in the *Record,* while reducing the pressure on time required for floor action. The device is especially useful when the House is considering an issue that is of great significance to one or two congressional districts, but is of little general interest, and is therefore to be approved or rejected by a voice vote. In effect, the right to extend makes the *Record* indicate what a member would have said had he been given time to say it, or how he would have voted had the question been put to a roll-call vote. However, revisions that affect the remarks of another member—especially an opponent in debate—are not permitted unless authorization is obtained from the other member involved as well as from the House. Thus, revisions that change the meaning of, place a different emphasis on, or in any way affect the remarks of another member customarily are called to his attention.

Procedure for obtaining permission. A member wishing to use this procedure obtains permission by requesting "unanimous consent that I be allowed to revise and extend my remarks." He may do this at the beginning or conclusion of his comments on the House floor. Permission to revise or extend while the House is in Committee of the Whole House is ordinarily limited to the member's own comments on the bill under consideration by the committee. If a member desires to include tables, editorials, or other extraneous but relevant material as a part of his contribution to the debate in Committee of the Whole, he may either request permission by unanimous consent before the House resolves itself into Committee of the Whole or as soon as possible after the committee rises and reverts back to the House.

Customarily, when time is limited and several members wish to extend their remarks on a bill without actually speaking, they pass such requests to their party's floor manager for the particular bill, and frequently a floor manager obtains "general leave" that all members have five or more legislative days in which to extend their remarks on the bill under consideration.

About an hour after a request for extension is made, the official reporter delivers to the member a transcript of his remarks. If he revises these in his office, he may return the edited transcript to the reporter by depositing it in one of the *Congressional Record* boxes on the guard's desk at each entrance to the House office buildings. It is customary to notify the clerk on duty in the official reporter's office whenever material is placed in a *Record* box late in the evening.

INSERTING OTHER MATERIAL

The statement or speech of a member's extended remarks appears in the body of the *Record* just as if it had actually been made on the floor during debate. The request to revise and extend is also used to insert material in the *Record* that is not directly related to the immediate legislative business before the House.

Unanimous consent required. A member wishing to insert material in either the body or the Extensions of Remarks requests "unanimous consent to extend my remarks at this point in the *Record*" at any time he is able to gain recognition; he then gives the material to be inserted to one of the official reporters. A number of advance permissions may be made in a single request. As described by a member, this is a convenient thirty-day checking account:

You can start a kind of blood bank of these. You can go down and make your request, make it for four or five or six insertions, and you have thirty days in which to use up these permissions to revise and extend in the Extensions of Remarks. And if you have something you want inserted in the Extensions of Remarks under a permission that you have obtained you can give it to the official reporters on the floor of the House, sitting there beneath the Speaker, or you can simply drop it in one of those boxes on the entrance guards' desks.

Permission to insert material also may be requested in behalf of another Congressman, and members customarily telephone requests from their offices to their parties' cloakroom attendant, who in turn conveys them to a member on the floor. And, to avoid interrupting legislative proceedings, each party frequently designates a member who requests permission to extend for all his colleagues desiring to insert material in the *Record* by obtaining a special order for a specific amount of time at the end of a particular day. During this time, the members involved may either give their statements to one of the official reporters, read part of their statements and give the remainder to the reporter, or read their entire statements.

Use of the Extensions of Remarks. As has been noted, members may insert materials in either the Extensions of Remarks or the body. Generally, the less pertinent or important items are placed in the Extensions, while the body is reserved for material dealing with current legislative action. Referring to use of the body of the *Record,* a more senior member suggests:

This should be . . . used only when you have something particularly pertinent you want to say about some legislative matters directly connected with the business of the Congress. I don't believe there is an enforced regulation with regard to insertions in the body of the *Record,* however.

Authorizing lengthy statements. The length of speeches and statements prepared by members themselves is not limited. Formerly, extraneous matter—material the member himself did not write or prepare—was not supposed to exceed two pages in the old Appendix, unless the House authorized otherwise. To obtain the necessary authorization, a cost estimate had to be secured from the Congressional Record Clerk, and unanimous consent had to be requested for inclusion of the material "notwithstanding the said cost." This procedure was abandoned during the 90th Congress—but most members are nevertheless reluctant to insert extremely long items of extraneous material.*

* In 1969 the Government Printing Office estimated printing costs for the *Record* at $119 per page. Some members cite the cost factor in turning down constituents' requests—which are not uncommon—for insertion of material.

Decorum and congressional ethics

MINIMUM STANDARDS of conduct are set out in House rules, including a Code of Official Conduct adopted in 1968, and in federal statutes. In addition, there are proprieties established by custom which recognize the need for parliamentary dignity, for courtesy, and for mutual respect among members. Observing these rules and traditions—on the floor in debate and elsewhere—is one key to effective House service. Ignoring them may have no immediate consequences, according to Representative John F. Baldwin, but repeated transgressions may hinder a member's legislative efforts:

. . . To establish a proper basis for your relationships with your fellow House members and to cause them to feel that you understand the proprieties of the House may be very important to you . . . when you are endeavoring to push through legislation, because they will either have a favorable reaction to you because of their past observations of your performance in the House or they will have an unfavorable reaction. And if they have an unfavorable reaction that may be quite a hindrance at some future time.

Establishing and maintaining a "proper basis for your relationships" with other members is not always easy. Legislative work is demanding physically and otherwise. Individual personality differences, the stresses of political life, the requirements of verbal combat, the stakes involved—all contribute to conflicts that occasionally violate traditions of courtesy, interrupt friendships of long standing, and diminish mutual respect among colleagues. But, in the view of Representative Burt L. Talcott, the House cannot function effectively if members indulge in personal animosity or vindictiveness:

The importance of the legislation, the enormity of the consequences of our deliberations, the pressures of politics, the demands of our constituents, and the earnestness of our convictions quite naturally arouse passions and strain tempers. The competitiveness of the professional athlete, the adversariness of the political arena, and the litigiousness of the trial lawyer are common ingredients of our floor debate and committee work. Few who have never served in the House can appreciate the strenuousness of our work, the onerous demands on our time, and the mental, physical, and emotional strains which are inherent in the discharge of our duties. . . .

We representative legislators cannot properly resolve the Nation's abrasive problems without occasionally exacerbating normal human tensions. But the House cannot continue to function effectively if Members permit personal animosity or vindictiveness to distort their perspectives or to disrupt their duties.

Members of Congress are as different from each other as their districts are different from one another. This ingredient of individualism enhances the legislative product. Congress is also a unit, "a body" whose Members are all working, perhaps not in unison, but toward the same goal—perfect Federal legislation. We must literally live and work together much of the time. Our philosophical differences, our political disagreements, our divergent approaches to problem solving, our various backgrounds, abilities, experiences, and temperaments are all understood and valued by each other. But these differences, which we respect and want to preserve, require special rules of order and personal behavior to enable us to work and to live compatibly with each other and still accomplish our legislative objectives.

Full explanation, trenchant questions, responsive answers, vigorous argument, thorough deliberation are all necessary to perfect legislation. The sharpness of spontaneous debate, so essential to good legislation, can cut to the quick, irritate, embarrass, even offend Members who are otherwise friends and mutual admirers.

We must foster incisive debate, yet preserve friendships. Debates on other issues, just as important, will follow closely. Later the same day, new advocates will be realigned with different adversaries, but with a constancy of purpose and continuation of mutual respect. This is the essence of that special relationship which we call "colleague"—tough contestants while debating issues, but tenacious allies in maintaining friendships.*

What is the cement that binds personal friendships? There is no codified list of do's and do not's, of course. Members frequently suggest, however, that charitable feelings can begin with the home folks. Representative Allard K. Lowenstein, as quoted in *The New Yorker*, explains:

In the House, as elsewhere, personal relations make a great difference if you want to get things done. A member may want you to speak at some function that one of his constituents has organized, or meet a delegation coming to see him, or simply come and have a drink. Then, too, if you're going to somebody's district, you try to tell him ahead of time and perhaps chat with him about your trip afterward. A while ago, when I marched in Charleston with the hospital workers, who were on strike, I called up Representative Mendel Rivers beforehand to tell him what I intended to do. It's no great secret that our political views are about as far apart as views can get, but our relationship has remained cordial.†

* "Precedents and Traditions for Decorum on the Floor of the House," in the *Congressional Record,* July 31, 1969, pp. H6671–6675.

† From "A Reporter at Large: New Member," by Flora Lewis in *The New Yorker*, January 10, 1970, p. 59. Reprinted by permission of the author and publisher.

Conduct on the floor*

Custom does not require new members to remain silent during debate on the House floor. Rather, it is recognized that they have a right and a duty to speak out, especially during consideration of matters of particular interest to their districts. It is generally agreed, too, that members are judged more by what they say and how they say it than by the number of times they speak. What is resented, in newcomers and experienced members alike, is speaking too frequently and saying too little in too many words:

I would just like to make this observation that the tradition as I learned it was not that you refrained from speaking in the House as a new member, but that you only spoke when you had something to say, something to contribute to the debate going on in the House. [If you will so guide your actions] you will find no one resents your taking the floor and stating your views.

RULES OF COURTESY

Courtesy is the practice in the House, whether on the floor or elsewhere, and it is against the rules to engage in personalities during debate. Accordingly, a member may not direct personal criticism toward another Congressman, nor may he question his motives, his character, or his honesty. Other members are always addressed in the third person. Thus, it is considered improper in the House to use the pronoun "you" in addressing another member or to refer to another Representative or Senator by name. *Jefferson's Manual* (section 361) states: "No member, in speaking, is to mention a member then present by his name, but to describe him by his seat in the House, or who spoke last, or on the other side of the question. . . ."

* This section follows closely the comments of the late Representative John F. Baldwin, of California, made during the 1959 and 1963 orientation programs for freshman Congressmen.

Forms of address. In addressing or referring to another member of the House, the proper usage is "The Gentleman from ————," naming his state. In the case of a woman member, the proper form is "The Gentlewoman from ————." On occasion, when it is clear to whom a member is referring or speaking, the shortened forms, "the gentleman" and "the gentlewoman," are permissible. Likewise, members of the Senate are referred to as "the senior (or junior) Senator from ————." In the House, the Senate is traditionally referred to as "the other body," rather than by name.

All statements including comments or questions directed to another member, are customarily begun by addressing the Chair. The proper form is to begin by saying either "Mr. Speaker" or "Mr. Chairman," depending upon whether the House or the Committee of the Whole is then sitting. If a woman member is presiding, the form is "Madam Speaker" or "Madam Chairman."

In referring to committees, the preferred form is the "Committee on Rules," not the "Rules Committee"; the "Committee on Ways and Means," not "Ways and Means," etc.

Guides to decorum. The House rules provide the basic guide to decorum on the floor, but practice has established unwritten rules that supplement them. House Rule XIV, section 7, states:

> While the Speaker is putting a question or addressing the House, no member shall walk out of or across the hall, nor, when a member is speaking, pass between him and the chair; and during the session of the House no member shall wear his hat, or remain by the Clerk's desk during call of the roll or counting of ballots, or smoke upon the floor of the House. . . .

The rule specifically prohibits passing between a member who is speaking and the Chair, but it is also considered bad manners to walk near him, especially if he is speaking from the well of the House. Occasionally, this is done by "somebody who may not have studied the rules," says Representative Baldwin, adding:

It doesn't look very good to have somebody walking right across in front of a speaker or right behind him, practically brushing past him, [when] he is in the middle of a serious talk. It is a propriety that can be observed with good judgment and I think that your fellow members of the House who have been here for some period of time will appreciate it if it is observed.

And although hats are the only article of clothing mentioned in House Rule XIV, it is generally understood that sports coats and sports shirts, or "loud" or extreme attire are not to be worn on the floor. Members need not dress like undertakers, but they are expected to wear suits and neckties. Smoking on the floor is prohibited (but is done behind railings at the back and sides of the chamber), and walking into the chamber with a cigar or pipe in mouth—lighted or not—is frowned upon.

Congressional newcomers are advised by their senior colleagues not to snack, put their feet on the chairs, or read newspapers on the House floor. The latter, although sometimes done, is not considered good form. Representative Baldwin explains why:

Once in a while you will see some House member violating these rules and nobody is going to come down and beat him over the head if he hangs his feet over the chair in front of him or if he is sitting on the floor of the House reading a newspaper. But it isn't good procedure and some of your senior members will probably observe it if you do it. Also, you never know when you have constituents in the House gallery. You will know part of the time because [if] constituents want to get passes to the House gallery they have to come to your office to get passes, but you may not always know when they are getting passes from your office. You may have left your office to go over to the floor and some constituents may drop in subsequently and ask for a couple of passes and come on over and go into the gallery. So you may have a couple of your own people watching to see what happens on that floor and watching you.

In addition, if they happen to come into the Capitol in the center corridor where the tours start out, they never have to come into your office to get a pass, because under standard procedure the person conducting the tours will take each group into the House gallery for about fifteen minutes. So you may have constituents on those tours. It is not just whether or not you may cause an unfavorable impression on your seniors but whether you may have constituents in the gallery unknown to you, and if you are sitting hanging your feet over the chair in front of you or reading a newspaper they may carry a report back to some of their friends that is not too favorable.

Order in the House. There is no prohibition against talking with other members on the floor, but speaking too loudly and interrupting normal procedure can be embarrassing:

. . . if you desire to speak to your neighbor you should certainly speak in a quiet tone of voice so that you aren't interrupting the proceedings. Don't cause so much noise that the recognized speaker becomes aware of it and is distracted by it. Don't speak so loudly that some other House member sitting near you, but not right next to you, is going to be bothered by the fact that you are talking so loudly that he can't hear what's going on. Now if this happens the member who is trying to hear has the right, under the rules of the House, to stand up and make a point of order that the House is not in order. The Speaker, who is in the chair, then has the function of sounding the gavel and requesting the House to come back to order. Certainly it is not advisable for you to be the one who is causing such commotion by talking so loudly that somebody near you finds this necessary in order for him to listen to what is going on.

Besides being discourteous and distracting to whoever is speaking and to those who are trying to listen, loud conversations also give the House an unruly, disorganized, inattentive appearance—especially when the Chair is forced to stop the proceedings and call for order. Hissing, jeering, and other such demonstrations are obviously out of order. The Chair has the responsibility of keeping order in the House, and the Speaker or Chairman usually can restore order simply by tapping his gavel. But he also may call a member to order by name, in which case the rules require that the member be seated immediately, unless he is permitted on motion to continue, and he may be censured or punished as the House deems proper.

Floor seating arrangements. Unlike the other body, where Senators have their own desks complete with engraved nameplates, members of the House do not have assigned seats in the chamber. They can and do sit where they please during regular sessions. Generally, however, members spend most of their time seated on their own party's side of the center aisle. The Democrats traditionally have the section to the Speaker's right, whether they are in the majority or the minority. Members may sit in the front rows regardless of seniority, except on such occasions as the President's State of the Union address, when the front seats are reserved for cabinet members and Supreme Court Justices.

PARTICIPATION IN DEBATE

House rules state that a member participating in debate "shall confine himself to the question under debate." But the Speaker, or Chairman of the Committee of the Whole, has great latitude and discretion in interpreting and applying this rule to particular situations. A member objecting to a bill calling for expenditures, for example, might discuss the size of the federal budget, the national debt, and other related factors that should be considered in any action taken on the new program.

If another member makes a point of order—that the discussion is not germane—and demands "the regular order," the Speaker or Chairman decides whether the comments in question are relevant to the pending bill or resolution. Moreover, a member desiring to make an important statement or announcement during the consideration of a bill or resolution may obtain time to discuss the pending bill and then ask unanimous consent to "proceed out of order." If his request is granted, he may speak on any subject.

Representative Baldwin describes this aspect of House operation and compares it with Senate procedure:

The rule of germaneness in the House means that if you are speaking on a bill you are supposed to speak on that subject. This is in contrast to the rules of the Senate. The rules of the Senate have no germaneness requirement.* You can speak on any topic at any time. You can get up and read the telephone book, and this has been done. But in the House, if you are speaking during a time that a bill is under debate, under the rule of germaneness you are supposed to speak on that subject unless you ask for unanimous consent to speak out of order. If you ask unanimous consent to speak out of order and that is given, then you can speak on any topic, even while the bill is still pending.

Gaining recognition. The proper method of gaining recognition to speak is specified in House rules:

When any member desires to speak or deliver any matter to the House, he shall rise and respectfully address himself to "Mr. Speaker," and, on being recognized, may address the House from any place on the floor or from the Clerk's desk. . . .

Only when the House itself is sitting is it proper to address remarks to the Speaker; when the Committee of the Whole is sitting, "Mr. Chairman" is properly addressed. In neither the House nor the Committee is embellishment of the salutation deemed appropriate. "Mr. Chairman, distinguished guests, reverend clergy, my fellow great Americans, and fair ladies" may be appropriate for openers at a Rotary Club banquet. But in the House it is likely to lose you your audience and gain you the scorn of your colleagues. The position of the mace—the symbol of authority in the House— indicates whether the House or the Committee of the Whole is sitting:

* The Senate adopted a rule on germaneness on January 23, 1964, but it has had little effect on Senate practice.

. . . if you come on the House floor and you are thinking about asking for recognition for some purpose—there is one simple rule you can follow in determining whether we are in the House of Representatives or what is called the Committee of the Whole House on the State of the Union. If the mace is fixed in its high position [on its pedestal] at the immediate right of the Speaker . . . then we are in the House of Representatives.

Now the mace is that, well it's sort of a club with an eagle on top of it. If you will watch closely, one of the House employees will move it up to its high position the moment the Speaker walks into the House, at the start of the House session each day. And while it is in that position, we are in what is known as the House of Representatives. Your proper request to obtain recognition is, "Mr. Speaker." When the House goes into the Committee of the Whole House on the State of the Union, the mace is removed to a lower position and from that time on if you want to obtain recognition the proper request is to say, "Mr. Chairman."

Although a member may speak from any place on the floor, it is customary to use the microphones placed in the chamber, as Representative Baldwin indicates:

. . . as a matter of procedure, if you want to be heard—unless you have a very loud voice—it is usually best to get close to a microphone. So you usually have a choice of going down in the well of the House and using one of the two mikes there or speaking from one of the mikes at the tables on both sides of the floor. You don't have to. Under the rules you aren't required to go to the mikes, but if you think you are saying something that is worth repeating on the House floor and worth hearing by others, then it is customary to get to a mike so that everybody else can hear what you have to say.

Before recognizing a member to speak, the Chair often asks, "For what purpose does the gentleman rise?" The Chair is governed by rules in recognizing members, and at certain times he is prohibited from recognizing members except for privileged questions or other matters taking precedence under the rules. Only if the member reveals in advance why he wants to speak can the Chair determine whether or not recognition is permissible. The Speaker (or Chairman, in Committee of the Whole) has sole jurisdiction over recognition. If he denies recognition, the ruling may not be contested.

Time limitations sometimes make it impossible for all interested members to speak on a bill. Members of the committee that reported the bill are given preference in recognition; members are then generally recognized on the basis of seniority. If a member feels strongly about a certain measure, however, or if it is vitally important to his district, he can usually get "on record" by asking the member in charge of the debate on his side to yield to him for a unanimous consent request to insert his statement in the *Congressional Record*. Representative Baldwin describes this procedure:

> . . . if some tax bill, or something that you have conducted a regular campaign on, comes up and by the time all the Democrats and all the Republicans of the Ways and Means Committee get their time allotted to them and all of their time is committed, and you go to the man who is handling your side and say you would like to speak on the bill, and he says, "My time is committed," then you are in the embarrassing predicament of having campaigned at home and saying you are going to get this bill passed. Yet here you may possibly be barred from speaking.

> Under these circumstances, the best out is to ask the person handling the debate on your side if he will just recognize you for a unanimous consent request. Normally the person handling the debate will do that. He can then recognize you, and you can simply say, "Mr. Speaker" or "Mr. Chairman," as the case may be, "I ask unanimous consent to insert my remarks in the *Record* at this point." Then you can put your two- or three-page speech in the *Record* and it will appear as a part of the debate in the *Congressional Record* the next day. This is

usually the best way to protect yourself if you can't get speaking time allotted to you.

During debate under the five-minute rule, when a bill is being read for amendments, members who feel that they must speak or go on record with a statement can gain recognition by offering a *pro forma* amendment. This is done by saying, "Mr. Chairman, I move to strike out the last word." After recognition is granted, the member may either speak for up to five minutes or simply ask leave to insert his statement in the *Record*.

A member of the House speaks as a matter of right after being recognized by the Chair. To conclude a speech with " I thank you" is therefore unnecessary—and suggests the amateurish notion that the member's words of wisdom may well be followed by applause, which seldom occurs.

Requesting colleagues to yield. Under House rules, the member who has the floor is not required to yield to anyone. This rule may present some problems for the newcomer who wants to participate in debate—but does not want to risk refusal of a request to yield. Representative Baldwin recommends advance consultation for those wishing to break in on floor debate:

. . . Sometimes you can actually ask [your colleague] in advance, "Say, I'd like to just get a shot at this and would you mind yielding to me. I just want to ask a question. Here's what it is." If he is a friend of yours you can work it out so you know he is going to yield to you. Sometimes it is a little bit embarrassing to get up and ask some committee chairman if he will yield to you and he just declines to yield or he doesn't even recognize you. And he doesn't have to either. He can just ignore you.

So it isn't always a good idea to start breaking the ice by getting up against a pretty tough committee chairman and asking him to yield at the first opportunity you have on the House floor. It might be a little easier to get somebody who is a friend of yours and call to his attention in advance that you just want to get a little opportunity to participate in House procedure and would he mind if he yielded to you and here is the question you are going to ask him. As long as you do it on that basis, you can obtain a first experience participating on the House floor that will be an easy one and one that won't let you down by having someone just ignore your existence. . . .

When a member yields to another, the time used by the second member is counted against the time alloted to the member holding the floor. And if the member to whom time was yielded offers a motion or proposes any other business, the member yielding loses possession of the floor. Generally, however, it is understood that the member who asks another to yield will not use the time for purposes other than asking questions or replying to the remarks of the member who has the floor.

Requests to yield are addressed to the Chair rather than to the member who is speaking. The proper form is, "Mr. Speaker (or Mr. Chairman), will the gentleman yield?" The member who has the floor, not the Chair, then responds, for the decision to yield or not is entirely his. He may decline to yield in order to avoid embarrassing questions. Usually, however, he yields when the request is made, or he offers to yield when he has completed his remarks. The latter response may, in effect, be a refusal to yield, for his time may expire just as he completes his statement. If a member refers to a colleague in his statement, however, it is considered only fair that he yield immediately at the request of the member referred to—or at least leave sufficient time for a reply after he completes his statement.

Points of order. A point of order is an objection that a certain proceeding is not in accordance with the rules. It may be raised by any member at any time. Raising a point of order usually stops all proceedings, except a roll-call vote, until a determination of its validity is made. When a member is not sure of his ground, according to experienced members, he should consult informally with the House Parliamentarian before making a point of order.

The proper form for raising a point of order is, "Mr. Speaker (or Mr. Chairman), I make a point of order that ————." The Chair may rule on the point of order immediately if he has the precedents at hand, or he may delay his ruling until he has had time to consider the matter. The Chair may also entertain debate on a point of order. For example, during debate in Committee of the Whole, a member might say, "Mr. Chairman, I make a point of order that the amendment is not germane." The Chair might then give the member proposing the amendment an opportunity to defend its germaneness and then again recognize the member who made the point of order to hear him further. Such debate is entirely within the discretion of the Chair; he can terminate it whenever he is ready to rule. Once the Chair has ruled, members may not debate the decision. They may appeal it by putting it to a vote but decisions of the Chair are seldom overturned.

Intemperate remarks. The procedure for dealing with intemperate remarks that violate the rules of the House is called "taking down words." If, for example, a member impugns the character or motives of a colleague in debate, the offended member or another may call him to order and demand that his words be taken down. The objectionable words are then read aloud to the House, and the Chair rules whether they are out of order. If the member who uttered the words denies that the language taken down is the exact language he used, the question is put to the House for decision. If the Chair rules the words as taken down to be out of order, the offending member may be permitted to offer an apology—or he may be prohibited from speaking for the remainder of the day.

FLOOR PRIVILEGES

The rules specify those who are entitled to admission to the floor while the House is in session. In addition to members, the list includes the President and Vice President and their private secretaries, Justices of the Supreme Court, U.S. Senators (House members also have Senate floor privileges), members-elect of Congress, members of the President's cabinet, foreign ministers, state governors, and former members of the House. Furthermore, Representative Baldwin points out:

Although the rules don't state this, by tradition members can bring their own small children on the House floor to sit with them a short time unless the Speaker has announced particularly that attendance is going to be limited to those who have the right to be on the floor, as he did for the joint session. Obviously, there would not have been space in the joint session to have children on the floor in addition to members. But other than those special occasions, by tradition, a member may bring his small children on the floor to sit with him for a few minutes. . . .

Various House employees and officials, including committee staff personnel when business from their committee is under consideration, also have access to the floor. But unlike Senate practice, members' personal staff employees are not admitted to the floor because of space limitations and existing congestion. Members may take individual constituents and other visitors onto the floor when the House is not in session, except during the fifteen minutes before a session begins and the fifteen minutes after it adjourns. House rules prohibit members—or the House itself, for that matter —from recognizing anyone in the gallery from the floor. Some state legislatures permit members to introduce delegations or important personages sitting in the galleries, but this is strictly forbidden in the House, and the Chair is prohibited from entertaining a request to relax the rule. A section of the gallery is set aside for the families of members of Congress, and another section is reserved for constituents and other visitors who are admitted only on presentation of a pass signed by a member of Congress. Sections are reserved for the press, for congressional staff employees, and for the President, members of his cabinet, Justices of the Supreme Court, foreign ministers, and members of their immediate families.

Only the Speaker or the Chairman of the Committee of the Whole may order the galleries cleared of all spectators.

Rules of decorum for spectators are strictly enforced, and members must comply when they are seated with constituents in the gallery. Representative Baldwin suggests that new members learn and abide by the gallery rules, particularly if they hope to make a favorable impression on their constituents:

The reason it's rather important to know some of the rules applicable in the gallery is that members frequently find that it is a desirable thing to take visitors up to the gallery and sit with them for a few minutes to explain some of the proceedings on the House floor. And if you are up in the gallery with constituents you have to comply with the rules of the gallery the same way anyone else does.

Now I learned the hard way. I never bothered to read the rules functioning in the gallery so on about three different occasions one of the doorkeepers in the gallery came down and tapped my shoulder because I was violating some rule. I am stating this just so you won't have the same kind of experience. I was sitting in the front row of the gallery with a couple of constituents one day, and put my hand on the rail as I was pointing out something on the floor. The doorkeeper came down and tapped my shoulder and said, "You are violating the rules. It is against the rules to put your hands on the rail in front of the gallery."

And, he adds wryly,

. . . if you are a Congressman and your constituents think you know everything and you violate a rule of the House gallery, that does not always cause you to feel you have impressed your constituents too favorably.

In addition to the prohibition against placing hands or feet on the front railing, gallery rules prohibit the following activites:

★ Reading

★ Writing or taking notes

* Sleeping

* Demonstrations of any sort, including cheering or applauding

* Carrying cameras, packages, books, or other items. (Women's purses are permitted in the gallery, but all other items must be checked at the desk outside.)

Ethics and conflict of interest*

As a member of Congress you are elected to represent a half million people. You take an oath to uphold the Constitution, do your duty and look out for the United States of America. You are an officer of the United States; trust is imposed in you. You are expected to be aware of and to put first the interest of all the people of the United States. Now, if you get in a situation where your private interests could be or might be opposed to the interests of the United States, then you have a conflict problem. You have to decide what to do about it.

Conflict of interest, as described in the foregoing comment by Representative Udall during the 1963 Seminar, is a thorny problem. It arises because a Congressman is both a public official and a citizen with private assets and aspirations. Existing rules and statutes dealing with the problem are imprecise and difficult to apply to particular situations faced by individual members. Moreover, little uniformity of congressional practice exists in the handling of outside business interests. Accordingly, in a large area of ambiguity the member and his conscience must make the decisions.

Political scientist Ralph Eisenberg describes the gray zone of legislative behavior as the area "lying between behavior that is 'clean as a hound's tooth' and behavior obviously improper and

* For a thorough discussion of problems of congressional ethics, see James C. Kirby, Jr., Armin Rosencranz, and Ellen W. Ober, *Congress and the Public Trust: Report of the Association of the Bar of the City of New York Special Committee on Congressional Ethics* (New York: Atheneum, 1970).

illegal, involving such things as bribery, embezzlement and theft."
Included in the gray zone are such activities as promising government contracts in order to elicit campaign contributions, using
official position to gain special advantages or privileges, accepting
favors from lobbyists, investing on the basis of inside information,
and misusing stationery and various funds entrusted to a member's
management.

To further complicate the matter, actions that are perfectly
proper or legal may *appear* to be improper. Such actions may
undermine public confidence in the Congress or the individual member—or both. Like Caesar's wife, a member must not only avoid
sinning; he must shun anything that might appear to be sinful.

COMMITTEE ON STANDARDS OF OFFICIAL CONDUCT*

To provide guidance for members on questions of possible conflict
and other ethical questions, and to provide for systematized response to allegations of official misconduct, the House in 1968
established a new standing Committee on Standards of Official
Conduct. Cited as a "great step forward" and a "historic new phase
of ethical self-discipline" by the New York City Bar's Special Committee on Congressional Ethics, formation of the committee was
accompanied by adoption of rules and regulations applicable to
members—and staff—in the conduct of their official duties. Taken
together, these actions:

★ Set up machinery for the investigation of members, officers of
the House, or employees charged with official misconduct;

★ Empower the bipartisan committee to recommend disciplinary
action when it determines that misconduct has occurred;

* This section follows closely Frederick H. Pauls, "The House Committee on Standards of Official Conduct," Legislative Reference Service
multilith report, Washington, D.C., November 26, 1968.

★ Provide for a limited form of financial disclosure by members and certain officers and employees of the House;

★ Institute a procedure for members, officers, and employees to obtain advisory opinions on the propriety of current or proposed actions;

★ Establish a Code of Official Conduct.

Moreover, because it was recognized that no single set of rules or procedures could resolve for all time all ethical dilemmas inherent in the job of the Congressman, the committee was empowered to recommend additional rules, regulations, and guidelines to assist members, officers, and employees in serving as trustees for the public. Actions of the committee since its establishment have included issuance of Advisory Opinion No. 1, containing guidelines for members in conducting business with governmental agencies on behalf of constituents, and recommendations for additional financial disclosure requirements.*

Committee jurisdiction and procedure. The committee's jurisdiction embraces all measures relating to financial disclosure and the code of official conduct. Among other functions it may:

★ Recommend to the House such legislative or administrative actions as it deems appropriate for establishing or enforcing standards of conduct;

★ Investigate, *subject to limitations,* any alleged violation of the code of official conduct or of any law, rule, regulation, or other standard of conduct applicable to members, officers, or employees

---

* Advisory Opinion No. 1 of the Committee on Standards of Official Conduct appears in the Appendix, pages 369–372. For details of the committee's background, operation, and initial recommendations see *Report of the Committee on Standards of Official Conduct,* House Report No. 1176, 90th Congress, 2d Session. (Washington, D.C.: Government Printing Office, 1968).

in the performance of their responsibilities and, *after notice and a hearing,* recommend to the House, by resolution or otherwise, such action as it deems appropriate;

★ Report, with the approval of the House, to appropriate federal or state authorities, any substantial evidence of a violation of any law by a member, officer, or employee of the House applicable to the discharge of his duties and responsibilities;

★ Consider a request of a member, officer, or employee for an advisory opinion respecting the general propriety of any current or proposed conduct by him, and, with safeguards to assure his privacy, publish its opinion for the guidance of other members, officers, and employees.

These functions are subject to the following limitations, however:

★ No resolution, report, recommendation, or advisory opinion may be made, and no investigation of conduct undertaken, unless approved by the affirmative vote of at least seven members of the committee.

★ Except when the committee undertakes an investigation on its own initiative, it may undertake an investigation only (1) upon receipt of a complaint, *in writing and under oath,* made by or submitted to a member of the House and transmitted to the committee by that member, or (2) upon receipt of a complaint, *in writing and under oath,* directly from an individual not a member of the House if the committee finds that the complaint has been submitted to at least three members of the House who have refused, in writing, to transmit it to the committee.

★ No investigation may be undertaken of any alleged violation of a law, rule, regulation, or standard of conduct not in effect at the time of the alleged violation.

Code of Official Conduct. In its report, the committee made clear that the Code of Official Conduct was not intended to be the "last word," that it would be subject to revisions and additions as experience demonstrated the need. As incorporated into House rules, the code contains eight principles.

A member, officer, or employee of the House shall—

★ Conduct himself at all times in a manner which shall reflect creditably on the House;

★ Adhere to the spirit and the letter of the Rules of the House and to the rules of its committees;

★ Receive no compensation nor shall he permit any compensation to accrue to his beneficial interest from any source, the receipt of which would occur by virtue of influence improperly exerted from his position in the Congress;

★ Accept no gift of substantial value, directly or indirectly, from any person, organization, or corporation having a direct interest in legislation before the Congress;

★ Accept no honorarium for a speech, writing for publication, or other similar activity from any person, organization, or corporation in excess of the usual and customary value for such services.

And a member of the House shall—

★ Keep his campaign funds separate from his personal funds; shall convert no campaign funds to personal use in excess of reimbursement for legitimate and verifiable prior campaign expenditures; and shall expend no funds from his campaign account not attributable to bona fide campaign purposes;

★ Treat as campaign contributions all proceeds from testimonial dinners or other fund-raising events if the sponsors do not give clear notice in advance that the proceeds are intended for other purposes;

★ Retain no one from his clerk-hire allowance who does not perform duties commensurate with the compensation he receives.*

Financial disclosure requirements. Members, officers, principal assistants to members and officers, and professional committee staff personnel must file financial reports with the Committee on Standards of Official Conduct annually by April 30. These reports— which must include the interests of the spouse when these are in effect controlled by the member or employee—are in two parts.

Part A is maintained on file with the committee and *is made available at reasonable hours to responsible public inquiry,* subject to the committee's regulations (such as requiring the inquirer to supply identification and notifying any member whose report is inspected). This part of the report must contain—

★ The name, instrument of ownership, and any position held in any business entity doing a substantial business with the federal government or subject to federal regulatory agencies, in which the ownership by the person filing is in excess of $5,000 fair market value as of the date of filing or from which income of $1,000 or more was derived during the preceding calendar year. It is *not* necessary to list any time or demand deposit in a financial institution or any debt instrument having a fixed yield unless it is convertible to an equity instrument. (Time deposits are savings accounts; demand deposits are checking accounts; debt instruments not convertible to equity instruments are financial investments, such as the purchase of corporation bonds.)

★ The name, address, and type or practice of any professional organization in which the person reporting, or his spouse, is an officer,

---

* A provision of the 1967 Postal Revenue and Federal Salary Act prohibits the hiring of any relative by a government official, including a member of Congress. This proscription did not apply to relatives already on a member's staff at the time. However, a member may temporarily hire a relative in an emergency situation if the Civil Service Commission so rules.

director, or partner, or serves in any advisory capacity, from which income of $1,000 or more was derived during the preceding calendar year.

★ The source of each of the following items received during the preceding year:

Any income for services rendered (except from the U.S. government) exceeding $5,000;

Any capital gain from a single source exceeding $5,000, other than from the sale of a residence occupied by the person reporting;

Reimbursement for expenditures (except from the U.S. government) exceeding $1,000 in each instance.*

Campaign receipts are *not* to be included in this financial report.

Part B of the report is sent to the committee in a sealed envelope. It may be opened, in the event of an investigation, if at least seven members vote to do so *and* after the member involved has been notified of the committee's intention. This part of the report must contain detailed information relating to items disclosed in Part A, including:

★ The fair market value of each item listed under the first section of Part A (a business entity doing substantial business with the federal government or subject to its regulation in which the filer maintains ownership exceeding $5,000 or from which he realizes annual income of $1,000 or more);

★ The amount of income derived from each item listed in the second and third sections of Part A (income exceeding $1,000 from any professional organization of which he or his spouse is a mem-

---

* Added by an amendment in 1970 were (1) disclosure of sources of honoraria of $300 or more, and (2) listing of each creditor to whom the person reporting was indebted, without the pledge of specific security, for $10,000 or more for ninety days or longer in the preceding calendar year. These additional disclosure requirements were to become effective January 1, 1971.

ber; fees for services rendered exceeding $5,000; capital gains from a single source exceeding $5,000; nongovernment reimbursement for expenditures exceeding $1,000 in each instance).

Reports are required whether or not the member or employee has interests subject to the disclosure rules. Those who do not have such interests simply state this in their reports.

Publishing disclosure statements. Some members voluntarily publish, in the *Congressional Record* or elsewhere, full disclosure of their sources of income and financial holdings. Said one who has made a practice of doing so, in a private conversation:

> It is one thing to be a director or large stockholder of a firm vitally interested in a bill and go to committee or the floor in debate and argue that the national interest requires passage without telling your colleagues and constituents the facts; it is quite another to lay the facts on the line for all to see—and then do exactly the same things.

Published disclosure practices vary widely in the completeness of the financial statement, the manner of its publication, and the stage at which it is introduced into the record. Some of the more common practices are:

★ In a general statement placed in the *Congressional Record,* usually at the beginning of a Congress, a member may list his assets, outside income, directorships, financial interests in businesses subject to federal regulatory agencies, etc. (A form for such a statement appears in the Appendix, page 375.)

★ In lobbying among colleagues, in committee deliberations, or in debate on the floor, a member may state the facts of a particular personal interest in the subject of the legislation and thus insulate himself from subsequent criticism.

★ In contacting Executive agencies for particular administrative actions, a member may include in his letter or statement a declaration that he has a specific interest in the subject matter of the proposed action. In such cases some members add a sentence requesting that "this letter be made a part of the public file," thus making sure that no one will ever successfully charge that a private interest was concealed.

VOTING IN CONFLICT SITUATIONS

In situations involving voting on bills in which members have a direct personal or pecuniary interest, Rule VIII states:

> Every member . . . shall vote on each question put, unless he has a direct personal or pecuniary interest in the event of such question.

Discussing this rule, *Jefferson's Manual* (section 376) states:

> Where the private interests of a member are concerned in a bill or question he is to withdraw. And where such an interest has appeared, his voice has been disallowed, even after a division. In a case so contrary, not only to the laws of decency, but to the fundamental principle of the social compact, which denies to any man to be a judge in his own cause, it is for the honor of the House that this rule of immemorial observance should be strictly adhered to.

The precedents of the House make it clear, however, that no one has the power to force a member to vote or to prohibit him from voting, and in such cases it is entirely for the member to make the decision. If he decides his situation is covered by the rule, he should state, "Mr. Speaker, I have a personal interest in the matter under consideration and therefore answer, 'present.' "

Although it occurs infrequently, members can and do answer "present" in cases in which only an apparent conflict exists. In 1965, for example, a member with extensive real-estate interests possibly affected by urban renewal laws answered "present" on the Omnibus Housing Bill, explaining:

> There was nothing the bill could do for me. However, I wanted to avoid even the suspicion there was any conflict of interest. If the bill passed by a close vote, mine among them, I could be criticized.

Application of Rule VIII. There are situations in which Rule VIII is clearly applicable—for example, with a private relief bill benefiting a member's immediate family. Or, as Representative Udall puts it:

If there is a bill for the relief of several members, including himself, and other purposes, that seeks to appropriate public funds of $2,000 apiece because of our distinguished services in this body, obviously there might be some impropriety suggested if I go down and lobby for the bill, if I vote for it, if I vote for it in committee or otherwise. This is [an] obviously ridiculous hypothetical situation. But it sometimes happens that a member will have a direct interest in a matter that's being voted on.

The situation becomes considerably more complex when a member's vote favors not only his own private interests but—clearly—the public interest as well. A Congressman may, for example, represent a constituency whose prosperity depends on copper. He may also be an officer or large stockholder of a copper-mining company. Should the member vote on a bill that affects the taxation or other treatment of his industry? It can be argued that, in good conscience, the member's private interests require him to withhold his vote. On the other hand, this action would deprive his constituents of representation on a matter important to their economic well-being.

In discussing this problem, Representative Udall suggests guidelines based on a distinction between benefiting from legislation as an individual and benefiting as a member of a large group of citizens similarly situated:

. . . I would think that if you are a member of a class—you are a taxpayer, you have children in school, and federal aid to education comes up—surely this doesn't constitute a conflict. If you're an automobile user, you take your car out on the road, and the highway bill comes up—you are merely a member of a class. All of us are veterans. We have [to vote on] all kinds of veterans' legislation. So I think we can draw one line that everyone will agree upon, and that is, if you are directly benefited and the bill is for your relief—[your] direct benefit—you should not vote. If it's for the relief of a class or affects a class to which you belong this is probably all right.

CRIMINAL STATUTES

A number of criminal statutes prohibit certain acts by members of Congress. (See Appendix, pages 373–374.) Included are statutes making it unlawful for members to:

★ Accept anything of value which is offered with intent to affect his official action, vote, or decision.

★ Either directly or indirectly "undertake, execute, hold or enjoy in whole or in part, any contract or agreement made or entered into in behalf of the United States or any agency thereof."

★ Solicit or receive compensation directly or indirectly for services rendered on behalf of another person, either by himself or a partner, before a government department, agency, or U.S. Court of Claims.

Special problems of lawyers. Prior to election to Congress, many members are attorneys and have partnerships (about half of those elected in 1964 were lawyers).* They, like other members, are often uncertain just how long they will wish to remain, or be permitted to remain, in Congress. Federal statutes and legal ethics create problems for the lawyer member, for although the statutes do not prohibit him from practicing law when the practice is

* In the 90th Congress the number of members with various professional backgrounds was as follows, according to the 1967 *Congressional Quarterly Almanac:*

Agriculture	39	Law	246
Business or Banking	161	Medicine	3
Education	57	Organized Labor	2
Engineering	6	Religion	3
Journalism	39		

(Total exceeds the House membership because some members have multiple professional backgrounds.)

divorced from service as a member of Congress, he quite clearly commits a criminal violation if he appears as a lawyer for private clients before any government agency or department, or the U.S. Court of Claims. And, because a law partnership is an agency relationship in which one partner acts for all members of the firm, the appearance of his partner in such cases may be similarly illegal.

To avoid the possibility of conflicts, some members withdraw from their law partnership arrangements. Others, perhaps not financially able to quit practicing altogether, follow different courses of action, as described by Representative Udall:

> Now this [problem] is resolved by lawyers in different ways. Some of them simply quite practicing and withdraw from the firm. Others [remain in] the firm with the understanding that [the] firm will handle no matter concerning the federal government. No criminal cases, no agency appearances, no appearances before the Internal Revenue—this is difficult for a big firm to do. Some [establish] two firms. . . . All those in one firm with the member handle nonfederal cases. There is another firm consisting of the identical bodies in the same building, but the Congressman doesn't belong to that firm. That firm handles the federal matters.*

Exercise of special privilege

Questions of propriety and ethics arise in the exercise of a number of special privileges extended to Congressmen.

* The American Bar Association has recently dealt with the question of use of a public official's name by a law firm in which he is not personally active. Disciplinary Rule 2–102 (B) of the Code of Professional Responsibility, as revised in 1969, states: ". . . a lawyer who assumes a judicial, legislative or public executive or administrative post or office shall not permit his name to remain in the name of a law firm or to be used in professional notices of the firm during any significant period in which he is not actively and regularly practicing law as a member of the firm, and during such period other members of the firm shall not use his name in the firm name or in professional notices of the firm."

IMMUNITY FROM LIBEL PROSECUTION

Perhaps the most significant privilege extended to members of Congress is immunity from prosecution for libel and slander. The Constitution states that "for any speech or debate in either House they [members of Congress] shall not be questioned in any other place."

The courts have construed this privilege liberally so that members of Congress will be able to execute the functions of their office without fear of prosecutions, civil or criminal. Absolute protection has been afforded to anything a member says in speech or debate on the floor of the House or Senate, anything inserted in the *Congressional Record* even though not actually said on the floor of either house, and anything said in committee while the committee is acting within its authorized province or jurisdiction.* This privilege also applies conditionally to unofficial distribution of the *Congressional Record,* and to reprints as well, provided that distribution or reprinting is not done with malicious intent.

LIMITED IMMUNITY FROM ARREST

The Constitution states that members of Congress "shall in all Cases, except Treason, Felony, and Breach of the Peace, be privileged from Arrest during their Attendance at the Session of their Respective Houses, and in going to and returning from the same. . . ."

This clause has been construed in a manner that excepts all

---

* *United States* v. *Johnson,* 383 U.S. 169, 86 Supreme Court 749, 15 L. Ed. 2nd 681, a leading case, involved two House members charged under federal conspiracy and conflict of interest statutes with accepting a large sum of money allegedly as payment for seeking to influence the U.S. Justice Department with respect to pending private matters. One of the members was convicted on evidence that as a part of a conspiracy he was paid to deliver in the House a speech designed to bolster confidence in the Maryland Savings and Loan industry. The U.S. Supreme Court reversed the conviction principally on a broad interpretation of the scope of the member's immunity under this constitutional provision.

indictable crimes: thus, as a general rule, the privilege applies only to arrests in civil suits. In the case of traffic violations, a member may not claim the privilege in an arrest for a traffic offense that is punishable under state law as a criminal offense. In states in which violation of a municipal ordinance is treated as a civil action, a member arrested for a traffic violation may properly claim privilege. In practice, however, the attendant publicity may act to limit the utility of this provision.

Immunity from court summonses. The privilege also protects a member of Congress from being summoned to court as a witness or juror in any matter. A summons to appear in court and testify has been held to constitute a breach of privilege, and the House has declined to make a general rule permitting members to waive their privilege, since "the privilege of a member is the privilege of the House." Any member who receives a summons to appear before a court must apply for and receive permission of the House before doing so, except when the House is not in session. A resolution usually is adopted before each adjournment authorizing members to appear in courts between sessions in response to subpoenas.

PERSONAL PRIVILEGE

Under the rules of the House, a member may take the floor to answer certain charges attacking his conduct or impugning his integrity, character, or honor. The privilege is set forth in Rule IX:

> Questions of privilege shall be, first, those affecting the rights of the House collectively, its safety, dignity and the integrity of its proceedings; second, the rights, reputation, and conduct of members, individually, in their representative capacity only; and shall have precedence of all questions, except motions to adjourn.

A member may interrupt ordinary legislative business to address the House on a question of personal privilege, but he may not interrupt a call of the "yeas" and "nays" or take the floor from another member who has been recognized for debate.

As the rule states, the privilege extends only to charges relating to a member's conduct as a member of the House of Representatives, not to charges concerning his conduct before becoming a member. Nor does the privilege necessarily extend to vague charges in news stories or to misrepresentation of a member's speeches or acts. And as a practical matter there is a major drawback to the use of personal privilege. In answering scurrilous attacks, the Congressman also gives them wider circulation, because in order to be recognized he must state for the record the exact language of the attack.

★ 9 ★

Parliamentary practice in the House

PARLIAMENTARY PROCEDURE IN the House of Representatives is highly refined and technical. Some find it confusing as well. But, according to Lewis Deschler, House Parliamentarian since 1928, "complications give way to logic and confusion gives way to order" when the rules that govern procedure are viewed in their proper context. As the Parliamentarian sees it:

The system of rules and precedents of the House has been built up neither to complicate nor to confuse, but to protect the rights of the minority to be heard and of the majority to work its will. The function of the Congress is to pass legislation that the majority wants. And as Mr. Speaker Reed of Maine once remarked, all of the rules of the House are intended to expedite business and not to retard it. All the rulings of the chair ought to be in harmony with that idea. . . .

One of the first committees appointed after a quorum was established in the first Congress on April 1, 1789, was a committee to formulate rules of procedure. Some of the rules then adopted are still in use. Some have been discarded. Many have been amplified and broad-

253

ened when changes were required to permit the majority to work its will. Today, the rules of the House are the most finely adjusted, scientifically balanced, and highly technical rules of any parliamentary body in the world. . . .

The rules of the House can be and are changed from time to time, suggesting that, although they are "finely adjusted" and "scientifically balanced," the adjustment process is a continuing one.* Sources of detailed information on the rules, including their historical development, are indicated by Parliamentarian Deschler:

There are four cardinal sources of parliamentary procedure in the House. First, the Constitution; second, the rules adopted by the House; third, *Jefferson's Manual;* and fourth, previous decisions of the Speakers and Chairmen of the Committees of the Whole. The Constitution directs the House to do certain things in a specified manner. As examples, Article I provides that a majority shall constitute a quorum to do business, that the "yeas" and "nays" on any questions shall at the desire of one-fifth of those present be entered on the journal, that when a Presidential veto is considered the vote shall be determined by the "yeas" and "nays," and that to override a veto a two-thirds vote of both Houses is necessary. To perform the functions not specifically detailed in the Constitution, each House is vested with the power to determine the rules of its proceedings. . . .

* At the beginning of the 89th Congress, for example, the following rules changes were adopted: (1) amendment of Rule XI, clause 23, to reintroduce—with modifications—the Twenty-One Day Rule (which had been in effect in the 81st Congress), permitting the House to act on bills that the Rules Committee has not cleared within three weeks; (2) amendment of Rule XX, clause 1, to provide a method for sending bills directly to conference by majority vote (previously unanimous consent was required, and if a single member objected the Rules Committee was empowered to decide whether a bill passed in different forms in House and Senate was to go to conference and, ultimately, on to final passage); and (3) amended Rule XXI, clause 1, eliminating a provision which permitted a single member to delay action on a bill by demanding the reading in full of the engrossed copy. The first of these, the Twenty-One Day Rule, was in effect only during the 89th Congress, however. It was deleted in rules adopted for the 90th Congress.

In the early history of the House, the membership frequently found it difficult to accomplish the purposes upon which they had determined. Quite naturally they turned to practices of the British Parliament for guidance. Thomas Jefferson recognized this need and, when he was President of the Senate, he prepared a manual based on the rules of the House of Commons. *Jefferson's Manual,* a handbook of parliamentary guidance, contributed greatly to procedure of the House, although it was not until 1837 that the House adopted a rule providing that *Jefferson's Manual* would be applicable in the House to cases not covered by specific rules. Rule XLII contains that provision.

The rulings of the Speakers of the House and the Chairmen of the Committees of the Whole are to the rules of the House what the decisions of the courts are to the statutes. It is rare indeed for a question of parliamentary procedure to arise that has not been decided at some time in the past. These rulings were compiled up to 1936 by the Honorable Ashley C. Hinds and the Honorable Clarence Cannon, former Parliamentarians of the House. Decisions from 1936 up to date are cited in the House Rules and Manual, which is updated at the beginning of each new Congress. However, because space will not permit, they are not in as great detail as the eleven volumes that cover the period from 1789 to 1936.

A brief introduction to House parliamentary practice is attempted in the following sections, which describe basic procedures —from calendar to enactment—used during the 91st Congress.*

Legislative calendars

In House practice a legislative calendar is a docket or list of measures that are ready for consideration by the House. There are five House calendars—the *Union* Calendar, the *House* Calendar, the *Private* Calendar, the *Consent* Calendar, and the *Discharge* Calen-

---

* For the operation of the rules, their impact on legislative strategy, and the substance of legislation, see Lewis A. Froman, Jr., *The Congressional Process: Strategies, Rules, and Procedures* (Boston: Little, Brown and Co., 1967).

dar—which are updated daily while Congress is in session and are published in a single document, *Calendars of the United States, House of Representatives and History of Legislation.*

Each of the five calendars has a particular use or purpose. Initially every bill reported by the standing committees is first placed on either the Union (revenue bills), House (nonrevenue), or Private Calendar, depending on the provisions of the bill. Thereafter, a bill on the Union or House Calendar may also be placed on the Consent Calendar, if a member seeks to use the short-cuts permitted under Consent procedures. Bills reported and referred to on the Private Calendar appear only on that calendar. Bills or resolutions discharged by petition only appear on the Discharge Calendar.

THE DAILY CALENDAR

The daily *Calendars of the United States* is often referred to simply as "the Calendar." The Calendar contains, in addition to the five legislative calendars, information relating to the status of reported legislation. It includes a brief history of action taken on each reported bill or resolution and the public or private law number, when enacted, along with similar Senate bills when messaged to the House. Other useful information includes:

★ Special orders to consider particular bills at particular times, or granting members permission to address the House on specific days. These items appear on the cover sheet.

★ A statement of unfinished business before the House.

★ A list of special legislative days for consideration of certain kinds of business.

★ A list of committees with dates on which they may be called to bring in bills under the rules.

★ A list of bills pending in conference with the Senate.

★ Lists of all public and private laws enacted during the current Congress.

Each Monday the Calendar carries a complete index of all reported, passed, enacted, and Senate-referred matters in the current Congress.

UNION CALENDAR

The calendar system of the House makes a basic distinction between public bills that raise revenue or make or authorize a monetary charge against the United States (Union Calendar) and those that do not (House Calendar). Examples of the first type are appropriations bills; bills to impose, raise, or lower federal taxes (all of which originate only in the House); and bills that authorize appropriations for various functions. Bills that neither raise revenues nor cause an expenditure of federal funds (e.g., a bill to name an existing federal dam "Truman Dam") are of the second type and would appear on the House Calendar. The vast majority of public bills involve money and appear on the Union Calendar after being reported.

Under House rules, Union Calendar bills must first be considered in a Committee of the Whole House on the State of the Union. The mere reporting of a bill by a standing committee, however, does not guarantee action or consideration by the House. To obtain consideration a Union Calendar bill must generally:

★ Be placed on the Consent Calendar; or

★ Be brought up by unanimous consent; or

★ Be brought up by motion to suspend the rules; or

★ Be brought up under the Calendar Wednesday rule; or

★ Be brought up by a special resolution from the Committee on Rules.

Although bills appear on the Union Calendar in chronological order as reported to the House from the standing committees, they are seldom considered in that order, for legislative scheduling and fixing of priorities is a function of the majority leadership.

HOUSE CALENDAR

The House Calendar contains only bills that are public and non-revenue in nature. Measures on this calendar are not normally considered in the Committee of the Whole but are taken up directly by the House. With this exception, procedures for considering and scheduling House Calendar bills are similar to those for measures on the Union Calendar.

PRIVATE CALENDAR

All bills of a private nature (bills, for example, permitting immigration of specific persons, allowing private claims by specific persons or corporations against the United States, transferring public lands to a private company or person, and so forth) are placed on the Private Calendar. The Private Calendar is called only on the first and third Tuesdays of each month, and bills are considered in the order in which they are reported by the committees. Most private bills are approved quickly and without debate. If two or more members object to a private bill, it is automatically recommitted to the committee that reported it. A member who is uncertain whether to object may ask unanimous consent that a bill be "passed over without prejudice," but no reservation of objection can be entertained by the Speaker.

CONSENT CALENDAR

When a bill has been reported by a committee and placed on either the House or the Union Calendar, any member may have it placed on the Consent Calendar by filing a written request on a form provided by the Clerk of the House. Such requests are often made when a bill is reported unanimously by the committee having jurisdiction and there is no known opposition. Bills on the Consent Calendar are considered only on the first and third Mondays of each month. To be eligible for consideration a bill must have been on the calendar for three legislative days* prior to the Monday on which the calendar is called.

Bills are called in the order placed on the calendar, and are often approved either by unanimous consent or without debate. If one member objects to consideration of a bill the first time it is called on the Consent Calendar, it remains on the calendar and is called again on the next Consent day. When called the second time, it will be considered unless three or more members object, in which event it is stricken from the calendar and may not be called up under this procedure again until the next session of Congress (except in an omnibus bill).

Passing over without prejudice. A member who has reservations or questions about passage of a Consent or Private bill may wish neither to object nor to remain silent and let the bill pass. In this case he may ask unanimous consent that the bill be "passed over without prejudice." The granting of such a request merely carries the bill forward to the next Consent or Private Calendar day, when it is considered as though it had not been called on the first occasion.

Similarly, when the sponsor of a bill knows that objection will be made, he may himself ask unanimous consent that the bill be passed over without prejudice. Requests of this kind are also entertained with respect to Private Calendar bills. Sponsors ordinarily try to determine in advance whether an objection will be raised to their Consent or Private bills—and they customarily try to meet privately with the other members involved to answer their questions, remove their doubts, or attempt to work out amendments that would ameliorate objections.

---

* Days on which the House holds any session. This concept is an important one in dealing with House rules, many of which provide for the performance of an act within —days (i.e., calendar days of the year) and others within —"legislative days." In computing action under the latter, one counts only the days on which the House has held a session.

Official objectors' committee. Although any member may object to unanimous consent passage of any bill appearing on the Consent or Private Calendar, most members have insufficient time or interest for advance study of such legislation. To protect the House and the country against passage of unwise legislation, each party delegates three of its members as "official objectors" for each of these calendars.

The duty of those serving in this capacity is to make careful, advance study of measures about to be called up. Sponsors of bills on the Consent and Private Calendars frequently contact members of the objectors' committees at least a day in advance to resolve questions that one or more objectors may have about the pending legislation.

Over the years, general guidelines have been developed by objectors' committees, and in 1965 the six members of the Consent Calendar objectors summarized them and described in some detail the operation of their committee. (See the Statement on Rules of Operation Adopted by Consent Calendar Committee, Appendix, pages 396–398.) Under the guidelines set by this committee, objection ordinarily is made if a bill:

★ Involves an aggregate expenditure of more than $1 million.

★ Changes national or international policy of the United States.

★ Affects the districts of a majority of members of the House of Representatives.

★ Has not been cleared by the Bureau of the Budget, the government departments affected by it, and neither the chairman of the committee that reported the bill nor its sponsor appears to justify this deficiency.

DISCHARGE CALENDAR

Four of the legislative calendars contain only bills that have been reported by a standing committee. In general, the Discharge Calendar contains only bills that have *not* been reported by a committee. In such cases, the signatures of a majority of the House membership (218) on a discharge petition constitute a substitute for committee approval, and the matter is then brought before the House for action. The Discharge Calendar is called only on the second and fourth Mondays of each month, and a petition must have the necessary signatures and be on the calendar for seven days before it is eligible for consideration by the House. The motion is privileged and any member who signed is eligible to move to call up the petition, although the usual practice is for the Speaker to recognize the member who will manage the bill on the floor. If the House votes to discharge the committee, the bill is considered under the regular rules of the House.

Obtaining floor action

In a typical session the standing committees act favorably on many more bills than can possibly be scheduled for debate by the House. It is necessary, therefore, to have a system and procedures for the establishment of priorities.

Some bills are noncontroversial or of minor impact and can be scheduled for action on the Private and Consent Calendars. Occasionally, a bill may be taken up by unanimous consent. But the vast majority of important bills which reach the Union or House Calendars are considered under one of four procedures. A *rule*, or resolution, from the Committee on Rules is the route most commonly followed. In addition there are three special procedures: *Discharge Petition, Calendar Wednesday,* and *Suspension of the Rules.*

RULES COMMITTEE ACTION

The Committee on Rules acts as a legislative committee on matters pertaining to the House rules and the creation of select committees. Its principal function, however, is to recommend which of the many public bills reported by other committees should receive consideration, and to recommend the amount of time and other conditions of debate necessary to a fair consideration and disposition of each of them. And, with few exceptions, an important public bill reaches the House floor only after the Rules Committee votes a special resolution—commonly called a "rule"—for its consideration.

The reporting of such a rule by this committee does not necessarily mean that the bill will be scheduled for debate. The Speaker and the Majority Leader determine when—or even whether—to call up the rule for floor action. Thus, following the granting of the rule, the chairman of the committee that reported the bill, or others who may serve as floor managers for it, contact the Speaker and the Majority Leader and seek to arrange a suitable time for scheduling the debate.

Hearings on the rule. Ordinarily, the chairman of a committee which has reported a bill and desires its passage requests the Rules Committee chairman to schedule a hearing for consideration of reporting a rule on his bill. He may do so either verbally or in writing, or both. If Rules Committee hearings are held, the committee chairman, ranking minority member, chief sponsors, and principal opponents of the bill appear to testify. In addition, other members may be heard, but public witnesses are rarely permitted. Testimony before the Rules Committee is usually directed to these questions:

★ Is the bill a product of proper hearings and careful consideration in the committee involved?

★ Is it sufficiently important to require taking the time of the House for debate?

★ If so, what is a reasonable amount of time for debate? and

★ Should the rule prohibit the offering of any germane amendments?

The Rules Committee may decline to grant a rule for any reason, and usually its hearings include considerable testimony and discussion on the merits of the legislation, as proponents attempt to persuade a majority of committee members that passage of the bill is desirable. If the full Rules Committee—ten from the majority party and five from the minority—is present and voting, eight votes are required to report a resolution making the bill privileged for the debate stage.

Conditions specified in the rule. Rules generally specify: (1) that upon the rule's adoption by the House it shall be in order for the House to resolve itself into the Committee of the Whole House on the State of the Union for consideration of the bill; (2) that general debate shall continue for not more than a specified number of hours, the time to be equally divided and controlled by the chairman and ranking minority member of the reporting committee; (3) that amendments are, or are not, to be in order under the five-minute rule; and (4) that various motions or other special procedures are, or are not, permitted. (An example of a rule appears in the Appendix, page 399.)

Rules usually are either *open*, permitting germane amendments to be offered and adopted by majority vote of the House, or *closed*, prohibiting the offering of amendments and thus requiring that the bill either be accepted or rejected as reported. Except for revenue raising measures, most rules are open. And even a closed rule usually permits the offering of amendments sponsored by the committee that reported the bill. In addition, both open and closed rules ordinarily permit the offering of one motion to recommit. This motion may take the form of a motion to recommit with instructions. Through such a motion it is possible, in effect, to propose one amendment or group of amendments *en bloc* which can be voted up or down. The right to recognition for recommittal motions is generally claimed by the minority party. Frequently the principal test of support for the heart of a bill will come on the recommittal motion rather than on final passage.

When a bill has been granted a rule and is scheduled for action, the House first debates adoption of the rule for debate not to exceed one hour. This debate is managed by majority and minority members of the Rules Committee. If the rule is adopted, the House, on a motion by the bill's sponsors, may then resolve itself into the Committee of the Whole House on the State of the Union for debate of the bill itself, under the terms fixed by the rule.*

DISCHARGE PETITION

The Discharge Petition is designed to permit a majority of the House to debate and act on specific bills when the standing committee having jurisdiction has failed or refused to act. This procedure may be initiated only when the measure has been pending for thirty days in the committee to which it was referred. The requirement is seven legislative days if the petition is for discharge of the Committee on Rules, and a petition may move for discharge of either the legislative or the Rules Committee. Any member may file a petition with the Clerk, in effect requesting the House to discharge the committee involved from further consideration of the measure.

* Under House practice and rules, some bills are privileged and need not face any further procedural hurdles after committee approval. (See Rule XI, Clause 22, for a list of the committees which have the right to call up particular matters without first obtaining a rule from the Rules Committee.) Examples are general appropriations bills reported by the Appropriations Committee, general pension bills from the Committee on Veterans' Affairs, and bills for the admission of new states from the Interior and Insular Affairs Committee. Under Rule XXIV, Section 8, the Committee on the District of Columbia also may call up legislation without first obtaining a rule. The Committee on Ways and Means is entitled to call up general revenue measures in similar fashion, but the privilege is seldom exercised, because this procedure would open its bills to amendments. In modern House practice, general revenue measures are considered under closed rules, obtained from the Rules Committee, and barring all amendments except those offered by the Ways and Means Committee. The theory generally accepted in the House is that tax legislation is so complex that it should not be written on the floor of the House.

The petition takes effect only when it is signed by a majority (218) of the full House membership. While the petition is pending on the Clerk's Desk—and before 218 members have signed—any member who has signed may remove his name. Once a majority has signed, however, the petition is immediately entered in the *Journal*, printed in the *Record* with the names of those signing, and placed on the Discharge Calendar. After the measure has been on the calendar for seven days any member who signed may move on any subsequent Discharge day that it be called up for consideration. Twenty minutes of debate are allowed on the motion and, if carried, the House proceeds to debate the bill under its general rules, or under such special ground rules as are provided in the resolution of discharge of the Rules Committee.

The Discharge Petition procedure is seldom successful. From 1910 to 1970, only nineteen bills were passed by means of it, and of these only two eventually became law. But the threat of using it sometimes brings about favorable committee action.

CALENDAR WEDNESDAY

The discharge procedure is used to permit House action when a standing committee has refused to act. Calendar Wednesday—another rarely used procedure—is designed to permit a committee that has approved a bill to get it debated in situations in which the bill is not privileged and either the Rules Committee or the majority leadership is blocking action.

Under House Rule XXIV (7), every Wednesday is Calendar Wednesday unless waived by a two-thirds vote. In practice, the Majority Leader customarily asks and receives unanimous consent each week to dispense with Calendar Wednesday proceedings. When used, the Calendar Wednesday procedure is as follows: The Clerk calls in alphabetical order the roll of the standing committees. As each committee is reached its chairman either "passes" or calls up for consideration any one bill previously reported by his committee and currently pending on either the House or Union Calendar. General debate on a measure called under this rule is limited to two hours. The usefulness of this procedure is limited, because:

★ Opponents of a measure can often persuade chairmen of committees that occur early in the alphabet to call up bills in order to consume time; and

★ If action is not completed on the Wednesday on which the bill is called up, it cannot be carried over to the next day, or to a subsequent Wednesday, until all other committees have been called.

SUSPENSION OF THE RULES

Bills considered under the procedures previously discussed in this chapter are passed either (1) by what is in effect unanimous vote or consent, as in the case of Consent Calendar bills, or (2) by majority vote of those present and voting. About midway between these extremes is Suspension of the Rules, a procedure permitting a two-thirds majority to suspend the rules and pass a bill that has been approved by a standing committee.

This procedure is designed to permit a short-cut for bills that have minimal opposition but are favored by a large majority of the House. Suspension of the Rules may be used only on the first and third Mondays of each month following disposition of Consent Calendar business and daily during the last six days of a session. Certain special restrictions apply to action under Suspension of the Rules:

★ The Speaker has complete control and discretion as to whether to recognize or refuse to recognize a member to move for suspention of the rules and passage of a bill. Sponsors who wish to use this procedure customarily consult the Speaker and attempt to persuade him that the bill is both sound and necessary and should be called up, and that, because it enjoys so much support and so little opposition, the bill is likely to receive a two-thirds majority.

★ No amendments are permitted under the suspension procedure. The bill must be approved or rejected in the form reported by committee.

★ Debate cannot exceed forty minutes, divided equally between proponents and opponents. When a bill is called under this procedure it may be put to a vote immediately unless a member demands a second, in which case the forty minutes for debate is allowed.

DISTRICT MONDAY

A final special procedure applies only to bills reported from the District of Columbia Committee. In addition to being Discharge days, the second and fourth Mondays of each month are commonly called "District days," and on those days the District Committee may call up such measures as it cares to present for disposition by the House. District Committee bills are privileged and do not require rules from the Rules Committee for their consideration.

Debate and amendment procedures

In debating and disposing of bills from the House and Union Calendars, the House may operate from time to time in one of three established forms:

The House itself, under regular House Rules that—

★ Make no provision for general debate;

★ Require the presence of 218 members to form a quorum;

★ Do not permit the very useful five-minute rule on amendments; and

★ Allow a member who is recognized to proceed for one hour.

The Committee of the Whole, in which all members of the House sit as a committee rather than as the House of Representa-

tives. Technically there are two Committees of the Whole—the
Committee of the Whole House on the State of the Union, for
Union Calendar bills, and the Committee of the Whole House, for
Private Calendar bills. The latter is seldom used except on the first
and third Tuesdays, and generally the term "Committee of the
Whole" refers to the former. Sitting as a committee has these ad-
vantages—

★ A specified time for general debate can be fixed, with the time
divided as needed among the main proponents and opponents.

★ The five-minute rule on amendments can be utilized;

★ Less time is wasted on quorum calls or dilatory procedures because a quorum is made with only one hundred members present;

★ Votes are taken quickly by voice, division, or tellers, and time-
consuming roll-call votes are not permitted; and

★ It is also easier to obtain teller votes, since one-fifth of a quorum
(twenty) may demand tellers, whereas in the House the minimum
for such a demand is forty-four.

The House as in Committee of the Whole, a short-cut procedure occasionally used on minor bills or those involving little controversy. The main features of this procedure are—

★ There is no general debate period, but the five-minute rule can
be utilized;

★ This forum may be used only by unanimous consent or special
order;

★ A quorum is 218 members; and,

★ It saves the time required for initially resolving into Committee
of the Whole, appointing a chairman, general debate, and then resolving back into the House for engrossment, third reading, and
passage.

COMMITTEE OF THE WHOLE HOUSE ON THE STATE OF THE UNION (COMMITTEE OF THE WHOLE)

In general, this device was created to provide for thorough consideration of major legislation on the Union Calendar and to avoid the obstacles involved in regular House procedures. It is a tried and proven procedure for debating and acting on proposed changes in a measure. However, action by the Committee of the Whole is tentative. Official and final approval of amendments and actual passage of the bill occurs when the Committee completes its work ("rises") and reports back to the House of Representatives. Occasionally, the House, on a roll-call vote, reverses or disapproves amendments that have been adopted by the Committee of the Whole.

When a motion to resolve into Committee of the Whole is carried, the Speaker designates an experienced member as Chairman and leaves the chair. The Chairman then presides from the Speaker's chair and is addressed as "Mr. Chairman," not as "Mr. Speaker." When both general debate and the amendment processes have been completed, the committee "rises," the Speaker resumes the chair, and the Chairman of the Committee of the Whole is recognized to report to the House the action taken in committee. Proceedings in Committee of the Whole are divided into two main parts—general debate, for a time ordinarily fixed by the rule, and the amendment stage, controlled by the five-minute rule.

General debate. General debate is the first step in considerations by the Committee of the Whole. The time allowed by the rule or by unanimous consent can be as little as one hour or as much as several days. Important bills frequently are given four to six hours of general debate, and usually the rule allocates the time equally between the majority and minority. Half the time is controlled by the chairman of the committee reporting the bill and the other half goes to the ranking minority member of the same committee.

Experience has proven the value of centralizing control of the time in the hands of the chief opponent and proponent of a bill. These two members may in turn yield specific amounts of their time to themselves or to other members of their party who wish to be heard. Those wishing to participate in the debate customarily arrange this directly with either of the two members in charge of the time. Preference ordinarily is given to members of the committee that reported the bill. Members obtaining time must confine their remarks to the bill or subject under discussion, unless they obtain unanimous consent to proceed out of order, in which case any subject may be discussed.

Time allocated by the chief opponent and proponent of a bill cannot be further subdivided into specific minutes. Thus, on an appropriation bill, for example, the committee chairman usually controls the time allotted to the majority side. He may yield Member A five minutes of that time. During his five minutes, Member A may yield to other members for comments, observations, or questions, but he may not yield two of his five minutes to Member B. The same example applies to debate under the five-minute rule on amendments.

An assistant on the Parliamentarian's staff keeps an accurate running account of time consumed by both sides. When the time allowed by the rule or agreement has been used, the Chairman terminates the debate. The manager of the bill for the majority usually reserves for himself the final few minutes to close the debate.

Amendment stage. When the time for general debate has expired, the Committee of the Whole proceeds to "second reading," and the bill is read for amendments. Ordinarily the Reading Clerk reads the bill paragraph by paragraph or section by section, unless the rule permits reading of the bill by title only. As soon as a section has been read, it is subject to amendment by any member. Frequently several members rise at the same time to offer amendments, and the presiding Chairman decides whom to recognize first.

By custom, in such cases preference usually is given to members of the standing committee that reported the bill, with seniority often a factor. The Chairman of the Committee of the Whole has wide discretion in this matter, however.

The five-minute rule technically permits only a total of ten minutes of debate on each amendment, five for the member offering it and five for the chief opponent—usually the originating committee's chairman or floor manager. But through the "motion to strike the last word" device any member usually may obtain five minutes on each amendment offered.

When there are no further amendments to the paragraph or section under consideration, the Clerk begins reading the next section. At this point, the previous section is deemed complete, and amendments to it, or to any prior section, are not permitted except by unanimous consent.*

Amendments permitted. Amendments offered must be germane to the bill, and a point of order will be sustained against those that are not. The rules permit oral amendments but require them to be presented in writing on demand. In practice, oral amendments are rarely offered, and experienced members advise their junior colleagues to submit amendments in writing to the Clerk's desk. Amendments by proxy are not permitted. Once rejected, an amendment may not be offered in identical form again, but proposals even slightly different are permitted. Once an amendment has been approved, an amendment to change it or strike it out is not in order. The title of a bill may be amended only after the amending process is complete and the bill has passed.

Amendments in the form of substitutes for a section of a bill or for the entire bill are permitted. However, the substitute must be

---

* In the infrequent cases in which the House itself acts on a bill, the *entire* bill is read under second reading and then is deemed open for amendment at any point, with one hour allotted to the sponsor of each proposed change.

germane—intended to accomplish the same end—and may not be foreign to the nature of the bill or to the portion it is intended to replace. A substitute amendment that involves an entirely different method of accomplishing the same purpose as the bill or section will usually be out of order.

The third-degree rule. House Rule XIX prohibits amendments in the third degree. An amendment to an amendment is permitted, but not an amendment to an amendment to an amendment. This rule is complicated by the fact that a substitute amendment to the original amendment is permitted, and one amendment can also be offered to the substitute. Thus, four amendments may be pending at the same time:

(1) The original amendment;

(2) An amendment to that original amendment;

(3) A substitute amendment to replace the original; and

(4) An amendment to the substitute amendment.

When this situation occurs, as it occasionally does, the order of disposition is as follows:

★ The vote first comes on (2), on the theory that the original amendment should first be perfected, in order that a more intelligent decision can be made on any substitute;

★ The next vote is on (4), in order that members may see both the perfected amendment and the perfected substitute, before choosing between them;

★ Next, the substitute (3), as perfected is accepted or rejected;

★ And finally, the original amendment (1), which may now have been replaced by the substitute, is approved or rejected.

Offering and voting on amendments. In the Committee of the Whole (as in the House) amendments are first put to a voice vote.

Any one member dissatisfied with the declared result may demand a division, and those for and against stand to be counted. If one-fifth of a quorum—only twenty if a minimum quorum of one hundred is present—are still dissatisfied, they may demand and obtain a teller vote. While roll-call votes are not permitted in Committee of the Whole, an amendment approved in the committee is subject to a vote on demand of any one member after the committee has resolved itself back into the House. However, the defeat of an amendment in Committee of the Whole ends the matter; a subsequent and separate vote is not permitted in the House.

A member who intends to offer an amendment usually checks it for technical correctness with a member or staff expert of the committee that reported the bill, or with the Office of Legislative Counsel. Although not required by rule, it is considered courteous —and wise—to give advance copies to the Reading Clerk, the presiding officer, and the floor manager of the bill. Floor managers often successfully oppose an amendment on the sole ground that there has been no opportunity to study it.

When the proper time to offer an amendment has arrived, the member stands and addresses the Chair. The Chair asks, "For what purpose does the gentleman rise?" and the member responds, "Mr. Chairman, I have an amendment at the Clerk's desk." The Chair directs the Clerk to read the amendment, and its sponsor is then recognized for five minutes to speak in its behalf.

THE FIVE-MINUTE RULE

Rule XXIII (5) states that:

. . . [A] member shall be allowed five minutes to explain any amendment he may offer, after which the member who shall first obtain the floor shall be allowed to speak five minutes in opposition to it, and there shall be no further debate thereon, but the same privilege of debate shall be allowed in favor of and against any amendment that may be offered to an amendment. . . .

This rule is probably the single most important aspect of procedure in Committee of the Whole, and in this forum it is most widely and effectively used. It is also used in the House as in Committee of the Whole, but it is never used in the House itself. The rule limits debate on any one amendment to a total of ten minutes—five minutes for each side. In cases in which an amendment to an amendment or an amendment in the form of a substitute is offered, an additional ten minutes is allowed for each. But under the "motion to strike the last word" procedure, debate dealing with a particular amendment can be extended considerably with the offering of *pro forma* amendments.

Special limitations apply. When the five-minute rule is in effect, the following special limitations apply:

★ Remarks must be confined to the subject under discussion, unless unanimous consent is obtained to proceed out of order.

★ A member recognized for five minutes *may* yield to a colleague or various colleagues for questions or comments, but he *may not* yield any specific part of his time. Thus, a member recognized for five minutes to speak in opposition to an offered amendment may properly say, "I yield to the gentleman from ———." If the latter's comments consume the full five minutes, this is entirely proper. But the recognized member cannot, except by unanimous consent, announce that "I yield my five minutes (or two of my five minutes) to the gentleman."

★ The five minutes is charged against the member who is recognized regardless of how briefly he speaks; if he yields the floor before his time has expired, another member may not claim the remainder.

★ A member offering or opposing an important amendment occasionally may ask and receive unanimous consent to proceed for an additional five or more minutes. But experienced members suggest that this courtesy should not be sought too often or without good cause.

MOTION TO STRIKE THE LAST WORD

House rules are the product of experience. Early in the history of the five-minute rule it was found that ten minutes were often inadequate to fully develop the argument, and the *pro forma* amendment was invented to extend the time. Under this procedure, when the ten minutes allowed to debate an amendment have been used, another member obtains recognition and moves to "strike the last word." He is then recognized for five minutes.

Technically, this is a motion to amend the amendment by striking the last word. Because this would often violate the third-degree rule, it is treated as a *pro forma* amendment, which obtains five minutes to discuss not the merits of the last word in the pending amendment but the merits of the amendment itself. If further extensions of the debate are required, another member moves to "strike the last two words," then "three words," and so on. Members often simply move to "strike the requisite number of words" in order to avoid confusion.

In theory, the member who uses these motions should, at the conclusion of his remarks, withdraw the *pro forma* amendments he has offered, but in practice this is not done. Except by unanimous consent, a member offering a *pro forma* amendment to "strike the last word" may not yield a specific part of his five minutes to any other member.

Recording views on a bill. Although any number of members may offer a *pro forma* amendment to a pending amendment and obtain five minutes, no member may offer more than one such motion. Members unable to obtain time during general debate often use the *pro forma* amendment procedure to go on record with their

views on the bill, and through the "revise and extend" procedure
may have extensive remarks appear in the official report of the
debate.

The *pro forma* amendment procedure could be used until
every member has spoken for five minutes. But a limiting practice
has evolved by which the manager of the bill, when it appears that
the arguments have been fully developed, either asks unanimous
consent or moves that all debate on the pending amendment close
in a specified number of minutes. If he desires to restrict debate
more rigorously, he may move that all debate close at a set time,
for example, five o'clock. When this is ordered, the remaining time
is distributed equally—usually in segments of one or two minutes
each—to those members seeking recognition.

MOTION TO STRIKE THE ENACTING CLAUSE

Another procedure occasionally used in Committee of the Whole
to obtain time for debate is the motion to "strike the enacting
clause." After all time has expired for the discussion of an amendment, a member still desiring to be heard may obtain five minutes
by moving that the Committee of the Whole rise and report the bill
to the House with the recommendation that the enacting clause be
stricken. This is a preferential motion that must be in writing. It
allows only five minutes of debate for the sponsor and five minutes
for one opponent, with no *pro forma* amendments permitted. If the
motion carries, the bill under consideration is killed, although the
action of the committee can be reversed when it resolves itself back
into the House.

Use is limited and risky. As a device for gaining time to speak,
the motion to strike the enacting clause is of limited use. It cannot
be offered a second time unless the bill has been changed by amendment. And there are risks involved. Proponents of a bill have used
this device to gain five minutes to announce their support, only to
have their motion backfire by carrying—and killing the bill:

It can be a very dangerous motion because the effect of the motion is to kill the bill. I recall some twenty-five or thirty years ago a member who was very much in favor of a bill to provide for 3.2 beer—he came from New York City, incidentally—and all the time had expired under the five-minute rule. He was frantically trying to get recognition because he thought he had to say something about that bill. So he got up and he gave this motion to strike out the enacting clause and, lo and behold, it carried, much to his embarrassment. I use that as an illustration to point out the danger.

MOTION FOR THE PREVIOUS QUESTION

Moving the previous question, which is not permitted in Committee of the Whole, is the only method of closing debate in the House. When ordered, it terminates all debate and amendments and brings the House to a direct vote upon the pending question, whatever it may be. On a debatable motion, if there has been no debate prior to ordering the previous question, forty minutes is automatically allowed; the time is evenly divided between proponents and opponents of the measure. But if any debate, however brief, precedes the motion for the previous question, then no further debate is allowed. A motion for the previous question is not debatable, and must be put to a vote. The motion is privileged and does not require a second. While any member has the right to make this motion, it is usually offered by the member in charge of the bill under consideration. The previous question may be asked and ordered upon a single motion or upon a series of motions allowable under the rules, or may be made to embrace all authorized motions and amendments and include the bill to its passage or rejection.

Procedure for final passage

When the Committee of the Whole has acted favorably on a bill, several formal steps must be completed before the measure is officially passed by the House:

First, report of the Committee of the Whole. After the Committee of the Whole rises, the member who served as chairman is recognized and reports that "the Committee of the Whole House has had under consideration the bill H.R. ———— and directs me to report the same back to the House with sundry amendments, with the recommendation that the amendments be agreed to and that the bill as amended do pass."

Second, agreeing to the previous question. The usual rule under which the Committee of the Whole debates a bill provides that, upon its Chairman reporting to the Speaker, "the previous question shall be considered as ordered on the bill and all amendments thereto to final passage." If the rule has no such provision, or the bill was considered as privileged under Clause 22, Rule XI, the manager of the bill may move the previous question, or the Speaker may say, "without objection the previous question shall be considered as ordered." Agreeing to the previous question is important because until this is done the bill is open to amendments offered in the House, including amendments defeated in Committee of the Whole, and the sponsors of any such amendments would be entitled to recognition for one hour.

Third, voting on amendments. When the previous question has been agreed to, the next pending matter is the amendments adopted in Committee of the Whole. At this point, any member can demand a separate vote on any such amendment. The vote is first by voice, but division, teller, or roll-call votes can be requested. If there is no demand for separate votes on any of the amendments adopted in the Committee of the Whole, the Speaker puts the question on all the amendments *en bloc.* If a separate vote is requested only on one among several amendments, or several among many amendments, the Speaker thereafter calls for a vote on the remaining amendments *en bloc.*

*Fourth, engrossment and third reading.** At this point the Speaker announces, "The question now is on the engrossment and third reading. As many as are in favor," and so forth. If the question is agreed to, the bill is considered engrossed, and the Reading Clerk proceeds to third reading. Third reading is by title only. Until the 89th Congress, any one member had the right to demand a reading in full of the engrossed copy of a House bill. Because considerable time is required to officially engross and print the final bill, such a demand nearly always delayed action until the following day. A rule change in January 1965 eliminated this provision.

Fifth, motion to recommit. Immediately after the third reading, a motion to recommit is in order. This important procedure is discussed in detail below.

Sixth, passage of the bill. Unless a motion to recommit has carried, the House proceeds immediately to vote on final passage. The vote may be by voice, division, tellers, or roll call.

Seventh, motion to reconsider. Passage of a bill by the House is not final or conclusive until there has been an opportunity to reconsider. Immediately after a bill's passage or defeat the Speaker ordinarily announces that, "without objection a motion to reconsider will be laid on the table." If the Speaker does not do so, the manager of a passed bill usually moves to reconsider the vote and a colleague moves to table that motion. This *pro forma* procedure makes the action final and effectively blocks any future attempt to reverse the vote.

---

* The first, second, and third procedures apply only to bills considered in Committee of the Whole and are unnecessary with bills handled in the House itself or in the House as in Committee of the Whole. The fourth, fifth, and sixth steps are necessary in all cases.

MOTION TO RECOMMIT

The motion to recommit usually is made by the minority and occurs just before voting on the question of passage. In effect, it sends a bill back to the committee that originated it. It can take one of two forms:

Simple recommittal. "That the bill be recommitted to the Committee on ———." If approved, this motion in effect kills the measure insofar as further House consideration is concerned. When simple recommittal is voted by the House, the committee that originated the measure must begin anew, and all previous action by the Rules Committee, the Committee of the Whole, and the House is void. A committee may, however, re-report a previously recommitted bill.

Recommittal with instructions. "That the bill be recommitted to the Committee on ——— with instructions to report it back to the House forthwith with the following amendments . . . ," etc. Whereas simple recommittal is designed to kill a bill, recommittal with instructions is intended to amend a bill. When such a motion carries, the chairman of the committee to which the bill was recommitted rises and reports, "Mr. Speaker, in accordance with the instructions of the House, and in behalf of the Committee on ———, I report back to the House the bill H.R. ——— with amendments as follows. . . ." The House then proceeds to vote on the amendments, and then on to passage.

By tradition and custom the right to offer the recommittal motion belongs to the minority. The ranking minority member, or the minority floor manager for the bill, is usually recognized if he desires to make such a motion. Former Speaker Gillett declared, "The whole purpose of the motion is to provide a record vote on the program of the minority." Since there are no roll-call votes in Committee of the Whole, and separate votes in the House usually can be obtained only on amendments approved by the Committee, without this procedure the minority might never have a roll-call vote on the bill as it would have drafted it. Additional features of the "motion to recommit" procedure are as follows:

★ The ordinary procedure permits only one motion to recommit;

★ The motion must be in writing, and the member making the motion must be recognized for that purpose;

★ In recognizing a member to make this motion, preference must be given to members who are opposed. The Speaker inquires whether a member proposing to offer the motion is opposed to the bill and thus qualifies for the preference; and

★ Members of the majority party, when opposed, are recognized to make such a motion only if no minority member in opposition wishes to do so.

Voting and pairing

All votes are decided by a simple majority except in the following instances, in which a two-thirds majority is required: resolutions proposing Constitutional amendments; motions to suspend the rules, to dispense with Calendar Wednesday, to dispense with the call of the Private Calendar, to consider a special rule immediately, to override a Presidential veto, or to expel a member.

METHODS OF VOTING

Votes are taken in four different ways—by voice, by division, by teller, and by "yeas" and "nays." Only the yea-and-nay vote, also called a roll-call vote, is a matter of record.* Members may not vote by proxy, and although House Rule VIII states that every member shall vote on each question unless he has a direct personal or financial interest in the outcome, precedent has established that the

* The Legislative Reorganization Act of 1970, provides for recording the members for and against on teller votes upon request by one-fifth of a quorum.

House has no authority either to compel a member to vote or to prevent a member from voting. A bell signal is used to announce teller and roll-call votes for members who are not on the floor. The party leadership, whip systems, and various informal groups provide advance notice of important votes. The bell signals are:

One Bell	Teller Vote
Two Bells	Yeas and Nays
Three Bells	Quorum Call
Four Bells	Adjournment
Five Bells	Recess
Six Bells	Civil Defense Warning

Voice vote. The Chair says, "As many as are in favor of the question, say 'Aye,' " and, "As many as are opposed, say 'No.' " The Chair alone decides which side received the larger number of votes. However, if the Chair or any member is in doubt, he may demand a vote by division.

Division vote. This is a standing vote, which is ordered by the Chair on the demand of any member. The Chair first directs, "Those in favor of the motion (amendment, etc.) will rise and remain standing until counted," and then, "The 'ayes' will be seated and the 'noes' will rise." The Chair does the counting and announces the result. A member dissatisfied with the outcome of the division may then demand a teller vote, and if one-fifth of the members present support the demand by rising to be counted, a teller vote is ordered.

Teller vote. In this vote tellers, rather than the Chair, count those favoring and opposing a question. The Chair appoints one teller for each side, usually the sponsor of an amendment or motion and its chief opponent, who place themselves at the head of the center aisle. At the Chair's direction, first, members favoring the question walk between the tellers and are counted; then those opposed follow suit.

A teller vote usually is demanded in the hope that a divison or voice vote can be reversed by members who are not on the floor at the time but are nearby in the cloakroom, corridors, dining room, or elsewhere in the Capitol building. One bell is sounded to signal a teller vote, but members in the office buildings rarely have time to reach the floor and be counted. The result of a voice vote is final unless a division or teller vote is immediately requested, but upon such request the first result is only tentative and can be reversed by the outcome of the subsequent voting procedures.

Yea-and-nay vote. The yea-and-nay or roll-call vote is the most precise voting procedure and in case of conflict prevails over all other forms. Many bills and questions are disposed of by voice or division vote; except for the "automatic" roll calls, the yeas and nays are generally ordered only when one member demands them and his demand is seconded by one-fifth of those present standing to be counted by the Chair. When this vote is ordered, the Clerk first calls the names of all members in alphabetical order. Then a second call is made of those members who failed to respond on the first. Following this, members who failed to answer either the first or second calls may appear in the well in front of the Speaker's desk and announce their vote. The Tally Clerk hands the totals for and against the question to the Speaker, who declares the result. Two bells are sounded to signal a roll-call vote, and the entire process described above ordinarily consumes twenty to twenty-five minutes, giving members sufficient time to reach the floor from the House office buildings.

CHANGES AND CORRECTIONS OF VOTES

A member may change his vote at any time before the result is declared by the Chair. A member who doubts whether the Tally Clerk recorded his response correctly may proceed to the well at the end of the second roll call, but before the vote result is announced, and inquire, "Mr. Speaker, how am I recorded?" The

Reading Clerk will announce his vote as recorded, and the member may then change it by stating, "Off 'Aye,' on 'No,'" or the opposite. If a member, on reading the *Congressional Record* on a day following a vote, finds that he was incorrectly recorded, he may obtain a correction of the *Record* and the *Journal* through a unanimous consent request. However, the request must be made within thirty days of the date of the vote.

Recapitulation on close votes. Changes may reverse the outcome of a close vote, but instances of this happening are rare. In order to protect against such a possibility, the Chair usually grants a request for recapitulation of close votes after the count has been announced. In a recapitulation, a Clerk reads the names of all those recorded as voting in the affirmative. The Speaker asks if there are any corrections. Then the names of all those voting in the negative are read, and corrections are requested. Thus, during a recapitulation, a member who is incorrectly recorded may have his vote changed, and the vote count also changes, even though the result has been previously announced by the Chair. A member not recorded may not vote. The Chair will usually refuse a recapitulation if the yeas or nays prevail, as announced, by four votes or more.

AUTOMATIC ROLL-CALL VOTE

Under Rule XV, a roll-call vote is automatic if on a voice or division vote a quorum is not present and a point of order is made on that ground. In such cases a member obtains an automatic roll-call vote by getting recognition and stating, "Mr. Speaker, I object to the vote on the grounds that a quorum is not present, and make a point of order that a quorum is not present." The Chair first counts to determine whether a quorum is present; if not, two bells are sounded and the Clerk calls the roll. Instead of answering "present," however, members vote for or against the pending question.

PAIRING

Pairing is an informal arrangement used by members who are unable to be present when votes are taken in the House. A pair is not counted as a vote; its only value is to indicate how a member would have voted if he had been present.

Pairing is essentially a gentleman's agreement on the part of individual members. The House exercises no jurisdiction over pairs, but the rules do provide for their announcement and publication. Thus, the terms of a pairing agreement rest exclusively with the members involved, and disputes relating to pairs are not subject to mediation by the House. Both parties provide Pair Clerks for the convenience of members. The clerks are normally in the chamber during sessions and are customarily consulted by members desiring to pair. Forms to facilitate pairing also are available at these clerks' desks.

Although in theory a member may not be paired except by written agreement, in practice members often indicate orally to the Pair Clerk the position they desire to take, and after noting his other requests and consulting with the clerk of the opposite party he pairs the members as requested. There are many different pairing arrangements, but they most often take one of these forms:

The live pair. A "live pair" is arranged when one member of the pair is present and the other is absent. By pre-arrangement the present member votes when his name is called. At the conclusion of the roll call and before the vote is announced, he goes to the well and, upon being recognized, states, "On this question I voted 'aye.' I have a live pair with the gentleman from ————. If he were present, he would have noted 'no.' If I were at liberty to vote I would vote 'aye.' I therefore withdraw my vote and answer 'present.' "

Specific pairs. When an important vote on a specific matter is scheduled for a day on which a member knows he is going to be absent, he may contact a colleague opposed to his position who is also going to be absent. These two members sign a pair form directing that they be announced as, "Mr. A for (the question), and Mr. B against." Or, as frequently happens, Member A tells the Pair Clerk of his party of his proposed absence when the question is to be voted and his support for it. The Pair Clerk consults with his opposite number, and they pair Member A with Member B.

General pairs. Two members who are generally in opposition to each other's point of view may both intend to be absent for several days. And because they are unable to determine which questions or bills will be voted upon, they sign or instruct the Pair Clerks to list them as a "general pair" on all matters for a stated period of time. The *Congressional Record,* after printing the list of those voting and those having live and specific pairs, simply lists, "Mr. A with Mr. B." More frequently, a member planning to be absent instructs the Pair Clerk to pair him for a specific period of time. Without instructions as to specific votes, the clerk, as each vote occurs, makes a general pair of this member and some other member—usually, but not always, of the opposite party. This form of pairing does not indicate how either would have voted.

Some members advise against the use of general pairs on the grounds that they can be misleading. Readers of the *Congressional Record* who find "Mr. A with Mr. B" may assume that Member A was for the question and Member B against, whereas this form of pairing is not intended to indicate the position of either. And, if Member A is publicly known as an opponent of the question, Member B's constituents may assume from the general pairing that he was in favor. Instead of using the general pair technique, some members prefer to obtain an official leave of absence and/or to insert upon their return a statement in the *Record* indicating the reason for the absence and their position on any votes taken.

In the live and specific pairing arrangements, members are paired two in the affirmative against one in the negative if a vote relates to a question where a two-thirds majority is required to pass a measure.

LEAVE OF ABSENCE

Members absent because of sickness or death in the family, or on official business, may obtain an official leave of absence. Most members apply for leave only when they will miss an important vote and want the *Record* to contain some explanation as to why they failed to vote on the issue. Requests for leave are not made orally from the floor of the House, but by filing the proper application form with the Clerk of the House. The Speaker presents the request to the House for unanimous consent approval, which is almost invariably granted. When a member does not know whether an important vote will occur while he is away, he may give his completed application for a leave of absence to a colleague or to his party whip rather than filing it with the Clerk. Should a vote then occur, the colleague or whip submits the request on the absent member's behalf.

★ 10 ★

Political survival in a democracy

Almighty and everlasting God, source of human rights and framer of eternal laws, we beg Your blessing upon this House.

O Supreme Legislator, make these gentlemen ever distinguished by fidelity to Your word. Make seniority in Your love ever germane to their conduct. Make them consistently vote yea in the cloakroom of conscience that at the expiration of life's term they may feel no need to revise and extend. Make them attentive to the gavel of honor and respectful to the mace of Your law that they may always yield personal and party considerations when the welfare of this Nation and its citizens is threatened.

When the congress of life is adjourned and they answer the final quorum call, may the eternal committee report out a clean bill on their lives.

Finally, by unanimous consent of the heavenly house, may the Infinite Speaker recognize them on both sides of the aisle with this reward: "Well done, good and faithful servants of my people." Amen.

Prayer offered in the House
by the Rev. Elmo L. Romagosa, March 2, 1966

A RECURRING THEME throughout the preceding chapters is the Congressman's concern for political survival. "First take care of your

289

district," says the senior member to his junior colleagues. "Become a statesman later." To some, such advice may seem cynical, if not damaging to the republic. But many students of government argue that the politician's concern for survival is a prerequisite— not a necessary evil—of democracy. Washington attorney Max M. Kampelman* expressed this view cogently in remarks concluding the 1965 Seminar for Freshman Congressmen:

Coming to Washington for the first time is an abrupt experience. Adlai Stevenson tells the story of the little girl who said in her prayers, "God bless mother and father, and sisters and brothers, and now this is good-by, God. We're moving to Washington."

To a large extent I think it is somewhat presumptuous for somebody who has never been elected to public office to give advice to those of you who have gone through the crucible of campaign fire, which somebody called the Dance of Democracy. I say that because, in my judgment, one of the most important sets of values which must guide you in your behavior as members of Congress should be the recognition that you must survive—and by that I mean that you must always keep your eye on the next election.

Some of you may be fortunate enough to come from geographical areas where you can afford to be more carefree and act like the candidate who, when a heckler said, "I wouldn't vote for you if you were the angel Gabriel," quickly replied, "If I were the angel Gabriel, you wouldn't be in my precinct." For most of you, however, you recognize that modern American politics is today increasingly heavy combat politics, whether it is in the primary or in the general election.

* A Washington lawyer, political scientist, and former congressional staff employee (legislative counsel to Senator Hubert H. Humphrey, 1949–1955), Mr. Kampelman was Treasurer of the American Political Science Association from 1956 to 1968.

Political survival is, therefore, quite understandably a matter of constant concern to members of Congress.

The point I desire to make in that connection is not merely to point out the obvious. It is rather to assert that this concern with survival—which many might consider selfish—is, in fact, [a] prerequisite of democratic government. It is a concern that must be recognized as a legitimate one in our society and not one to be lamented as a necessary evil. Our democratic society is not based on a search for philosopher-kings whose only concern is with achieving excellence in public service. Noble and essential as the pursuit of excellence may be, it must be tempered by a concern for survival if we are to avoid the totalitarianism of a philosopher-king society and strengthen our democratic life.

It is this concern with survival which permits the Congress to serve as a decided link between those who are governed and our government in Washington. Certainly the tremendous volume of mail and requests that will pour into your offices is a reflection of the vital role that a member of Congress plays in translating the meaning of government to his constituency and in acting as the point of reference between the citizen and his government.

The pupil's typographical error in a geography class, to the effect that Washington, D.C., is hounded on all sides by the United States of America, will fast become a harsh reality to you. In all likelihood, you will not reply to the constituent that our government is one of separation of powers, that the problem he is raising with you refers to the Executive branch of the government and not the Legislative branch, and that, therefore, he ought to write to somebody else—that is, you will not write such a letter if you are concerned with survival.

Those who are concerned with democratic government are concerned about the growing disassociation that takes place between people and the government. The extent to which the institutions of the Congress, through its mail and errand boy functions, help to provide some method of association—to that extent is democratic government strengthened.

There is one other related point that I consider to be relevant here. It refers to survival as it relates to the word "compromise." T. V. Smith once said that "Politics is the art of compromising an issue without compromising yourself." Senator Fulbright stated the same problem in yet another way when he said, "To be prematurely right is to court what, to the politician, at least, is a premature retirement."

The give and take of legislative debate is the essence of preserving Congress as an institution. I suppose one of the most profound lessons that I learned after arriving in Washington in 1949 to serve as a staff member of the Senate was the overpowering presence of the color gray within these halls. There are black and white issues, but they are not as evident as they once were to me. The variations of background, experience, and problems of geography among your colleagues is an impressive fact of life which cannot be ignored.

There are forces on the outside—and I am included among them—who will be urging this or that solution to the many problems of the day that face our country and the Congress. I choose to think that I am probably right about my solutions, but I am fully aware of the fact that it is not I who vote. Somebody once said that a reformer is a person who wants his conscience to be your guide. But you must always remember that there are no "maybe" votes in the Congress—no "yes but" or "no and" votes that you will be permitted to cast. This sense of finality and responsibility, knowing that you in the end are held accountable for those votes, of necessity injects a distinguishing characteristic which can be experienced by nobody else not in your shoes.

Now, for one final word about the Congress as an institution: I speak to you not only as a lawyer and an observer, but as a political scientist.

I started my talk by referring to those of us who give you free advice. . . . [Many feel they] can tell what is wrong with Congress as an institution, why its rules ought to be modernized, why it is failing as an institution.

I stand here in a dissenting role. I urge you not to feel inferior about this institution of which you are now a part. I know of no parliamentary institution in the history of man which has fulfilled its responsibilities as conscientiously and as seriously as the Congress of the United States.

It is fair game to attack the Congress. . . . In one sense this is so because you are politically a representative body. Unlike the President and members of the Supreme Court, you do not walk separated from your fellow man by the Secret Service or by black robes. You are a part of ordinary man—people just like us with our strengths and our weaknesses. You are fair game for attack.

Congress is also attacked, however, because of some strange drive within our society toward easy solutions, which takes the form of a drive for greater centralized power in the hands of the President—a drive which unfortunately in recent years has been as much a characteristic of my fellow liberals as it has traditionally been considered an illiberal doctrine. Certainly the Congress debates, considers, and may even have the temerity to alter legislative proposals submitted by the President. This is as it should be. I remind you that the Congress, almost alone among the world's legislatures, has withstood the absolutism of the Executive and has remained the coordinate branch which our democratic philosophy means to be.

Yours is a great privilege. Be proud of your role and your Congress. May you fulfill your trust with dignity and honor.

Appendix

★ Salaries for members of Congress 1789–1969

FOLLOWING IS SELECTED historical information on compensation of members of Congress, 1789–1969, prepared by the office of the Sergeant at Arms and presented by the Clerk of the House in testimony before the House Subcommittee on Legislative Branch Appropriations on February 17, 1970:

Act of Sept. 22, 1789	$6 a day ($7 a day for Senators during extra sessions). $12 a day for the Speaker.
Act of Mar. 10, 1796	Previous act repealed; $6 a day set for both Members and Senators.
Act of Mar. 19, 1816	$1,500 annually ($3,000 for the Speaker). Repealed Feb. 6, 1817.
Act of Jan. 22, 1818	$8 a day for members ($16 a day for the Speaker).
Act of Aug. 16, 1856	$3,000 annually ($6,000 for the Speaker), payable monthly.
Joint Res. Dec. 23, 1857	$250 a month for members.
Act of July 28, 1866	$5,000 annually for members ($8,000 for the Speaker).
Act of Mar. 3, 1873	$7,500 for members ($10,000 for the Speaker).
Act of Jan. 20, 1874	Previous act repealed and $5,000 annually restored to members ($8,000 for the Speaker).

297

Act of Mar. 4, 1907	$5,000 to $7,500 for members ($12,000 for the Speaker).
Act of Mar. 4, 1925	$7,500 to $10,000 for members ($15,000 for the Speaker).
Act of July 4, 1932	*Decreased* from $10,000 to $9,000 (Speaker from $15,000 to $13,500). Economy Act.
Act of Apr. 1, 1933	*Decreased* from $9,000 to $8,500 (Speaker from $13,500 to $12,750). Economy Act.
Act of Apr. 4, 1934	Increased from $8,500 to $9,000 (Speaker from $12,750 to $13,500). Partial restoration.
Act of July 4, 1934	Increased from $9,000 to $9,500 (Speaker from $13,500 to $14,250). Partial restoration.
Act of Apr. 1, 1935	Increased from $9,500 to $10,000 (Speaker from $14,250 to $15,000). Final restoration.
Act of July 3, 1945	$2,500 annual expense allowance (tax free) retroactive to January 3, 1945.
Act of Aug. 2, 1946	$10,000 to $12,500 for members. ($15,-000 to $20,000 for the Speaker), effective January 3, 1947.
Act of Jan. 20, 1949	$20,000 to $30,000 for the Speaker (and $10,000 tax-free expense allowance).
Act of Oct. 20, 1951	Expense allowance amended, effective Jan. 3, 1953 (Public Law 183, 82d Congress), to make accountable for tax purposes but not subject to withholding tax.
Act of Mar. 2, 1955	$12,500 to $22,500 for members ($2,500 expense allowance repealed). $30,000 to $35,000 for the Speaker ($10,000 expense allowance for Speaker retained).
Act of Aug. 14, 1964	$22,500 to $30,000 for members ($35,-000 to $43,000 for the Speaker), effective at noon on Jan. 3, 1965 (beginning of the 89th Congress) $10,000 expense allowance for Speaker retained.

Act of Oct. 29, 1965   Compensation of the majority and minority leaders of the House and Senate was raised from $30,000 to $35,000 per annum, effective Oct. 1, 1965. (Public Law 89–301, sec. 11(e).)

Act of Dec. 16, 1967 $30,000 to $42,500 for members. Salary Commission established (by Public Law 90–206) recommended certain adjustments to the President. President, under the act, recommended $42,500 in his 1970 budget, and under the law, this went into effect Mar. 1, 1969, with respect to members.

Act of Sept. 15, 1969   So-called leadership pay bill. Speaker, from $43,000 to $62,500; majority and minority leaders of House, from $35,000 to $49,500, effective Mar. 1, 1969. Bill also covers Vice President and Senate leaders.

★ House Office Building Commission rules for assignment of office space

SELECTION AND ASSIGNMENT of office space in the House Office Buildings is regulated by law. In order to clarify and simplify the selection and assignment process, the House Office Building Commission has adopted the following rules and procedures.

VACANCIES DURING SESSION

Rule 1. If an office shall become vacant during a session of Congress, it shall not be assigned for a period of ten days beginning at 12 o'clock noon from the day of vacancy. During this period the Superintendent of the House Office Buildings shall accept in writing applications for the vacancy from members, and at 12 o'clock noon on the tenth day the office will be assigned to the member or member-elect with the longest continuous service. In the case of members of equal service the one whose application was first received shall prevail; and if applications from members of equal service are received at the same time, priority shall be determined by lot.

RE-ELECTED AND FORMER MEMBERS

Rule 2. (a). At noon on Monday following election day on the even years (or the next day if Monday is a Legal Holiday) applications for vacant offices will be received in writing by the superintendent

300

of the House Office Buildings from re-elected members and former members re-elected to the House of Representatives. These applications will be listed in the order they are received. The period for filing these applications shall expire at noon on December 1 following (or the next day if it comes on Sunday). Allotments shall be made in accordance with the provisions of Rule 1 where applicable. The Superintendent of the House Office Buildings shall deliver a copy of this memorandum to each re-elected member on Thursday following the election, and it shall then become incumbent upon each re-elected member to file for an office by December 1 following (or the next day if it comes on Sunday), if he wishes to move. At the same time the Superintendent of the House Office Buildings shall mail a copy of this memorandum to each re-elected former member.

MEMBERS-ELECT DRAWING

(b). Between the hours of 9 A.M. and 12 noon on December 5 (or the next day if it falls on a Sunday) members-elect without prior service, or their representatives, will draw numbers from a box to determine the order of their choice of an office from those remaining available. One individual may represent any number of members-elect without prior service, but he must draw a separate number for each person he represents and he must submit written authority from the member-elect he represents. The numbers drawn will be recorded immediately, and the card bearing the number drawn must be inscribed with the name of the member-elect without prior service for whom it is drawn. This card is to be retained by the member-elect without prior service or his representative and presented to the Superintendent of the House Office Buildings at 1 P.M. the same day when offices will be assigned in the numerical order of the numbers drawn. If more than one number is drawn out of the box at one time, the higher number shall prevail and the other numbers replaced in the box.

MEMBERS WHO MISS DRAWING

Rule 3. Members-elect without prior service or their accredited representatives who have not participated in the drawing will make their applications for offices in writing with the Superintendent of the House Office Buildings. Allotments shall be made in accordance with the provision in Rule 1 where applicable.

OUTGOING MEMBERS CHECK-OUT TIME

Rule 4. Members of Congress who will not be members of the succeeding Congress must vacate their offices by 12 o'clock noon on January 1 before the new Congress convenes.

SUPERVISION

Rule 5. The Superintendent of the House Office Buildings is authorized to carry out the provisions of these rules.

★ The congressional office work load

FOLLOWING ARE EXCERPTS from findings of a congressional office survey conducted by John S. Saloma III, of the Massachusetts Institute of Technology. The survey was carried out during the 89th Congress under auspices of the American Political Science Association's Study of Congress Project. Results are based on a tabulation and preliminary analysis of 158 questionnaires returned by congressional offices.

Pressures on a Congressman's time

1. The average Congressman reported that he spent 59.3 hours per week at his job during a typical work week while Congress was in session. The average work week was broken down as follows:

15.3 hours on the floor (25.8%)
7.2 hours on legislative research and reading (12.1%)
7.1 hours in committee (12.0%)
7.2 hours answering mail (12.1%)
5.1 hours handling constituent problems (8.6%)
4.4 hours visiting with constituents in Washington (7.4%)
3.5 hours on committee work outside of committee (5.9%)
2.4 hours on leadership or party functions (4.0%)
2.7 hours on writing chores, speeches, magazine articles, etc.
    (4.6%)

303

2.3 hours with lobbyists and lobby groups (3.9%)
2.1 hours on press work, radio, and TV (3.5%)

2. The average Congressman spent 5.6 days per month in his district while Congress was in session. He had an average of 2.1 speaking engagements outside Washington (other than district) per month.

3. Congressmen reporting made an average of 7.3 *radio* appearances per month while Congress was in session.

Number of broadcasts	0–5	6–10	11–20	21–30	31 or more
Number of members	99	20	10	1	7

4. Congressmen reporting made an average of 3.5 *television* appearances per month while Congress was in session.

Number of broadcasts	0–5	6–10	11–15	16–20	21 or more
Number of members	107	6	7	3	3

5. In the initial sample of 158 questionnaires, 82 members replied that they report regularly to their constituents by radio or TV. Thirty-six members replied that they do not report regularly by radio or TV.

6. While Congress is in session, the average member reads 5.0 daily newspapers; 8.4 weekly newspapers; 5.5 periodicals, and 1.8 nonfiction books per month. Frequently his staff marks or clips additional newspapers for him.

7. During the 88th Congress, 89 congressional offices reported re-

ceiving a total of 134,404 visitors, or an average of 1,511 visitors per office.

Number of visitors	0–750	750–1,500	1,500–2,250	2,250–3,000	3,000 or more
Number of offices	29	30	14	9	7

The average percentage of visitors seen personally by the member during the 88th Congress was 52.0%.

Percentage	0–20%	21–40%	41–60%	61–80%	81–100%
Number of offices	22	14	23	26	17

8. The following "excessive demands" were cited by three or more members: poor floor procedure (including quorum calls, excessive and irrelevant debate); committee work (especially legislative study and research); visitors in the office during working hours (several cited visitors from outside the district); constituents with unrelated personal business and requests (favors, jobs); political problems from the district; telephone calls at all hours; correspondence (including mail cranks); banquets, dinners, and parties (social functions were the most frequently cited single "excessive demand"); demands of reading (including requests to edit, read, or review material for publication).

Office work load and facilities

1. The average mail count per week reported was 521 pieces, broken down into the following categories:

   a. 64 letters involving casework (constituent problems)
   b. 154 pressure or opinion letters (views pro and con on issues, legislation)
   c. 51 opinion ballots (preprinted by an organization)
   d. 44 requests for information (such as government bulletins, etc.)

    e. 77 miscellaneous letters from constituents

    f. 120 letters received from outside the district

    g. 11 letters referred to member by other members of Congress

The distribution between these categories varied considerably from office to office. The average percentage of mail received in each category:

a. 12.3%; *b.* 29.6%; *c.* 9.8%; *d.* 8.4%; *e.* 14.8%; *f.* 23.0%; *g.* 2.1%

2. Peak and low mail counts varied dramatically. A typical office with a light volume of mail (210 per week) reported a range of 100 to 300 pieces per week. A typical office with a heavy volume of mail (800 per week) reported a range of 500 to 1,000 pieces per week.

3. The average percentage of mail received which related directly to the committee assignment of the member was 13.7%.

4. The estimated percentage of total volume of mail handled by the district office was 6.3%.

5. In responding to pressure or opinion mail, 138 members reported that they use "form" or "key" letters; 7 members reported that they do not use "form" or "key" letters. Autotypers are used by 125 members; 17 members reported that they do not use autotypers.

6. In handling requests for information, members used the following sources:

	Never	Seldom	Occa-sionally	Fre-quently	Very Often
a. Office of the Coordinator of Information	25	78	41	9	1
b. Legislative Reference Service	0	6	58	72	19
c. Liaison Offices	0	1	15	71	69
d. Other contacts in govt. depts. and agencies	1	3	25	85	41

Staff assistance for legislative duties and research

1. Members used the following staff resources in drafting public bills:

	Never	Seldom	Occasionally	Fre-quently	Very Often
a. Office of the Legislative Counsel	2	11	48	44	41
b. Committee or subcommittee staff	14	30	41	38	21
c. Government agencies and departments	31	48	33	16	5
d. Sources outside the government	41	58	33	6	0

2. Members used the following staff resources in drafting private bills:

	Never	Seldom	Occasionally	Fre-quently	Very Often
a. Office of the Legislative Counsel	11	17	37	34	40
b. Committee or subcommittee staff	29	25	30	35	18
c. Government agencies and departments	64	40	18	4	5
d. Sources outside the government	72	36	14	4	1

3. Sixty-three members replied that they have a full-time legislative assistant; 91 members replied that they do not. (Two members

answering "yes" considered their administrative assistant equivalent to a legislative assistant.)

4. The following estimates were made of legislative research done for the member (average percentages):

    a. by himself, 30.0%
    b. by the legislative assistant, 24.4%
    c. by other members of the staff, 20.6%
    d. by the Legislative Reference Service, 8.8%
    e. by committee staff, 10.9%
    f. by department and agency staff, 3.4%

These percentages varied markedly between offices. For example, one member reported that 100% of his research is done by committee staff. Another replied that he does 50% of his research himself and relies on his office staff (which does not include a legislative assistant) for the other 50%.

5. The following estimates were made of work done in preparation for the member's committee meetings and hearings (average percentages):

    a. by the member himself, 60.9%
    b. by the member's office staff, 15.5%
    c. by committee staff, 20.9%
    d. by the Legislative Reference Service, 1.4%

Again, percentages varied markedly with individual members.

6. The following estimates were made of work done in preparation for floor debate and voting:

    a. by the member himself, 60.1%
    b. by the member's office staff, 28.4%
    c. by committee staff, 8.8%
    d. by the Legislative Reference Service, 2.9%

Newsletter operation, questionnaires, etc.

1. In the initial sample of 158 offices, 121 members replied that they send a newsletter to their constituents on a regular basis; 29 replied that they do not.

2. Of these members, 32 reported that they circulate more than one kind of newsletter.

3. In distributing their newsletters, 12 members mail to all postal patrons, 98 members distribute by mailing list, and 14 members do both.

4. The circulation figures for congressional newsletters (counting the larger circulation when more than one kind of newsletter is sent out) breaks down as follows:

Circulation	Number of members
0–5,000	11
6,000–15,000	25
16,000–30,000	20
31,000–60,000	17
61,000–90,000	11
91,000–120,000	16
121,000–150,000	12
Over 150,000	4

5. Members reporting spent an average of 5.7 hours on preparation of each newsletter.

6. An average of 28.5 total staff hours was required for the preparation and mailing of each newsletter. Eighty offices reported they use an addressograph or its equivalent; 32 offices reported they do not.

7. In reproducing the newsletter, 28 offices use a mimeograph; 84 offices use photo offset; and 4 report they use both methods.

8. In responding to the question, "Does your office allowance cover the cost of your newsletter operation?," 31 members replied "yes," 89 replied "no."

9. Asked if their newsletter was reprinted in district newspapers, 51 members replied "yes," 65 replied "no."

10. In the initial sample of 158 offices, 48 members reported that they write a separate news or opinion column for newspapers; 94 reported that they do not.

11. Eighty-nine members reported use of mail questionnaires.

12. The circulation figures for members' questionnaires break down as follows:

Circulation	Number of members
0–30,000	7
31,000–60,000	11
61,000–90,000	14
91,000–120,000	19
121,000–150,000	18
Over 150,000	6

The average constituent response to members' questionnaires was 14.3%.

13. Members and staff reported spending on the average 19.6 hours in preparation of the questionnaire. Two members reported using the assistance of outside groups (university, etc.) to prepare their questionnaires.

14. A total of 117.9 staff hours, on the average, was required to tabulate the questionnaire responses. Twenty members reported using an outside group or firm for tabulation (and are not included in the 117.9 figure).

15. Of the 89 members who mailed questionnaires to their con-

stituents, 49 reported that they notified their constituents of the results.

16. Members reporting cited the following frequency in use of *Congressional Record* remarks mailed to constituents:

Never	*Seldom*	*Occasionally*	*Frequently*	*Very Often*
5	46	66	32	3

★ Initial office staff organization and salary schedule*

Washington staff	Basic	Gross annual salary
Administrative assistant	$ 5,750	$20,974
Legislative assistant	4,420	16,013
Case specialist– stenographer	2,050–2,435	7,757–9,002
Stenographer	1,840–2,280	7,012–8,501
Clerk-typist	1,450–1,840	5,811–7,012
Night man (filing, autotyping)	5–500	1,287–2,972
District staff		
District representative (part-time)	1,065–1,505	4,805–6,006
Clerk-typist (part-time)	5–500	1,287–2,972

Total basic used $16,585–19,230

* Allowances in effect in the 91st Congress, Second Session.

312

1971 PAYROLL CONVERSION

Under terms of the Legislative Reorganization Act of 1970, conversion from the *basic* system to a *gross* salary system becomes effective on January 3, 1971. The new system provides:

★ Members who represent fewer than 500,000 people are authorized up to $133,500 per year for payment of staff salaries.

★ Members whose districts are certified by the Bureau of Census as having an estimated population of more than 500,000 are authorized up to $140,500 per year.

The Act specifies that the monthly office payroll cannot exceed one-twelfth of the annual gross allowance. Thus, the *monthly* payroll of a member who represents fewer than 500,000 people may not total more than $11,125 (the *monthly* payroll maximum for those representing larger districts is $11,708).*

The Act leaves unchanged the limitations in effect during the 91st Congress on the total staff that may be employed at any one time: twelve for those who represent fewer than 500,000 people and thirteen for those who represent larger districts. The maximum salary a member may pay his top aide also remains unchanged—$27,343.

Members may establish—by written notice to the Clerk of the House—titles for positions of staff employees as he sees fit. Staff rearrangements and changes of salary schedules are certified in writing to the Clerk.

---

* The initial salary schedule on page 312, computed on the basic rate system, is well within these *monthly* payroll limitations, providing for eight employees at a total cost of from $5,412 to $6,196 per month.

★ Informal titles given House staff employees

A MULTIPLICITY OF titles is in use informally to describe various congressional staff positions. Following are those listed for House offices in an unofficial publication, the *Congressional Staff Directory,* for the first session of the 89th Congress.

Aide

Administrative Aide
Congressional–
Departmental–
District–

Field–
Legislative–
Press–

Assistant

Administrative Assistant
Administrative-Legislative–
Clerical–
Departmental–
Deputy–
District–
Executive–
Executive Secretary-
 Administrative–
Field–

Legislative and Research–
Office–
Press–
Public Relations–
Publicity–
Research–
Special–
Staff–
State–

Caseworker

Secretary-Caseworker

Clerk

Administrative Clerk
Assistant–
File–

Legislative–
Stenographer–

Consultant

Labor Consultant
Military–

Director

Assistant District Director
District Liaison–

Liaison

District Liaison
Government–
Public Relations–

Manager

Assistant Office Manager
District Office–
Office–

Receptionist

Clerk-Receptionist
Secretary–

Representative

Assistant Representative
District–
District Office–
Field–

Secretary

Administrative Secretary
Appointments–
Appointment and Personal–
Congressional–
Departmental–
Departmental Assistant and–
District–

Assistant–
Case–
Clerk–
Liaison–
Personal–

(*Secretary,* continued)

District Office–   Private–
Executive–   Press–
Field–   Public Relations–
Home–   Receptionist–
Legislative–   Resident–
Personal and Legislative–   State Office–

Stenographer   ### Typist

Clerk-Stenographer   Clerk-Typist
Secretary–

Miscellaneous

Assistant Researcher   Legislative Analyst
Case Specialist   Legislative Counsel
District Administrator   Press
Fiscal Adviser   Public Relations
Government Activities   Research Associate
In Charge   Staff

★ Housekeeping and maintenance services

OFFICE DECORATIONS

Various services and supplies for decorating offices are available, including:

★ Drapery-hanging service from the House Property Custodian's Office. (Draperies are furnished only for the member's room; those for other rooms must be supplied by the member.)

★ Picture-framing from the House Carpenter Shop.

★ Potted plants and cut flowers from the Botanic Gardens.

★ Scenic photographs from the National Park Service.

HOUSEKEEPING ITEMS

The House Building Superintendent's Office is responsible for replacing light bulbs and other general office maintenance—cleaning, carpentry, plumbing, heating, painting, and air conditioning. His office also supplies water glasses, soap, towels, hairbrushes, combs, dust cloths, and similar housekeeping items. On request, his office delivers ice by the bucket. Each suite of offices is cleaned every night.

Office keys. The Superintendent's Office is the keeper of keys to office doors in all three House office buildings. Many members give the Superintendent a list of individuals to be let into their offices in the event they misplace or forget keys. Keys for all movable furniture are supplied by the Property Custodian, who also is responsible for moving all furniture within and to and from offices.

Police and fire. A single House extension is set aside for police and fire calls. In summoning police assistance, if the caller does not wish it known that the police are being contacted, he simply gives his room number when the officer answers the phone. A policeman will then be dispatched immediately to that office.

REPAIRS AND MAINTENANCE

The House Property Custodian's Office is responsible for maintenance and repair of furniture, rugs, draperies, and venetian blinds. Installation and repair of telephone equipment is arranged through the chief operator, Telephone Office.

★ Description of filing system for congressional correspondence

FOLLOWING IS A description of a filing system established especially for congressional correspondence. This system, developed with the help of the Library of Congress, provides for the filing of correspondence with constituents according to the various subject titles listed. Concurrently, a 4" x 6" card should be made for every constituent who has any dealings with the member's office. This card lists address, political affiliation when available, and other pertinent personal information. When the constituent writes the member, the location of the letter and the reply, along with the date of each, is entered on the card. For example, if the constituent writes to inquire about a problem he is having with the Bureau of Employment Compensation, his inquiry and the answer will be filed in file number A10a, and so listed on the 4" x 6" card. Using this system, the member can tell at a glance the date on which the constituent wrote, the subject of his letter, the date of the reply, and the disposition of the matter.

A. Executive—Federal

A1. Executive Offices
   A1a. President's
      Commissions
   A1b. Office of Management
      and Budget

A2. Judiciary

A3. Department of Agriculture

A4. Department of Commerce

319

A5. Department of Defense

A6. Department of Air Force
     (except cases) *
     A6a. Jones AFB
     A6b. Smith AFB
     A6c. Early Warning
           Station

A7. Department of Army
     (except cases) *
     A7a. Fort Sam Jackson
     A7b. Camp Boredom

A8. Department of the Navy
     (except cases) *
     A8a. Marine Corps

A9. Department of Health,
     Education, and
     Welfare
     A9a. Social Security
           Administration*
     A9b. Office of
           Education

A10. Department of Labor
     A10a. Bureau of
           Employment
           Compensation*

A11. Postal Service

A12. Department of State
     A12a. Foreign Relations
     A12b. AID and Alliance
           for Progress
     Annex—AID newsletters,
           releases
     A12c. Passports and Visas
     A12d. Peace Corps

A13. Department of the Treasury
     A13a. Internal Revenue
           Service

A14. Department of the Interior

A15. Department of Justice
     A15a. U.S. Penal System
     A15b. Immigration and
           Naturalization

A16. Civil Service Commission
     (except cases) *

A17. Department of Housing and
     Urban Development
     A17a. Federal Housing Ad-
           ministration
     A17b. Metropolitan Devel-
           opment
     A17c. Renewal and Hous-
           ing
     A17d. Intergovernmental
           Relations

A18. Department of
     Transportation
     A18a. Coast Guard
     A18b. Federal Aviation
           Agency

A19. Office of Economic Oppor-
     tunity
     A19a. Job Corps
     A19b. Community Action
     A19c. VISTA

A20. Veterans Administration
     (except cases) *

A21. General Services
     Administration

* Cases are in individual folders marked with the file number and the number of the month of the year. For example, a January 1963 Air Force case is labeled A6–1/1963; February Veterans Administration A20–2/1963, etc.

A22. National Aeronautics and
　　　Space Administration

A23. Railroad Retirement Board

A24. United States
　　　Information Agency

A25. Other Independent Agencies

B.　Legislative—Federal

B1.　Agriculture

B2.　Appropriations

B3.　Armed Services

B4.　Banking and Currency

B5.　Education and Labor

B6.　Foreign Affairs

B7.　Government Operations

B8.　House Administration

B9.　Interior and Insular Affairs
　　　B9a.　Establish Gooney
　　　　　　　　Bird National
　　　　　　　　Seashore

B10. Interstate and Foreign
　　　Commerce

B11. Judiciary
　　　B11a.　Prayer Decision
　　　B11b.　Prayer Amendment

B12. Merchant Marine and
　　　Fisheries

B13. Post Office and Civil Service

B14. Public Works

B15. Rules

B16. Internal Security

B17. Veterans' Affairs

B18. Ways and Means

B19. District of Columbia

B20. Science and Astronautics

B21. Select Committee on
　　　Small Business

B22. Special, Select, and
　　　Joint Committees

C.　District Projects

C1.　Rivers and Canals

C2.　Harbors and Bridges

C3.　Highways

C4.　Individual Projects

C5.　Reserve Training Centers

C6.　Federal Employee Transfers

C7.　Absentee Ballots

C8.　Schools

C9.　Airports

C10. Access Road

C11. Airline Service

C12. Peace Corps Program

C13. Post Office
C14. City Development
    C14a. Manpower
           Retraining
    C14b. Mass Transit
    C14c. Urban Job Corps—
           OEO
C15. Vets Building

    C15a. Hospital
C16. Federal Building
C17. ARA—Area
      Redevelopment
      Administration
C18. Wage Board Employees
C19. Promotion of District

D.   State and Local Executive

D1. Councilmen and County
    Commissioners
D2. District Attorney and
    Police
D3. Housing Authority
D4. Mayor's Office
    D4a. City Manager's Office
D5. River Authority
D6. School System
D7. University and College
    Systems

D8. Other Departments
D9. State Legislators
D10. State Board of Pardons
     and Paroles
D11. State Department of
     Public Welfare
D12. State Employment
     Commission
D13. State Governor's Office
D14. Other Departments

E.   Academies

E1. Air Force (general only)
    E1a. Cadets
    E1b. Nominations
         (by years)
E2. Army (general only)
    E2a. Cadets
    E2b. Nominations
         (by years)

E3. Coast Guard
E4. Merchant Marine
E5. Navy (general only)
    E5a. Cadets
    E5b. Nominations
         (by years)

F.   Public Relations

F1.   Appreciation,
         congratulations, and
         condolences

F2.   Biographies, pictures

F3.   Birth lists

F4.   Invitations (a–l by month)
         F4a. January, etc.

F5.   Mailing list and newsletter

F6.   Naturalization lists

F7.   Newsletter

F8.   News releases

F9.   Press, radio, and TV

F10. Speeches

F11. Staff publications

G.   Office Techniques

G1.   Bills and invoices

G2.   Clerk of the House

G3.   Congressional accounts

G4.   Library of Congress

G5.   Office staff
         G5a. Applicants

G6.   Other

H.   Office Services

H1.   Agriculture yearbooks

H2.   Congressional records,
         directories, calendars,
         flags

H3.   Congressional referrals

H4.   Employment assistance
         H4a. Employment
                 opportunities

H5.   Gallery passes and
         White House tours

H6.   Government publications

H7.   Legislative bill requests

H8.   Patronage and nominations
         H8a. Post Office positions

H9.   Recommendations

H10. State delegation

Miscellaneous

@ a1. For unfillables
@ b1. Crackpot mail
@ c1. Campaign, congressional
@ d1. Domestic issues
@ e1. Foreign policy
        (nonspecific)
@ f1. Personal
@ g1. Honors received
@ h1. Medicare
@ i1. News clippings

@ j1. Opinion ballots
@ k1. Bouquets and praise
@ l1. Local politics
@ m1. State politics
@ n1. National politics
@ o1. Rights—Civil
@ p1. Taxes (nonspecific)
@ q1. Tax cut and reform letters
@ r1. United Nations
@ s1. Well-wishers

★ Publications available for distribution to constituents

FOLLOWING IS A partial list of government publications available in quantity for distribution by members of Congress to their constituents:

AGRICULTURE YEARBOOKS

Each member is automatically allotted four hundred yearbooks annually. The books are credited to the member's account in the House Folding Room and will be sent to his office or mailed out as he directs. The agriculture yearbook is especially useful to agriculture teachers, students, and 4-H Club members. Each yearbook is devoted to a special subject: Titles since 1936 have included *Grass, Trees, Crops in Peace and War, Insects, Plant Diseases, Marketing, Water, Animal Diseases, Soil, Land, Food, Power to Produce, Seeds, After a Hundred Years, A Place to Live, A Farmer's World, Consumers All, Protecting Our Food, Outdoors U.S.A., Science for Better Living,* and *Food for Us All.*

FARMERS' BULLETINS

There are more than two hundred different farmers' bulletins covering a variety of topics of interest to both rural and urban residents. The Department of Agriculture prepares separate lists of popular bulletins for members representing rural districts and those representing urban districts. Members may obtain copies of the bulletin lists in quantity to mail to constituents so that they can make their own selection of publications. (However, it is considered advisable to limit the number of bulletins a constituent may receive.) Each member is allowed a total of 10,000 farmers' bulletins annually. Quotas are cumulative indefinitely.

PACKETS FOR BRIDES

This is a package of ten publications designed especially for young homemakers and enclosed in an attractive but inexpensive folder. For each packet furnished to a member, a deduction of ten is made against his farmers' bulletin quota account.

OTHER PUBLICATIONS

The Department of Agriculture has many other publications available to members for distribution to constituents. Included are home and garden bulletins, marketing bulletins, marketing research reports, home economics research reports, production research reports, and technical bulletins. The number supplied is charged against the farmers' bulletin quota.

INFANT CARE

This is a publication of the Health, Education, and Welfare Department and is designed for new parents. Members may obtain up to five hundred copies per month, and the allotment will be sent automatically to the House Folding Room.

NOTE: The Department of Agriculture will mail its publications directly to constituents unless the member prefers to have them sent to his office first in order to stamp his name on them. Furthermore, members may expand their quotas of various publications by securing transfers from colleagues who do not use all of theirs. When such an arrangement is made, a letter must be sent to the Department of Agriculture, Office of Information, Congressional Section, directing that a specified number of publications be transferred from one member's account to another.

PUBLICATIONS FOR OFFICE VISITORS

Each member of the House is allotted copies of educational publications describing aspects of the American governmental system:

	Allotment
Our American Government	2,000
How Our Laws Are Made	500
The Capital	1,000
Our Flag	500

These publications are made available to the member on order from the House Folding Room. Other sources of printed brochures and lists useful to visitors include:

★ *Brochures of national monuments,* public gardens, parks, and places of historic interest. Available on request from the National Park Service, Department of the Interior.

★ *Map of Capital,* showing points of interest, list of public tours, motel and hotel booklet, where to eat and shop pamphlet, list of public buildings and other places to visit including hours each is open. Available on request from the Washington Convention and Visitors Bureau.

★ *Road maps of Washington area,* including Maryland and Virginia suburbs. Available on request from oil companies. Address request to the company's main office in Washington rather than to an individual service station.

★ *District and state tourist promotional materials.* Chambers of Commerce in district, banks, and other major industries, state promotional offices.

★ Maps available for official, constituent use*

MEMBERS MAY OBTAIN various kinds of maps for their personal use or to send to constituents and schools through several sources. As a general rule, members are advised to call the Map Information Office of the Geological Survey, Department of the Interior, or the Map Division of the Library of Congress for information on where to obtain particular maps. However, following is a list of some of the sources and the types of maps available.

GEOLOGICAL SURVEY

Geological Survey will provide maps for official needs or to meet requests of constituents or schools. Available are detailed topographic-contour maps of quadrangles throughout the country, large and small maps of the United States, maps of individual states, and maps of special areas. They are of varying scales and include such types as base maps, geologic maps, relief maps, and outline maps. Geological Survey maps are issued in unmounted form only. Each member has a quota against which he may draw. The quota is based on the number and type of maps published during his term of office and therefore varies from year to year.

* This section follows closely *Congressional Secretaries Club Handbook: 1964 Edition* (Washington, D.C.: Congressional Secretaries Club, 1964), pp. 25–26.

LIBRARY OF CONGRESS

The Library of Congress has large maps of states and counties (as well as other maps and atlases on all parts of the world) available for temporary use only in a member's office.

BUREAU OF LAND MANAGEMENT

The Bureau of Land Management will provide members with outline maps of the United States for their personal use only. Maps come in two sizes, 30″ x 45″ and 16″ x 25″ and are not available for general distribution.

POST OFFICE DEPARTMENT

The Map Section of the Post Office Department will provide members with unmounted State Post Route maps.

BUREAU OF PUBLIC ROADS

The Bureau of Public Roads provides large highway maps of the United States.

DEPARTMENT OF AGRICULTURE

The Department of Agriculture allots a limited number of county soil maps to members whenever such are printed. Available maps may be purchased from the Government Printing Office.

FOREST SERVICE

The Forest Service will provide maps of national forests as part of a folder that includes descriptive matter about recreational facilities in the area. Check with the Forest Service Division of Information and Education.

CENSUS BUREAU

The Geographic Division of the Census Bureau will provide maps of county census divisions which include the enumeration districts in each division. However, members may have to pay the cost of having the maps photostated, depending upon the amount involved.

NAVAL OCEANOGRAPHIC OFFICE

Published materials can be furnished to members for their official use upon request. This office prepares and prints nautical and aeronautical charts for international waters and foreign coasts.

U.S. ARMY TOPOGRAPHIC COMMAND

TOPOCOM publishes maps of foreign areas, and will make available selected issues for congressional use without cost.

ENVIRONMENTAL SCIENCE SERVICES ADMINISTRATION

A quota of 100 publications is provided each member for each Congress. The ESSA publishes daily weather maps, climatological charts, and nautical and aeronautical charts of the U.S. and its possessions.

DISTRICT OF COLUMBIA ENGINEER DEPARTMENT

The District Engineer Department can provide members with a large wall map of Washington showing all city streets.

★ Use of the congressional frank and correction of mailing lists

ON DECEMBER 26, 1968, the Post Office Department's general counsel, Timothy J. May, issued a policy statement on determination of "proper use" of the congressional frank, as follows:

The Congress has by statute (39 U.S. Code §4161) determined the nature of material which a Congressman may send free of charge under his congressional frank. This statute simply says that the privilege is available for "correspondence . . . upon official business." This statute, rather than being a directive to the Executive branch, is really more of a guideline for the conduct of its own members. Congress nowhere expressly enjoins the Post Office Department to police the behavior of individual members of Congress in their use of their franking privilege.

The Post Office Department has traditionally performed the function of interpreting, through General Counsel opinions, the meaning of "correspondence . . . upon official business," as that term is applicable to different types of mailings.

The Post Office Department is not vested with any authority by Congress to make binding determinations as to what is and what is not the "official business" of a member of Congress. The Post Office Department has no financial interest in the matter. Congress each year appropriates a specific amount of money to cover the Department's costs in the handling of franked mail. In that sense, the use of the frank by a member in no way contributes to the postal deficit.

The General Counsel of the Post Office Department for a number of years has rendered advisory opinions both to members of the Congress and members of the public, upon request, as to whether certain material was entitled to use of the congressional frank. It is the position of the department that the General Counsel's opinion is merely that—an opinion. It is not and cannot be binding upon the member of Congress. It has some weight because it is presumably a disinterested opinion. Many Congressmen seek some independent guidelines so that they may exercise the franking privilege strictly within the limits intended by the Congress. For these Congressmen the General Counsel performs a genuine service in rendering such advice.

It is the Department's position, however, that the final judge as to whether or not the franking privilege has been properly used must be the Congressman himself. When inquiry is made, the General Counsel will continue to furnish advisory opinions with which the member may agree or may disagree. But the member is himself in the best position to know whether or not, in the light of all the circumstances, he has abused his privilege and, therefore, owes postage to the Treasury. In the past the department has requested payment of postage in those instances where, in the opinion of the General Counsel, the frank was improperly used, although no effort was made to enforce payment. That will no longer be this department's policy. We believe it neither to be an obligation of nor a proper course of conduct for the department to seek to collect monies from a member of a separate branch of the government.

Finally, the department is of the view that franking laws are a matter purely of interest to the congressional branch. Congress created the privilege for its own members, and it is the responsibility of the Congress to insure the proper and lawful exercise of that privilege by its own members. Our advice will be available when requested; if after considering our opinion, and possessed of knowledge of all relevant circumstances, a member concludes that a particular mailing should have carried postage and, therefore, a member believes he owes monies to the Treasury, we will, of course, be glad to receive such payments from that particular member. On the other hand, it is beyond our authority to tell a member that he owes postage and most certainly beyond our authority to proceed to collect such postage.

This has been the first occasion for Postmaster General Watson to examine the policy questions presented by the department's involvement in franking rulings. This involvement has grown over the last several years from an occasional inquiry to the point where the mailings of a substantial number of Congressmen are being questioned on a continuing basis. We believe that the policy outlined in this statement, which admittedly is a departure from past policy, is compelled, lest we otherwise find the Executive branch becoming increasingly involved in the conduct of the official duties of the Congress, even to the point of engaging in censorship. We do not believe that this would be at all proper or conducive to good relations between the two branches of government and it might, in fact, raise constitutional questions.

SUMMARY OF LAWS

Following is a brief summary of laws pertaining to the franking privilege:

★ U.S. Code 39:4161 authorizes certain officials including members and members-elect of Congress to use the franking privilege, until June 30th following expiration of their respective terms of office, to mail official matter not exceeding four pounds in weight to any person.

★ U.S. Code 39:4162 authorizes certain officials including members of Congress to use the franking privilege to mail all public documents printed by order of Congress.

★ U.S. Code 39:4163 authorizes members of Congress to use the franking privilege to mail the *Congressional Record*, or any part thereof, or speeches or reports contained therein.

★ U.S. Code 39:4164 authorizes members of Congress to use the franking privilege to mail seeds and agricultural reports emanating from the Department of Agriculture.

★ U.S. Code 39:4166 makes it unlawful for anyone entitled to use a frank to lend it or permit its use by any committee, organization, or association, or to permit its use by any person for the benefit or use of any committee, organization, or association. This section does not apply to any committee composed of members of Congress.

★ U.S. Code 44:733 authorizes the Public Printer to furnish printed blank franks for mailing of public documents to members of Congress without cost. It also authorizes the Public Printer to print upon franks or official envelopes the facsimile stamp of the Congressman, providing that the member pay for the extra expense involved. It also authorizes the Public Printer to print on official envelopes the member's name, the date, and the topic or subject matter, not to exceed twelve words.

★ U.S. Code 44:907 authorizes the Public Printer to furnish to members of Congress, without cost, envelopes for mailing the *Congressional Record* or parts thereof.

HANDLING OF FRANKED MAIL

Franked mail is handled virtually the same as other mail. No franked mail will be admitted to the mail unless admissible as ordinary mail. Franked mail is forwarded like any other mail; once delivered to the addressee, it may not be remailed without payment of postage. None of these provisions prohibit sending franked envelopes to an individual, or firm, who is to address and mail them on the member's behalf.

Weight restrictions. A number of weight restrictions limit the use of the frank:

★ Official correspondence to other than a government official cannot exceed four ounces.

★ Official correspondence to a government official may weigh up to four pounds.

★ Public documents may be sent under frank, even if their weight exceeds four pounds. They may not exceed the general postal maximum of seventy pounds, however, nor may any package mailed under this provision include any matter besides public documents.

★ Official files of a member, addressed to himself, cannot exceed four pounds.

Simplified addresses. Members of the House may use simplified forms of address, such as "postal patron" and "occupant," on mail intended for general distribution within their congressional districts, although street addresses are required on mail to certain urban recipients. The privilege of using the simplified address form does not apply to Senators, but Representatives elected at large may send mail with simplified addresses to patrons throughout their state. Franked mail which is addressed to a recipient outside a member's congressional district (or state, in the case of an at-large member) must be addressed by name and post office address. General mailings require addresses as follows:

★ *Urban.* Franked mail intended for delivery in a city or village that has local carrier service must bear a specific street address (including apartment number, if any) or post-office box number. Such mail may be addressed to "postal patron," "occupant," "householder," or "resident" rather than to the intended recipient by name. Use of the city and state is optional. Designations such as "farmer," "voter," or "food-buyer" are not permitted.

★ *Rural.* Franked mail intended for delivery to each box-holder on a rural or star route, or to each family on a rural route (or any post office), or to all post-office box-holders at a post office that does not have city or village carrier service, need only be addressed to "postal patron—local" or to "rural route box-holder—local."

Preparation requirements. All pieces for the same post office must be tied, so far as practicable, in bundles of fifty. A facing slip must be attached showing the distribution desired (for example, rural route, post-office box-holders, etc.). If the pieces are bundled in quantities other than fifty, the number must be indicated on the facing slip. If selective distribution is desired, enough pieces must be presented to cover the route or routes selected, and the route numbers must be shown on the facing slips.

Post office assistance. Advice on simplified addresses and general mailings is available through local postmasters, who also will furnish the following information on request:

★ Number of post-office box-holder patrons

★ Route numbers and numbers of box-holders on each rural and star route

★ Route numbers and numbers of families on each rural route

★ The number of possible deliveries or possible stops (with or without stores or office buildings) within the total delivery area or on particular carrier routes.

CORRECTION OF MAILING LISTS

The Post Office Department is authorized to correct mailing lists— including addition of zip coding—used by members of Congress without cost and as frequently as requested. Following are excerpts from regulations pertaining to this service:

Name and address lists. Typewritten or printed lists should be submitted to the post office that serves the addresses, on cards, one name and address to a card. Cards should be approximately the size and quality of a postal card. The owner of the list must place his name in the upper left corner of each card. At third- and fourth-class post offices, mailing lists may be submitted in sheet form. Lists should be submitted by mail only. Names to which mail cannot be delivered or forwarded will be crossed off; incorrect house, rural, or post-office box numbers will be corrected; initials will be corrected, and the head of the family will be indicated, if known, when two or more names are shown for the same address.

New addresses for patrons who have moved will be furnished when permanent forwarding orders are on file. If no change is necessary, an X will be marked in the upper right corner of the card. New names will not be added to a list.

Occupant lists. Lists of street addresses may be submitted on cards, one address to a card, or in sheet form, provided the sheets are made up separately by carrier routes and each street bears the list owner's name and address. Lists for mail addressed to "occupant" and street address will be corrected. Numbers representing incorrect or nonexistent street addresses will be crossed off, but numbers will not be changed or added. Business addresses will be indicated by inserting B opposite the number. Addresses on a rural route will be indicated by R. The number of separate family units will be indicated opposite addresses of apartment houses or other multiple dwellings. If no change is necessary, an X will be marked in the upper right corner of the card or sheet. Corrected cards or sheets will be grouped by routes when returned to the owner so that he may handle and label mailings by routes.

★ Publication distribution service

THE HOUSE FOLDING ROOM prepares material for bulk mailings and serves as a "bank" for various publications allocated to each member. Included among its services are:

★ *Bulk mailings.* The Folding Room Speech Section folds, inserts, and seals envelopes containing speeches, newsletters, and other bulk mailing material. Because of the section's heavy work load, a mailing schedule must be worked out in advance to allow ample time for processing. Work is handled in the order it is received. Envelopes must be in good condition—they cannot be stuck together, overlapping, or wrinkled—and must be addressed before they are sent to the Folding Room for stuffing unless gummed address labels are to be used. (Labels are not affixed until after the envelopes are stuffed and sealed.)

★ *Book bank.* The Folding Room Ledger Section serves as a bank for agriculture yearbooks, Session Laws, bound copies of the *Congressional Record*, and other books and documents allocated to members. Members may draw on their accounts at will. Each receives a statement of items credited to his account twice a year, and special statements are furnished on request.

★ *Book wrappings.* The Folding Room Book Section will wrap books, such as the agriculture yearbooks, for which official wrappers are furnished by the Government Printing Office. Members

338

who wish their names stamped on agriculture yearbooks may make an appointment for a member of their staff to do so. Ordinarily, the entire yearbook allotment is not stamped and wrapped at once, because the books then will not be accepted for exchange credit by the Government Printing Office. Instead, members usually stamp only as many books as are certain to be used.

★ *Wrapping service.* The Folding Room Mail Section wraps and mails packages and other materials from members' offices in accordance with written instructions.

★ *Delivery service.* The Folding Room Delivery Section will pick up work to be processed (and deliver it to members' offices if necessary), and will pick up and deliver requisitioned supplies and other items.

★ *Miscellaneous.* The Folding Room will also provide wrapping paper, twine, cardboard, mailing tags, mailing tubes, odd-size envelopes, and similar items. A paper-cutting machine and a paper-punch are also available in the Folding Room.

★ Services performed for members by the Legislative Reference Service

LRS DESCRIBES its services and suggestions for their use in material sent annually to each congressional office. Excerpts follow:

The Service will provide what you want in the way that you want it as nearly as possible. It can be:

a written report,
a quick telephone call,
a personal conference,
a background study,
a bibliography, or
a book borrowed from the Library's collection.

In any case, all work will be done in a nonpartisan, objective manner, and a confidential relationship will be preserved.

Inquiries may be placed in three ways:

★ *By telephone.* Best for brief, less detailed inquiries. . . . Here your request will be recorded and assigned to the appropriate LRS subject specialists. If you wish to speak directly to the specialist, the person recording the inquiry will either give you the necessary extension or have him return your call.

★ *By letter*. Best for more complex and detailed questions to insure that nothing is omitted or confused in telephone communication. Correspondence may be addressed to:

> Mr. Lester S. Jayson, Director
> Legislative Reference Service
> Library of Congress

★ *In person*. Best for the times when you or your staff wish to develop a particularly complex or technical question, chat with a researcher, or browse through our clipping files. The place to come to is ROOM 107, MAIN BUILDING, LIBRARY OF CONGRESS.

No matter which you choose the LRS can do a better job, if you can tell us—

★ How the answer will be used

★ How quickly it is needed

★ What length and form will be most useful to you

★ If for a constituent, the age level or nature of the organization requesting it.

Some of the kinds of services we can provide are as follows.

ANALYSIS OF ISSUES FACING CONGRESS
You may request an analytical study, general background report, specific factual information, alternative proposal for solutions to problems, or the arguments pro and con.

LEGAL RESEARCH AND ANALYSIS
We will examine the constitutionality or interpretation of existing or proposed legislation, provide summaries and analyses of court decisions, make surveys of federal or state legislation on given sub-jects, prepare legislative histories, and provide legal research on related topics.

CONSULTATION WITH COMMITTEE STAFFS

We can assist with many aspects of committee work, among them: helping with preparation for hearings, suggesting appropriate "outside" specialists as possible witnesses, briefing staff on issues involved, noting questions that might be appropriate to ask witnesses, etc.

CONSULTATION WITH MEMBERS AND THEIR OFFICE STAFFS

You may wish to discuss a particular legislative issue or proposal directly with one of our subject specialists. We can help you evaluate the comment you have received from other sources or develop questions for further research on its public policy implications.

ASSISTANCE WITH STATEMENTS AND DRAFTS OF SPEECHES

The Service can provide background material for statements or speeches or—given sufficient time—will prepare drafts of appropriate content. For the latter, it is helpful to provide information on the occasion, the date, the viewpoint to be expressed, the length, etc.

GENERAL REFERENCE ASSISTANCE

On occasion, you may wish to have us assist you in your own research project, identifying and securing materials for your use. This can include searches of the *Congressional Record*, books, magazines, newspapers, and scholarly journals or the preparation of bibliographies or citations to federal or state law. If you wish, we will organize these materials for your use in the Congressional Reading Room or send them to you on loan from the Library's collections.

The LRS also provides while-you-wait or prompt call-back service on biographical information, addresses, identifying quotations, the identification and description of organizations, etc.

SPECIAL SERVICES

We have a number of services heavily used by members, which are somewhat specific and may not be recognized as a part of the generalized descriptions we have mentioned above. Among them are:

★ *Translations.* We can assist with translating your correspondence into or out of any of the major European, Latin American, or Asian languages.

★ *Charts, graphs, and maps.* The LRS has a graphics artist to help you with any statistical or geographic pictorialization which you may wish to use in congressional documents, hearings, presentations, etc.

★ *Congressional interns.* If you have assigned some research or study project to your staff interns, the Service can provide guidance in the use of the Library's resources, and the Stack and Reader Division . . . will make desk space available in both the Main and Thomas Jefferson Reading Rooms.

CONSTITUENTS

While we cannot undertake research for your constituents—please, no term papers or master's theses!—we do try to help with that portion of your constituent mail which can be answered with readily available material. Rather than telephoning each inquiry, many offices find it faster and more convenient to send the letters they think appropriate for the LRS directly to us. We will return them with the proper materials for transmittal to your constituents.

WORKING TOOLS FOR THE LEGISLATIVE PROCESS

The LRS has attempted to develop aids for the day-by-day work of congressional offices. Three of the most popular are:

★ *The "Bill Digest."* The Service prepares *The Digest of Public General Bills and Resolutions,* which furnishes brief synopses of all public bills and resolutions introduced in the current session. The "Bill Digest" is kept current by supplements and consolidations issued every two weeks. All issues have a subject index, and each consolidation gives the status of bills and resolutions acted on, a list of bills by sponsor, and by public law numbers.

★ *The Legislative Status Report.* While the "Bill Digest" is comprehensive (last year's grew to 2,296 pages), the "Status Report" is selective. In this, our subject specialists try to select the 200 most important bills, arrange them into subject groupings (veterans, agriculture, urban affairs, etc.), tell what they will do, and where they stand at the moment. The Report appears monthly and its "Legislative Status Checklist" appears weekly.

★ *"The Green Sheets."* The Service prepares several thousand background reports each year. From these we select those which seem to be of general interest and duplicate them in quantity. So your office may know what is available for general briefing on current legislative issues, speeches, and newsletters, we send you a list of these on "The Green Sheet" each month. After examining it, if you wish copies of any of the studies, you need only call . . . and order them by their serial number.

★ *The Congressional Reading Room.* This is a special room in the Library for use of members, their families, and their staffs. Located in Room 109 in the Main Building, it contains some 5,000 reference volumes and a browsing collection of recent books and magazines. It is open from 8:30 in the morning till 9:30 at night, Monday through Friday; 8:30 to 5 on Saturday and 1 to 5 on Sunday. At all times, it is staffed with reference librarians to answer your questions and charge material on loan you may wish to take with you.

★ *Loan Service.* Members of Congress may borrow books and other materials from the Library for their personal and official use. The borrowing privileges also extend to your immediate family, and you may recommend a limited borrowing privilege for specific members of your staff.

You may order books by telephone, either from the LRS . . . or, if you have a specific author or title, from the Loan Division. . . .

Books will be delivered directly to your office. When you wish them picked up for return, you may call the following Library Book Rooms located in the various Congressional buildings:

The Capitol—Room HB-4
    Capitol Ext. 3000
Senate Office Buildings—Room 34A
    Capitol Ext. 3550
Cannon House Office Building—Room B56
    Capitol Ext. 3170
Longworth House Office Building—Room 1039
    Capitol Ext. 2030
Rayburn House Office Building—Room B335
    Capitol Ext. 6958

Should you wish to place an inquiry after 5:15 P.M. Monday through Friday, or on Saturday, Sunday, or a holiday, calls will be taken in the Congressional Reading Room. . . .

A complete LRS Telephone Directory is available on request.

SERVICES THE LRS CANNOT PROVIDE

While we attempt to provide any information or analysis that will help you or your office with your legislative duties, there are a few things we cannot do.

The Service cannot prepare reports or speech drafts of a partisan nature or which deal with individual members or parties; its reports and drafts must be limited to issues and occasions.

The LRS cannot provide personal information relating to individual members of Congress except at the specific request of the member concerned.

We cannot accept rush or priority deadlines on constituent inquiries.

The Service cannot provide legal advice to constituents concerning their personal legal problems unrelated to action by federal government agencies.

We cannot provide translation services for constituents beyond a few lines of text and information on available commercial translating sources.

And although the Service does assist with preparing legislative proposals, it cannot draft legislation. Bill drafting is the function of the Offices of the Legislative Counsels.

✱ Assistance available from
the General Accounting Office

FOLLOWING ARE EXCERPTS, related to special assistance to Congress, from a report prepared by the General Accounting Office at the request of the Senate Committee on Government Operations: ✱

Assistance to the Congress

The U.S. General Accounting Office is a nonpolitical, nonpartisan agency in the legislative branch of the Government created by the Congress [in the 1921 Budget and Accounting Act] to act in its behalf in examining the manner in which Government agencies discharge their financial responsibilities with regard to public funds appropriated or otherwise made available to them by the Congress and to make recommendations looking to greater economy and efficiency in public expenditures. . . .

In addition, the 1921 act broadened the scope and objectives of the audit work. It requires the Comptroller General to investigate all matters relating to the receipt, disbursement, and application of public funds and to make recommendations looking to greater economy or efficiency in public expenditures; to make such investigations and reports as shall be ordered by either House of Congress or by a committee of either House having jurisdiction over revenue, appropriations,

✱ 87th Congress, Second session, Senate Document No. 96, May 29, 1962.

347

or expenditures; and, at the request of any such committee, to direct assistants from the General Accounting Office to furnish the committee such aid and information as it may request. . . .

Liaison with the Congress

Members of the staff of the Office of Legislative Liaison of the General Accounting Office are in constant contact with the committees of Congress and their staffs and with the Members of the Congress to confer with them and to supply such information as they may require in connection with the several hundred audit, investigative, and legislative reports submitted by the Comptroller General each year to the Congress or to its committees, Members, and officers. [These reports are available to members upon request.]

This staff also arranges for furnishing the various types of special assistance requested by the committees of Members of Congress. This includes arranging with the responsible operating divisions and offices for special audits, surveys, and investigations; for the assignment of personnel to assist congressional committees; and for the appearance of witnesses to testify before congressional committees on the subject matter of the audit and investigative reports, on legislative recommendations contained in the reports, or on bills before the committees for consideration.

Special assistance to the Congress

In addition to the work initiated by the General Accounting Office in carrying out its statutory responsibilities, the Office makes many special audits, surveys, and investigations at the specific request of congressional committees or individual Members of Congress. In many cases the requested work can be carried out in conjunction with other work and, if agreeable, may be reported on in a regular report. In many other cases, however, the work must be done as a special engagement and the report is sent solely to the committee or Member requesting the work. This type of work is given a very high priority and the performance of such work, particularly for congressional committees, has become a very important part of the work of the Office. Special audits, surveys, or investigations may also be undertaken as the result of (1) information obtained through the operations of various divisions and offices of the General Accounting Office or (2) information volunteered by other organizations, employees, or private individuals. A great number of requests are received from individual Members of Congress for information that can be supplied as the result of work already performed or for information relating to specific transactions that can be obtained readily. Many inquiries relate to the legality of specific transactions or to their conformance with existing regulations.

[The General Accounting Office receives numerous inquiries from members on claims of individuals for amounts alleged to be due from the government and on protests of proposed contracts awarded by bidders on government work. These cases are considered by GAO under its authority to settle claims for and against the government and to make final determinations on the legality of the expenditure of federal funds. Congressional action may be initiated based on a claimant's or protestor's letter without requiring legal representation and does not in any way limit the claimant's further petitioning the matter to the courts.]

Assignment of personnel to assist committees

Section 312(b) of the Budget and Accounting Act, 1921, in addition to requiring the Comptroller General to make such investigations and reports as shall be ordered by either House of Congress or by any committee of either House having jurisdiction over revenue, appropriations, or expenditures, requires the Comptroller General, at the request of any such committee, to direct assistants from his Office to furnish the committee such aid and information as it may request. In fulfillment of this responsibility, members of the professional staff of the General Accounting Office are frequently assigned on detail to congressional committees to assist the committees in conducting their studies and investigations.

Testifying before congressional committees

As a result of the widespread review by the Office of the activities of various departments and agencies of the Government, the Comptroller General or his representatives are often called upon to testify before congressional committees to provide information that might be of assistance to the committees and their members, and to testify on the reports which the Office has submitted to the Congress.

Furnishing comments on proposed legislation

An important part of the service which the General Accounting Office renders to the Congress consists of furnishing comments on proposed legislation. All bills introduced in the Congress are analyzed to ascertain whether the accounting, auditing, investigative, or legal work has provided information that might be useful to the congressional committees in their consideration of the bills. At the request of the various committees the General Accounting Office furnishes reports on several hundred bills during each session of the Congress. These are submitted in the form of letters to the chairman of the committee. The Bureau of the Budget also requests the General Accounting Office to submit comments to it on drafts of proposed legislation and to the President on enrolled bills.

*   *   *

In recent years, GAO has placed increasing emphasis on review of federal programs to determine whether congressional objectives are being achieved. This trend was described by the Comptroller General, Elmer B. Staats, in testimony before a subcommittee of the House Committee on Science and Astronautics in December 1969 as follows:

Role of the General Accounting Office

Section 312(a) of the Budget and Accounting Act of 1921 directs the Comptroller General to "investigate . . . all matters relating to the . . .

application of public funds. . . ." Section 312(b) of that Act directs that the Comptroller General "make such investigations and reports as shall be ordered by either House of Congress or by any committees of either House having jurisdiction over revenue, appropriations, or expenditures" and "at the request of any such committee, direct assistants from his office to furnish the committee such advice and information as it may request."

These provisions constitute a broad charter within which to serve informational needs of the Congress. Accordingly, we have extended our assistance to all committees of the Congress.

Section 312(a) clearly indicates, in our opinion, that the GAO is to be concerned with whether funds expended are achieving the program objectives intended by the Congress. Consequently, we have placed increased emphasis on reviewing Federal programs and activities from the standpoint of the extent to which congressional objectives are being achieved. This increased emphasis stems from various expressions of interest by the Congress and its committees and members in our doing more of this type of work as well as from our own desire to be of greater service to the Congress.

Because many of the programs and activities for which the Congress has authorized funds involve the promotion or control of technology, the application of technology to meet an existing problem or need, or the treatment of problems brought about by technological change or progress, our work necessarily involves us in the area which is the subject of these hearings. Our reviews of programs from the standpoint of achievement of objectives can and often do result in providing information which suggests the need to revise or strengthen a program or its administration to improve its effectiveness. In some cases this information leads us to recommend a change in the governing legislation itself. . . .

When we are called upon by committees of the Congress for information and assistance, the work requested often parallels work which we have undertaken or plan to undertake on our own initiative. Principally, our reviews involve examinations into programs or activities from various perspectives, such as the degree to which they have achieved intended results and the manner in which they have been administered. In other cases, a request may involve assistance to a committee in analyzing an executive branch proposal under consideration by the committee or alternatives which have been suggested.

I attach great importance to being responsive to requests for assistance and I am desirous of finding ways to increase our capabilities in this regard. . . .

In our assistance to the committees in their consideration of alternative proposals, our work and the work of legislative committees is made much easier if the background studies and analyses made by or for the executive branch in the development of its proposals for congressional consideration are made available. But we have found that executive agencies, in many cases, are reluctant or unwilling to provide the legislative branch with such studies or analyses or other material which contain communications, opinions, and argumentation which may or may not be consistent with the official position or decision of the agency or which may reveal prematurely executive branch determinations as to priorities.

For example, analyses of alternatives developed under the executive branch planning, programming, budgeting system (PPBS) which are designed to explore the potential results, side effects, and uncertainties involved in alternative courses of action, usually have not been made available. We understand that the executive branch, in response to increasing requests for such information, is now considering steps through which documentation resulting from the studies and analyses themselves would be maintained separate from documentation relating to policy recommendations and argumentation in order that it could be made available to the legislative branch upon request.

We do not believe that the Congress intended that the GAO initiate or be called upon to initiate new program proposals to deal with technological, social, economic, or other problems or needs. Nor do we believe it was intended that we initiate recommendations with respect to funding levels or budget priorities.

It is clear, however, that the GAO can and should direct its work in a way which will provide information concerning the results of authorized programs and activities which will be useful to the Congress and its committees in making judgments on these matters. Also, GAO can and should be available to assist committees on a case by case basis in analyzing information relating to alternatives considered by executive agencies and in reviewing the justification which prompted such agencies to propose specific research programs or other courses of action.

In September of this year, the role of the GAO in reviewing the results of Federal programs was discussed in considerable depth during hearings before the Subcommittee on Executive Reorganization of the Senate Committee on Government Operations. These hearings grew out of debate on several proposed amendments to the Military Procurement Authorization Bill which raised the question of the feasibility and desirability of the GAO playing a larger part in monitoring, analyzing, and reporting on progress and problems arising in the carrying out of existing programs and activities or analyzing and reporting on proposals under consideration by the Congress. During our appearance before the subcommittee, we outlined what we believed GAO's role should be in much the same terms as I have outlined above.

Also a special subcommittee of the House Rules Committee is now considering a proposed legislative reorganization bill which among other things would, in its present form, emphasize the role of the GAO along much the same lines.

In carrying out this role, whether it be in connection with work undertaken on our own initiative or work which may be requested by the Congress or its committees, we seek answers to questions such as:

(1) Is the program accomplishing the results intended as spelled out in the legislative objectives or implementing directives of the executive branch?

(2) Is the program or activity being conducted and are expenditures being made in compliance with the requirements of applicable laws and regulations?

(3) Does top management have the information and mechanisms essential to exercising supervision and control and to ascertaining directions or trends?

(4) Are there overlappings of jurisdictions and duplications of effort which serve no useful purpose?

(5) Have alternative programs or procedures been examined or

should they be examined for potential in achieving objectives with improved economic efficiency?

(6) Where alternatives have been considered, were studies—including cost benefit studies—lying behind executive branch proposals adequate from the standpoint of analyzing costs and benefits of alternative approaches?

. . . we are increasing our emphasis on work directed to ascertaining the extent to which programs and activities authorized by the Congress are achieving intended objectives and increasing our efforts to be responsive to the needs of the various committees of the Congress for reviews and staff assistance. These aims, of course, require that we give careful attention to the development of staff resources having the capability to perform the needed work in these areas. It has been my objective since assuming the Office of Comptroller General to increase the capability of our professional staff, particularly in the area of reviewing whether programs are yielding the results intended by the Congress.

Not only are we concentrating on increasing our staff of professional accountants and auditors, but we recognize the need to add professional staff educated and experienced in other disciplines—economics, business administration, mathematics, engineering, and systems analysis —to achieve the capability to more effectively review and evaluate Government programs. At June 30 of this year, about 300 members of our total professional staff of 2,665 involved in our accounting, management, and program review activities had educational or experience backgrounds in areas other than accounting or auditing. Many of these 300 staff members are recent graduates and therefore represent mainly potential for the future. . . .

★ Sample information sheet, candidate's statement, and application form for academy appointments

Sample information sheet

Consideration for appointment to the service academies can only be given to those young men who are LEGAL RESIDENTS OF THE_____ DISTRICT OF_____. A primary consideration upon which I base nominations to fill vacancies alotted to me is the candidate's grade on the Civil Service Placement Examinations which are given in July of each year, and which I require all applicants for my appointments to take. There is no limit to the number of times a young man may take the Civil Service Examination, even prior to his reaching the minimum age limit to one of the academies, inasmuch as I base my final consideration on the highest score attained by an applicant.

Candidates must be at least 17 years of age and must not have reached their 22nd birthday by July 1 of the year for which they seek admission to an academy. They must be single and must meet the specific requirements of the Academy to which they desire an appointment, as outlined in the respective air, naval, and military academy brochures. (Available on request from my office.)

I make my nominations to the various academies during the fall for classes beginning the following summer. Therefore, to qualify for nomination to next year's class, the applicant should take the Civil Service Placement Examination this July. I give letters to all applicants authorizing them to take the examination, and notify them of the day, hour, and place the examination is given in the community nearest their homes.

Young men interested in applying for nomination to one of the academies should address their inquiries as follows:

> Honorable_____
> U.S. House of Representatives
> Washington, D.C.   20025

Sample statement of academy applicants

> Representative_____
> U.S. House of Representatives
> Washington, D.C.   20025

NOTE: *Important.* Young men who are selected for training at one of the service academies receive an outstanding and costly education at the expense of the United States government. Graduates are required to serve a minimum of 4 years after graduation; however, some officers then resign and utilize their education in private occupations, resulting in the loss of valuable time received at public expense. In making my nominations I am most anxious to select young men who sincerely want a service career, and who intend to make it their life's work. For this reason I am requesting every applicant to sign the statement below:

Certificate

I, _____, a candidate for appointment to one of the United States service academies, do hereby certify that my application is motivated primarily by a desire to serve my country as a career officer. I further certify that it is my intention, if appointed, to graduate from the academy and make the military or naval service my profession and career. I make this certificate and pledge in good conscience and without mental reservation.

_____   _____
(Date)   (Signature)

Sample academy application form

ACADEMY APPLICANTS

Representative _____
U.S. House of Representatives
Washington, 25, D.C.

PERSONAL DATA SHEET

Name (in full)_____
                         (Last)   (First)   (Middle)

Permanent address_____
                              (Number and street)   (City)   (State)

Present mailing address_____
                              (Please advise me of any future change of address.)

Date of birth_____Place of birth_____
                                                           (City)   (State)

Parents or guardians (name both)_____

Parents' address_____
                              (Number and street)   (City)   (State)

Parents' legal residence_____
                                        (City)   (State)

Length of your residence in (state)_____

Name of high school (city and state)_____

Date of graduation_____

Present activity (if completed high school)_____

Probable activity next fall_____

Military service_____

Desire appointment to: Naval_____Military_____Air Force_____
             (Specify your preference in numerical order.)

I wish to enter the academy in_____
                                   (Year)

NOTE: Please attach to this sheet a complete summary of all extra-curricular activities during and since your high school years, including hobbies, sports, clubs, jobs, school activities, etc. While I am strongly influenced by the Civil Service Placement Examination, I also try to evaluate leadership qualities. You should, furthermore, obtain and send me three to six letters of recommendation from teachers, ministers, family friends, or civic leaders who have personal knowledge of your activities.

                                          _____
                                                (Signature)

                                          _____
                                                 (Date)

★ Suggestions for constituents in writing the Congressman

CONSTITUENT MAIL WILL be easier to answer—and more effective —if letter writers follow some ground rules. Following are guidelines from a newsletter sent to his constituents by Representative Udall:

The Right to Write: Some Suggestions on Writing Your Congressman

Surprisingly few people ever write their congressman. Perhaps 90 per cent of our citizens live and die without ever taking pen in hand and expressing a single opinion to the man who represents them in Congress —a man whose vote may decide what price they will pay for the acts of government, either in dollars or in human lives.

This reluctance to communicate results from the typical and understandable feelings that congressmen have no time or inclination to read their mail, that a letter probably won't be answered or answered satisfactorily, that one letter won't make any difference anyway. Based on my own six years' experience, and speaking for myself, I can state flatly that most of these notions are wrong:

> —Let me say that I read every letter written me by a constituent; a staff member may process it initially, but it will be answered and I will insist on reading it and personally signing the reply.
>
> —On several occasions I can testify that a single, thoughtful,

factually persuasive letter did change my mind or cause me to initiate a review of a previous judgment. Nearly every day my faith is renewed by one or more informative and helpful letters giving me a better understanding of the thinking of my constituents.

Mail to a modern-day congressman is more important than ever before. In the days of Clay, Calhoun, Webster and Lincoln congressmen lived among their people for perhaps nine months of the year. Through daily contacts in a constituency of less than 50,000 people (I represent 10 times that many) they could feel rather completely informed on their constituents' beliefs and feelings. Today, with the staggering problems of government and increasingly long sessions, I must not only vote on many more issues than early-day congressmen but I rarely get to spend more than 60 days a year in Arizona. Thus my mailbag is my best "hot line" to the people back home.

SOME FUNDAMENTALS

Here are some suggestions that apply to all congressional mail:

★ *Address it properly:* "Hon. ————, House Office Building, Washington, D.C. 20515." Or "Senator ————, Senate Office Building, Washington, D.C. 20510." This may seem fundamental, but I once received a letter addressed like this: "Mr. Morris K. Udall, U.S. Senator, Capitol Building, Phoenix, Arizona. Dear Congressman Rhodes . . ."

★ *Identify the bill or issue.* About 20,000 bills are introduced in each Congress; it's important to be specific. If you write about a bill, try to give the bill number or describe it by popular title ("truth in lending," "minimum wage," etc.).

★ *The letter should be timely.* Sometimes a bill is out of committee, or has passed the House, before a helpful letter arrives. Inform your congressman while there is still time to take effective action.

★ *Concentrate on your own delegation.* The representative of your district and the senators of your state cast *your* votes in the Congress and want to know your views. However, some writers will undertake to contact all 435 Members of the House and 100 senators, who cast votes for other districts and other states. If you happen to be acquainted personally with a Member from Nebraska, he might answer your letter, but there is a "congressional courtesy" procedure which provides that all letters written by residents of my district to other congressmen will simply be referred to me for reply, and vice versa.

★ *Be reasonably brief.* Every working day the mailman leaves some 150 or more pieces of mail at my office. Tomorrow brings another batch. All of this mail must be answered while I am studying legislation, attending committee meetings and participating in debate on the House floor. I recognize that many issues are complex, but your opinions and arguments stand a better chance of being read if they are stated as concisely as the subject matter will permit. It is *not* necessary that letters be typed—only that they be legible—and the form, phraseology and grammar are completely unimportant.

★ *Student letters are welcome.* Some of the most interesting letters come from high school and college students. Students may not vote, but many of them can be drafted, they must obey the laws we pass, and their opinions are important to me.

In the course of my years in Congress I have received every kind of mail imaginable—the tragic, the touching, the rude, the crank; insulting, persuasive, entertaining, and all the rest. I enjoy receiving mail, and I look forward to it every morning; in fact my staff people call me a "mail grabber" because I interfere with the orderly mail-opening procedures they have established. Whatever form your letter takes I will welcome it. But to make it most helpful I would suggest these "do's" and "don'ts".

DO'S

★ *Write your own views—not someone else's.* A personal letter is far better than a form letter or signature on a petition. Many people will sign a petition without reading it just to avoid offending the circulator; form letters are readily recognizable—they usually arrive in batches—and usually register the sentiments of the person or lobbying group preparing the form. I regret to report that form letters often receive form replies. Anyway, I usually know what the major lobbying groups are saying, but I don't often know of *your* experiences and observations, or what the proposed bill will do to and for you. And I often am not fully aware of new conditions and developments in Arizona. A sincere, well-thought-out letter from you can help fill this gap.

★ *Give your reasons for taking a stand.* Statements like "Vote against H.R. 100; I'm bitterly opposed" don't help much. But a letter which says "I'm a small hardware dealer, and H.R. 100 will put me out of business for the following reasons . . ." tells me a lot more. Maybe I didn't know all the effects of the bill, and your letter will help me understand what it means to an important segment of my constituency.

★ *Be constructive.* If a bill deals with a problem you admit exists, but you believe the bill is the wrong approach, tell me what the *right* approach is.

★ *If you have expert knowledge, share it with your congressman.* Of all the letters pouring into a congressman's office every morning, perhaps one in a hundred comes from a constituent who is a real expert in that subject. The opinions expressed in the others are important, and will be heeded, but this one is a real gold mine for the conscientious Member. After all, in the next nine or ten months I will have to vote on farm bills, defense bills, transportation bills, space, health, education, housing and veterans' bills, and a host of others. I can't possibly be an expert in all these fields; many of my constituents *are* experts in some of them. I welcome their advice and counsel.

★ *Say "well done" when it's deserved.* Congressmen are human, too, and they appreciate an occasional "well done" from people who believe they have done the right thing. I know I do. But even if you think I went wrong on an issue, I would welcome a letter telling me you disagreed; it may help me on another issue later.

DON'TS

My list of "don'ts" would include these:

★ *Don't make threats or promises.* Congressmen usually want to do the popular thing, but this is not their *only* motivation; nearly all the Members I know want, most of all, to do what is best for the country. Occasionally a letter will conclude by saying, "If you vote for this monstrous bill, I'll do everything in my power to defeat you in the next election." A writer has the privilege of making such assertions, of course, but they rarely intimidate a conscientious Member, and they may generate an adverse reaction. He would rather know why you feel so strongly. The reasons may change his mind; the threat probably won't.

★ *Don't berate your congressman.* You can't hope to persuade him of your position by calling him names. If you disagree with him, give reasons for your disagreement. Try to keep the dialogue open.

★ *Don't pretend to wield vast political influence.* Write your congressman as an individual—not as a self-appointed spokesman for your neighborhood, community or industry. Unsupported claims to political influence will only cast doubt upon the views you express.

★ *Don't become a constant "pen pal."* In a newsletter appealing for *more* constituent mail I don't want to discourage letters, but quality, rather than quantity, is what counts. Write again and again if you feel like it, but don't try to instruct your congressman on every issue that comes up. And don't nag at him if his votes do not match your precise thinking every time. Remember, he has to consider all his constituents and all points of view. Also, keep in mind that one of the pet peeves on Capitol Hill is the "pen pal" who weights the mail down every few days with long tomes on every conceivable subject.

★ *Don't demand a commitment before the facts are in.* If you have written a personal letter and stated your reasons for a particular stand, you have a right to know my present thinking on the question. But writers who "demand to know how you will vote on H.R. 100" should bear certain legislative realities in mind:

> On major bills there usually are two sides to be considered, and you may have heard only one.

> The bill may be 100 pages long with 20 provisions in addition to the one you wrote about, and I may be forced to vote on the bill as a whole, weighing the good with the bad.

It makes little sense to adopt a firm unyielding position before a single witness has been heard or study made of the bill in question.

A bill rarely becomes law in the same form as introduced. It is possible that the bill you write me about you would oppose when it reached the floor.

The complexities of the legislative process and the way in which bills change their shape in committee is revealed by a little story from my own experience. One time a couple of years ago I introduced a comprehensive bill dealing with a number of matters. I was proud of it, and I had great hopes for solving several perennial problems coming before Congress. However, after major confrontations in committee and numerous amendments I found myself voting *against* the "Udall Bill."

CONCLUSION

Here we are in January 1967, at the start of a new and drastically different 90th Congress. Before 1968 is history the House clerk will record my votes on more than 250 issues. But in a very real sense these will not be "my" votes; they will be yours too. There are more than 500,000 Americans in the 2nd Congressional District of Arizona, but when the clerk calls the roll, he calls only my name. Thus these 250 votes I cast will speak for you in the decisions our country must make in the next two years.

I need your help in casting those votes. The "ballot box" is not far away. It's painted red, white and blue, and it reads "U.S. Mail."

Morris K. Udall

★ Personal services available to members

FOLLOWING ARE SOME of the personal services and benefits available to members and their staffs.

HEALTH INSURANCE

Members and employees may obtain medical and hospitalization insurance through the Federal Employees Health Benefits Program. The program is partly paid for by the government and offers better rates and protection than can be obtained by individuals regardless of age and physical condition. The program is voluntary and offers a choice of various plans and options. However, to participate members must enroll in a plan within 31 days after the beginning of their term. Employees must enroll within 31 days from the date their employment begins. Brochures on the various plans and other information may be obtained from the office of the Sergeant at Arms.

REGULAR LIFE INSURANCE

A member may elect to be covered under the Federal Employees Group Life Insurance Act by filing the required form with the Sergeant at Arms. Payment of double indemnity is made for accidental death. Payment is made for accidental loss of one or more limbs or of eyesight. Life insurance is continued without further premiums if eligible for an immediate annuity on retirement after at least twelve years of service or because of disability. Otherwise, the insurance continues in effect for 31 days after termination from Congress, during which time an individual policy may be purchased at standard rates without a medical examination. Members are covered for $45,000 while in Congress. Upon retirement the insurance of a member over the age of 65 is reduced by two per cent for each month he is over the age of 65 until a reduction of seventy-five per cent is reached. The remaining twenty-five per cent stays in effect. A premium of $26.82 is withheld from the member's monthly salary for this purpose.

OPTIONAL LIFE INSURANCE

A member may elect to be covered by $10,000.00 optional life insurance by filing the required form with the Sergeant at Arms, but must pay the entire cost of this coverage. This election must be made within the first month of pay status, but may be canceled at any time. The premium is set according to age and increases at ages 35, 40, 45, 50, 55, and 60. These premiums are payable through the member's 65th birthday, even though he may retire before and meet the twelve years' requirement to continue this insurance. After age 65 and retired, this coverage will be reduced by two per cent each month until a reduction of seventy-five per cent is reached.

RETIREMENT AND DEATH BENEFITS

Members may join the Civil Service Retirement System by filing a form with the House Sergeant at Arms. Under present law an 8 per cent salary deduction is made each month and credited to the member's account in the retirement fund. Most previous federal service, including military service, is creditable. If a member terminates his congressional service, he may receive either a full refund of his contributions or annuity benefits whenever he becomes eligible. A similar program is available for staff employees. Further information and assistance may be obtained from the retirement consultant in the office of the Sergeant at Arms.

PHYSICIAN AND FIRST-AID ROOMS

A doctor maintains offices in the Capitol for the convenience of members. In addition, there is a first-aid room with a nurse on duty in each of the House office buildings.

ATHLETIC FACILITIES

Gymnasium facilities are available in the basement of the Long-worth House Office Building. Included are facilities for handball and paddle ball, exercising equipment, a steam room, and dry heat room. A swimming pool and additional gym facilities are available in the Rayburn House Office Building.

PARKING

Each member has a designated parking space in the Cannon or Rayburn House Office Building garages. In addition, each member is assigned two parking spaces in the garages for members of his staff. All inside and outside parking space is under the supervision of the House Special Committee on Parking. In addition, street areas around the Capitol are reserved for members and their staffs; the House Sergeant at Arms office, which has jurisdiction over all outside parking areas, issues tags permitting their use.

CONGRESSIONAL LICENSE TAGS

Members may obtain a special congressional license tag by applying (through the Sergeant at Arms) to the District of Columbia Director of Vehicles and Traffic. Each tag is separately numbered and is used in addition to the member's regular license plate. Similar tags are available to staff members. Among other advantages, congressional license tags permit parking in designated areas around various federal buildings.

IDENTIFICATION CARDS

An identification card certifying that the member is a duly elected member of the House of Representatives will be provided by the

Clerk of the House. Similar identification cards are available for staff employees.

DINING ROOMS

There are two dining rooms on the House side of the Capitol— one for members and their guests only, and the other for members, their staffs, House employees, and their guests. Private dining rooms also are available to members for special occasions. Included are the Speaker's Dining Room and the Joe Martin Dining Room. Details of dining-room and cafeteria use are contained in a booklet, "Standard Operating Procedure for House Restaurants," issued by the Select Committee on the House Restaurant.

CAFETERIAS

Cafeterias are operated in the Longworth and Rayburn House Office Buildings. Each is open from 8 A.M. to 2:30 P.M. Monday through Friday, and from 8 A.M. to 1:30 P.M. on Saturdays. Members are asked to avoid scheduling groups of visitors for luncheon in these cafeterias between 11 A.M. and 1:30 P.M. weekdays.

CATERING SERVICE

The House cafeteria will furnish catering service at reasonable cost to members for breakfast, luncheon, and receptions in special banquet rooms.

RAILROAD AND AIRLINE TICKETS

Both a railroad and an airline ticket office are maintained in the Capitol for the convenience of members.

CHECK-CASHING SERVICE

Both payroll and personal checks may be cashed at the Sergeant at Arms office in the Capitol. However, staff personal checks for $35 or more must be endorsed by the member.

★ Advisory opinion number one, Committee on Standards of Official Conduct

On the role of a member of the House of Representatives
in Communicating with Executive and
independent federal agencies
(January 20, 1970)

REASON FOR ISSUANCE

A number of requests have come to the Committee for its advice in connection with actions a member of Congress may properly take in discharging his representative function with respect to communications on constituent matters. This advisory opinion is written to provide some guidelines in this area in the hope they will be of assistance to members.

BACKGROUND

The first Article in our Bill of Rights provides that "Congress shall make no law . . . abridging the . . . right of the people . . . to petition the Government for a redress of grievances." The exercise of this right involves not only petition by groups of citizens with common objectives, but increasingly by individuals with problems or complaints involving their personal relationships with the federal government. As the population has grown and as the government has enlarged in scope and complexity, an increasing number of citizens find it more difficult to obtain redress by direct communication with administrative agencies. As a result, the individual turns increasingly to his most proximate connection with his government, his representative in the Congress, as evidenced by the fact that congressional offices devote more time to constituent requests than to any other single duty.

The reasons individuals sometimes fail to find satisfaction from their petitions are varied. At the extremes, some grievances are simply imaginary rather than real, and some with merit are denied for lack of thorough administrative consideration.

Sheer numbers impose requirements to standardize responses. Even if mechanical systems function properly and timely, the stereotyped responses they produce suggest indifference. At best, responses to grievances in form letters or by other automated means leave much to be desired.

Another factor which may lead to petitioner dissatisfaction is the occasional failure of legislative language, or the administrative interpretation of it, to cover adequately all the merits the legislation intended. Specific cases arising under these conditions test the legislation and provide a valuable oversight disclosure to the Congress.

Further, because of the complexity of our vast federal structure, often a citizen simply does not know the appropriate office to petition.

For these, or similar reasons, it is logical and proper that the petitioner seek the assistance of his Congressman for an early and equitable resolution of his problem.

REPRESENTATIONS

This Committee is of the opinion that a member of the House of Representatives, either on his own initiative or at the request of a petitioner, may properly communicate with an Executive or independent agency on any matter to—

★ Request information or a status report;

★ Urge prompt consideration;

★ Arrange for interviews or appointments;

★ Express judgment;

★ Call for reconsideration of an administrative response which he believes is not supported by established law, federal regulation, or legislative intent;

★ Perform any other service of a similar nature in this area compatible with the criteria hereinafter expressed in this Advisory Opinion.

PRINCIPLES TO BE OBSERVED

The over-all public interest, naturally, is primary to any individual matter and should be so considered. There are also other self-evident standards of official conduct which members should uphold with regard to these communications. The Committee believes the following to be basic:

★ A member's responsibility in this area is to all his constituents equally and should be pursued with diligence irrespective of political or other considerations.

★ Direct or implied suggestion of either favoritism or reprisal in advance of or subsequent to action taken by the agency contacted is unwarranted abuse of the representative role.

★ A member should make every effort to assure that representations made in his name by any staff employee conform to his instruction.

CLEAR LIMITATIONS

Attention is invited to United States Code, Title 18, Sec. 203 (a) which states in part: "Whoever . . . directly or indirectly receives or agrees to receive, or asks, demands, solicits, or seeks, any compensation for any services rendered or to be rendered either by himself or another (1) at a time when he is a member of Congress . . . , or (2) at a time when he is an officer or employee of the United States in the . . . legislative . . . branch of the government . . . , in relation to any proceeding, application, request for a ruling or other determination, contract, claim, controversy, charge, accusation, arrest, or other particular matter in which the United States is a party or has a direct and substantial interest, before any department, agency, court-martial, officer, or any civil, military, or naval commission . . . shall be fined not more than $10,000 or imprisoned for not more than two years or both; and shall be incapable of holding any office of honor, trust, or profit under the United States."

The Committee emphasizes that it is not herein interpreting this statute but notes that the law does refer to *any compensation, directly or indirectly, for services by himself or another.* In this connection, the Committee suggests the need for caution to prevent the accrual to a member of any compensation for any such services which may be performed by a law firm in which the member retains a residual interest.

It should be noted that the above statute applies to officers and employees of the House of Representatives as well as to members.

★ Criminal statutes proscribing conduct by members of Congress

★ *U.S. Code 18:201* makes it unlawful for anyone to "promise, offer, or give any money or thing of value . . . to any Member of either House of Congress . . . with intent to influence his action, vote, or decision on any question, matter, cause or proceeding which may at any time be pending in either House of Congress, or before any committee thereof. . . ."

★ *U.S. Code 18:203* makes it unlawful for any member of Congress to "directly or indirectly ask, accept, receive or agree to receive, any money or thing of value . . . with intent to have his action, vote, or decision influenced on any question, matter, cause, or proceedings, which may at any time be pending in either House of Congress or before any committee thereof. . . ."

★ *U.S. Code 18:431* makes it unlawful for a member of Congress to receive or agree to receive any compensation "for giving, procuring or aiding to procure . . . any contract from the United States or from any officer, department or agency thereof. . . ."

★ *U.S. Code 18:431* makes it unlawful for a member of Congress to either directly or indirectly "undertake, execute, hold, or enjoy, in whole or in part, any contract or agreement made or entered into in behalf of the United States or any agency thereof. . . ."

373

★ *U.S. Code 18:281* makes it unlawful for a member of Congress to receive or agree to receive compensation directly or indirectly "for any services rendered or to be rendered, either by himself or another, in relation to any proceeding, contract, claim, controversy, charge, accusation, arrest or other matter in which the United States is a party or directly or indirectly interested, before any department, agency, court martial, officer, or any civil, military or naval commission. . . ."

★ *U.S. Code 18:204* prohibits a member of Congress from practicing before the U.S. Court of Claims.

★ *U.S. Code 18:283, 205* prohibits officers or employees of the United States from prosecuting any claim against the United States.

★ *U.S. Code 25:70* prohibits a member of Congress from practicing before the Indian Claims Commission.

★ *U.S. Code 46:1223* makes it unlawful for any contractor or charterer who holds any contract made under the authority of the Merchant Marine Act to employ any member of Congress as an attorney either with or without compensation.

★ Sample statement for disclosure of business interests and assets

MR. SPEAKER: In order to help maintain public confidence in the legislative branch of our government and in me as a member thereof, I wish to make this public disclosure of my outside business and financial interests and income. My assets, holdings, affiliations, and outside income are as follows:

1. I own the following stock, bonds, and securities: (Some members have listed precise numbers of shares; others, only the names of the corporations in which they hold stocks or securities.)
2. I own, or have interest in, the following real estate: homes, buildings, lands, etc. (Some members give values and equities; others do not.)
3. I am a director or officer of the following commercial corporations and partnerships and associations:
4. I hold financial interests in the following corporations or partnerships which are directly or indirectly subject to federal regulatory agencies:
5. I have income other than my salary as a member of Congress from the following sources: *or,* My annual salary as a member of the House constitutes two-thirds (half, less than half, 90%, etc.) of my annual income from all sources.

375

★ Tax computations relating to congressional service

MEMBERS OF CONGRESS have a number of special problems and rules to consider in filing their income tax returns. Following is a *sample format* for reporting congressional reimbursement and expenses prepared by the Internal Revenue Service:

I. *Expenses deductible in arriving at adjusted gross income reimbursements* (*items to be included in gross income*)

A.	Travel expense		$ x
B.	Home office expense		x
C.	Telephone expense outside Washington, D.C.		x
D.	Stationery allowance		3,000.00
	Total		$ x

Less: Expenses

E.	Travel	$ x	
F.	Home office	x	
G.	Telephone	x	
H.	Stationery	x	
* I.	Cost of living, Washington, D.C.	3,000.00	x
	Adjustment[1]		$ x

* See affadavit attached.

[1] The excess of expenses over reimbursements is deductible as an "adjustment" in arriving at "adjusted gross income" even if itemized deductions are not claimed.

Explanations

ITEM A

This includes one round trip per year at $.20 per mile plus one trip per month while Congress is in session upon submission by a Member of his transportation costs to the House Disbursing Office. In lieu of the monthly trip, a Member may elect to receive a flat $750.00 per year allowance.

ITEM B

This item is limited to $300.00 per quarter and must be applied for by a Member from the Disbursing Office.

ITEM C

To receive this amount a Member must submit actual billings. This amount is limited to $300.00 per quarter.

ITEM D

This item is a flat $3,000.00 per year. It is automatically credited to a Member's account on July 1st of each year. The Member may withdraw from this account or expend it for stationery items. A Member is furnished monthly any yearly balances of this account by the Stationery Store.

ITEM E

This amount includes all non-campaign travel expense of a Member while on Congressional business except while in the Member's place of residence within his District or in Washington, D.C. Travel expense includes transportation, meals, lodging, local transportation, and personal laundry and cleaning.

ITEMS F AND G

The expenses shown under these headings will be the actual amounts expended limited to the amount of the reimbursements received. Expenditures in excess of the reimbursements received are deductible as itemized deductions.

ITEM H

This item is the actual amount expended in the Stationery Store, limited to reimbursement in arriving at adjustment. Any amount expended in excess of reimbursement can be deducted as an itemized deduction.

ITEM I

This amount is limited by statute (Sec. 162(a), IRC, 1954) to $3,000.00 per year. It is to pay for a Member's cost of living in Washington, D.C. Included in such cost are meals, lodgings, commuting expense, household laundry, maid service and so forth. An affadavit will be accepted as substantiation unless it appears unreasonable on its face.

II. *Expenses deductible as itemized deductions*

Entertainment of constituents	$ x
Newspapers & periodicals	x
Home office expense in excess of reimbursements	x
Telephone expense in excess of reimbursements	x
Stationery expense in excess of reimbursements	x
Public service broadcasts	x
Professional dues	x
Reimbursements to employees	x
Clipping service	x
Photographs	x
Other	x
Total[2]	$ x

[2] The total of these expenses is allowable only as an itemized deduction and may not be claimed if the standard deduction (in lieu of itemized deductions) is elected. The particular items listed reflect some of the more commonplace expenses which are incurred but the listing is not intended to be all-inclusive.

*Affidavit: I hereby certify that I was in a travel status in the Washington area, away from home, in the performance of my official duties as a Member of Congress, for_____days during the taxable year, and my deductible living expenses while in such travel status amounted to $_____.

★ Steps in the legislative process

THE FOLLOWING BRIEF outline indicates the usual steps in the legislative process, from introduction of a bill to enactment:

1. *Introduction* by a member, by placing the measure in the "hopper" on the Clerk's desk. Bill is numbered and sent to Government Printing Office to be printed and is made available next morning at Document Room.

2. *Reference to committee.* Bills are referred to a standing or select committee by the Parliamentarian under direction of the Speaker.

3. *Consideration by committee.* Usually involves hearings before either full committee or subcommittee and "mark-up" session during which members consider bill section by section and vote on changes.

4. *Committee approval.* Committee reports bill back to the House for consideration; bill is accompanied by committee report (which may be unanimous or include a minority report) explaining bill and changes made in committee.

5. *Placing on calendar.* All bills reported by committee are first placed on either the Union Calendar (revenue and appropria-

tion bills), House Calendar (nonrevenue bills), or Private Calendar (private bills only). Some are later transferred to the Consent Calendar.

6. *Obtaining consideration.* There are several ways in which bills are brought up for consideration by the House. Bills reported by certain committees are "privileged" and may be called up at any time or on certain days each month. Nonprivileged bills on the Union and House Calendars must be brought up under a special "rule" from Rules Committee or by special procedure (by Discharge Petition, Calendar Wednesday, or Suspension of the Rules). Bills on Private and Consent Calendars may be called only on certain days of each month in chronological order.

7. *General debate.* Bill is debated in general in either the House or the Committee of the Whole House, depending on type of bill. Debate time is limited and is usually divided equally between proponents and opponents.

8. *Amending process.* Bill is read in its entirety and opened for amendments. Debate on amendments under Committee-of-the-Whole procedure is limited by the five-minute rule. In House one-hour rule applies unless consent granted to use five-minute rule.

9. *Committee rises* (for bills considered in Committee of the Whole only). Committee resolves itself back into House and the chairman reports the bill and recommendation for passage to Speaker.

10. *Approval of amendments* (for bills considered in Committee of the Whole only). House votes approval of amendments made by committee, usually all at once and by voice.

11. *Engrossment and third reading.* Bill read by title only. Vote is usually by voice.

12. *Motion to recommit.* May be made by opponents only. If successful, bill is sent back to committee and is defeated, unless motion was to recommit for amendment. Vote is frequently by roll call.

13. *Passage.* Speaker puts the question of passage automatically if motion to recommit was defeated. Vote frequently by roll call.

14. *Transmission to Senate.* By message.

15. *Consideration by Senate.* Usually after reference to and report from committee, reading, debate, and opportunity for amendment.

16. *Return from Senate to House.* With or without amendment. If Senate rejects bill it so notifies House.

17. *Consideration of Senate version.* House votes on approval or disapproval of Senate amendments.

18. *Conference.* If House does not agree with all Senate amendments, members of the two bodies meet in conference to work out differences.

19. *Approval of conference report.* Compromise version of bill worked out in conference is put to vote of both House and Senate for approval.

20. *Enrollment on parchment paper.*

21. *Examination by committee.* Chairmen of the House and Senate committees which considered the bill must each certify that the enrolled bill is true and correct.

22. *Signing.* Always by the Speaker first and then by the President of the Senate.

23. *Transmittal to President of the United States.*

24. *Approval or disapproval by President.* Usually after referring it to department or agency affected for recommendation.

25. *Action on a vetoed bill.* If the President refuses to sign the bill, Congress may enact it if two-thirds of each house vote approval. Votes on overriding a veto must be by roll call.

★ Standing committees and subcommittees of the House during the 91st Congress, Second Session

AGRICULTURE

Cotton
Dairy and Poultry
Forests
Livestock and Grains
Oilseeds and Rice
Tobacco

Special Subcommittes on—
  Conservation and Credit
  Domestic Market and Consumer Relations
  Departmental Operations
  Family Farms and Rural Development

APPROPRIATIONS

Agriculture
Defense
District of Columbia
Foreign Operations
Independent Offices and Department of Housing and Urban Development
Interior and Related Agencies

Labor, Health, Education, and Welfare
Legislative Branch
Military Construction
Public Works
State, Justice, Commerce, and the Judiciary
Transportation
Treasury and Post Office

ARMED SERVICES

Subcommittees numbered 1–4
Special Subcommittees on—
  Air Defense of Southeastern U.S.

Antisubmarine Warfare
Armed Services Investigating
Central Intelligence Agency

Construction Costs
The Draft
Disturbances on Military
    Installations
Exchanges and Commissaries
Special Subcommittees on—
    M–16 Rifle
    Military Airlift

Military Construction
Military Installations
Real Estate
Retirement
Seapower
Service Academies
Supplemental Service Benefits

BANKING AND CURRENCY

Bank Supervision and Insurance
Consumer Affairs
Domestic Finance
Housing

International Finance
International Trade
Small Business
Ad Hoc Subcommittee on
    Urban Growth

DISTRICT OF COLUMBIA

Subcommittees numbered 1–5

EDUCATION AND LABOR

Special subcommittees on—
    Education (No. 1)
    Labor (No. 2)
General Subcommittees on—
    Labor (No. 3)
    Education (No. 4)

Select subcommittees on—
    Labor (No. 5)
    Education (No. 6)

FOREIGN AFFAIRS

Africa
Asian and Pacific Affairs
Europe
Foreign Economic Policy
Inter-American Affairs
International Organizations
    and Movements

National Security Policy
    and Scientific Developments
Near East
State Department Organization
    and Foreign Operations
Special Subcommittee for Review
    of the Foreign Aid Programs

GOVERNMENT OPERATIONS

Conservation and
  Natural Resources
Executive and Legislative
  Reorganization
Foreign Operations and
  Government Information

Government Activities
Intergovernmental Relations
Legal and Monetary Affairs
Military Operations
Special Studies

HOUSE ADMINISTRATION

Accounts
Elections
Library and Memorials
Printing

Special subcommittees on—
  Contracts
  Electrical and Mechanical
    Office Equipment
  Police

INTERIOR AND INSULAR AFFAIRS

Indian Affairs
Irrigation and Reclamation
Mines and Mining

National Parks and Recreation
Public Lands
Territorial and Insular Affairs

INTERNAL SECURITY

(No standing subcommittees)

INTERSTATE AND FOREIGN COMMERCE

Commerce and Finance
Communications and Power
Public Health and Welfare

Transportation and Aeronautics
Special Subcommittee
  on Investigations

JUDICIARY

Subcommittees numbered 1–5
Special subcommittes on—
  State Taxation of
    Interstate Commerce
  Submerged Lands

MERCHANT MARINE AND FISHERIES

Coast Guard, Coast and
  Geodetic Survey and Navigation

Fisheries and Wildlife
  Conservation

Merchant Marine

Oceanography

Panama Canal

Special Subcommittee on
  Maritime Education
  and Training

POST OFFICE AND CIVIL SERVICE

Census and Statistics

Compensation

Manpower and Civil Service

Position Classification

Postal Operations

Postal Rates

Retirement, Insurance, and
  Health Benefits

PUBLIC WORKS

Flood Control

Public Buildings and Grounds

Rivers and Harbors

Roads

Watershed Development

Special Subcommittee on—
  The Federal-Aid Highway
  Program

Special Subcommittee on
  Economic Development
  Programs

Ad Hoc Subcommittee
  on Appalachia

RULES

Special Subcommittee on
  Congressional Organization

SCIENCE AND ASTRONAUTICS

Advanced Research
  and Technology

Manned Space Flight

NASA Oversight

National Bureau of Standards

Science, Research
  and Development

Space Sciences
  and Applications

STANDARDS OF OFFICIAL CONDUCT

(No standing subcommittees)

VETERANS' AFFAIRS

Compensation and Pensions   Housing
Education and Training
Hospitals   Insurance

WAYS AND MEANS

(No standing subcommittees)

★ Conference committee rules and procedures

FOLLOWING ARE EXCERPTS of a *Congressional Quarterly* Fact Sheet describing rules and procedures of the joint committees of conference that are used to resolve differences between bills passed by the Senate and by the House:*

Closed conferences often wield legislative power

Unlike most national legislative bodies in the western world, the U.S. Congress is composed of two houses with roughly equal lawmaking powers. No bill may become law until it is passed in identical form by both houses.

Since Congress first met in 1789, it has used joint committees of conference to iron out differences between bills passed by the Senate and by the House of Representatives.

Little known to most outsiders because the committee meetings take place in virtual secrecy, conference committees frequently have almost dictatorial control over the final shape of important legislation.

Conferences are held after one chamber states formally that it is unable to accept the version of a bill that has been passed by the other chamber. Sometimes the chamber that originated the bill requests a con-

* Excerpts reprinted with permission of the publisher, Congressional Quarterly, Inc. For the full text of the Fact Sheet, see *Congressional Quarterly Weekly Report,* December 12, 1969, pp. 2573–2576.

ference after its bill has been amended by the other chamber. In other cases the chamber that considers the bill last assumes that its amendments will not be accepted by the other chamber and requests the conference on its own.

HOUSE, SENATE RULES

The House of Representatives generally requests or agrees to a conference either by unanimous consent or by majority adoption of a rule from the Rules Committee providing for a conference on a particular bill.

Until the beginning of the 89th Congress in 1965, the House could bypass the Rules Committee only by unanimous consent or by suspension of the rules, for which a two-thirds majority is required. Since then, a simple majority of House Members has had the power to request or agree to a conference with or without the consent of the Rules Committee, if the committee with jurisdiction over the bill wishes one.

The 1965 change was partially a result of Rules Committee reluctance to send some liberal House-passed bills to conference. In 1960, for example, both chambers passed an aid-to-education bill that never became law because the Rules Committee refused to grant a rule providing for a conference.

It is still common practice for the House to work through the Rules Committee in providing for conferences, despite the rules change. The measure adopted in 1965 has been used only twice. It is possible, however, that the Rules Committee is less willing to block conferences now because it knows it may be overruled by a simple majority of House Members.

A conference cannot take place until both chambers formally agree that it be held. In rare cases, one chamber has refused a conference request made by the other, preventing passage of any version of a bill.

Of nine bills in the conference stage during the first week of December 1969, only two were sent to conference following a request by the chamber originating them. The seven other conferences were requested by the second chamber in anticipation that its amendments would not be accepted by the chamber of origin.

A survey during the 88th Congress indicated that about 8 percent of all public and private bills passed by either house are sent to conference. The survey said that almost 95 percent of bills that go to conference eventually become law.

The Senate generally requests or agrees to a conference by unanimous consent. A roll-call vote may be taken if there is objection. There is no Senate body that serves a function comparable to that of the Rules Committee in the House.

Appointments. The two chambers have different formal rules for appointing conferees but follow similar practices. Senate rules say, "The Senate (acting as a body) may appoint its conferees if it sees fit to do so." Generally, however, the conferees are appointed by the presiding officer on the recommendation of the chairman of the committee that considered the legislation. The Senate has elected conferees only a few times in the 20th century, notably on the Muscle Shoals bill in 1925.

House rules grant the Speaker the right to appoint its conferees, but he, too, normally acts on the advice of the chairman of the committee involved.

In many cases the members selected by a committee chairman as conferees are the senior members from both parties in his committee. Junior committee members are often appointed if they are members of the subcommittee that first considered the legislation.

The practice of appointing subcommittee members as conferees regardless of their seniority is particularly common in appropriation conferences. For example, Democratic Senate conferees on the Legislative Branch appropriations bill of 1970 were Senators Joseph M. Montoya (N.M.), Ralph W. Yarborough (Texas) and William Proxmire (Wis.), the three lowest-ranking Democrats on the Appropriations Committee. They were chosen as conferees because their Subcommittee chaired by Montoya, had the initial responsibility for the bill.

It is rare for a chairman to recommend, or for a presiding offiicer to appoint, a conferee who is not on the appropriate committee. Occasionally, however, a committee chairman will reach outside the committee to enable the author of a bill to participate in its conference.

Size. In the 90th and 91st Congresses, conference committee delegations have varied in size from 3 to 18 members. Delegations from the two chambers need not be the same size, since a conference report must be approved by a majority within each delegation. In the Senate, the

various appropriations delegations are the largest, because members of
the committees that authorize the expenditures often join Appropriations
Committee members in conference.

As of Nov. 25, 1969, 10 conference committees were operating.
They averaged 15.2 members, of whom 8.1 were Senators and 7.1 were
Representatives. The average conference committee had 8.8 Democrats
and 6.4 Republicans. Thus the percentage of Democrats on conference
committees was 57.9 percent, as opposed to 56.5 percent in the House
as a whole and 57 percent in the Senate as a whole. . . .

Unenforced provision. The Legislative Reorganization Act of
1946 says that conferees must have demonstrated support for the legislation as passed in their chamber, but this provision is unenforced. In
1964, for example, Sen. Joseph Clark (D Pa. 1957–69), protested that
the conferees appointed to consider the Social Security Amendments bill
were not in sympathy with the prevailing views of the Senate. . . .

Instructions. Either chamber may instruct its conferees on how to
vote when they go to conference, but the conferees are not required to
follow the instructions. No conference report is subject to a point of
order on the grounds that it violates instructions given by the full chamber. Therefore, instructions to conferees are little more than guidelines
expressing the general position of the House or Senate. Conferences are
set up for the purpose of compromising differences, and a conference in
which the participants were bound in advance would serve little purpose. . . .

Although House and Senate rules do not force conferees to follow
instructions, they do place fairly strict limitations on the changes they
can make in bills. For example, Rule XXVII of the standing rules of the
Senate provides that "Conferees shall not insert in their report matter not
committed to them by either house, nor shall they strike from the bill
matter agreed to by both houses." In cases where the two houses disagree
on the amount of an appropriation, Senate conferees are directed by the
rules to find a compromise amount between the two extremes, but not
below the lower amount or above the higher one.

Additions, deletions. In both houses, conference reports are subject to points of order on grounds that they contain improper additions

or deletions. The job of the conference committee is made more complex, however, by the Senate rule that any bill may contain amendments not germane to the rest of the bill. This means that the Senate can amend a House-passed bill by voting to strike from it everything after the enacting clause and inserting entirely new legislation in its place. When this happens, there is no way for conferees to reach a compromise without designing a bill different from either of the versions they received. In such cases, House precedents say that conferees "may exercise a broad discretion as to details, and may even report an entirely new bill on the subject." Senate rules also permit wide latitude in such cases but require that conferees include only material germane to the subject matter of at least one of the original versions of the bill.

All conference committee meetings are held in executive session— closed to the public and to the press. No minutes are taken and no official records of debate or voting are kept. Staff aides are permitted to attend the meetings upon unanimous consent of the conferees. Traditionally, most conferences have taken place on the Senate side of the Capitol, but this is not always the case. . . .

House discharge. House conferees face one additional limitation not placed upon Senate conferees—they may be discharged by a majority vote of the House Members if after 20 calendar days of conference they have failed to make a report. This rule was adopted in 1931 to give the House greater flexibility over its conference committees. But it has rarely been invoked and has had little apparent effect on conference committees.

Reporting procedures. Here are several of the ways in which conferees can report back to their full chambers after a conference:

★ If they have reached agreement on legislation, they can present a conference report embodying their revisions and submit it to the chamber for a vote.

★ If they have been unable to reach agreement, but wish further instructions, they can ask the full chamber whether it desires to insist upon its own amendments or whether it will recede and concur with some or all of the amendments of the other chamber.

★ If they have reached agreement on some provisions but not on others, they can present a conference report embodying the agreements and ask the full chamber for instructions on the rest.

★ If they have been unable to reach agreement, they can simply inform the full chamber of this and allow it to act as it wishes.

Conferees are not obligated to make any report at all, however, and they may choose to let the bill remain in conference. If a bill is still in conference at the end of a Congress, it dies there.

HIGH PRIORITY

The house that suggested the conference is the latter to act on the report once the conferees have finished. Conference reports are presented on the floor of both chambers as highly privileged documents, and their presentation can interrupt any normal business except a vote or other roll call. A conference report can interrupt a Senate vote only by unanimous consent.

In the Senate, there is even a precedent for interrupting debate on one conference report so that another can be presented.

The House, though it does so infrequently, may send a completed conference report to its Rules Committee before the report reaches the floor. This has happened when conferees inserted into a bill new material that could make the conference report subject to a point of order. The Rules Committee, in such cases, can grant a rule prohibiting points of order against the report. This occurred in the consideration of a foreign aid bill in December 1963. . . .

Positive terms. In the Senate, after a conference report has been presented, the chamber votes on whether to consider it. If the Members agree to consider, a motion to adopt the report is in order. A Senator cannot move the consideration and adoption of a report at the same time.

In the House, there is no separate motion to consider a conference report. It is simply called up for discussion, and a motion to adopt it is then in order.

In both chambers, motions on the adoption of a conference report must be phrased in positive terms. It is not in order, in either chamber, to move the rejection of a conference report.

Nor is it in order in either house to amend a conference report—
and this is one of the greatest sources of conference committee power.
Both chambers must vote on a conference report exactly as presented
by the conferees.

FLOOR ACTION

Options. These are some of the options the Senate and House have in
dealing with conference reports. They can:

★ Accept a report in its entirety.

★ Reject a report in its entirety.

★ Reject a report and vote to send it to a new conference, either with the
same conferees or with a different group.

★ Table a report.

★ Recommit a report to the same conferees, with or without instructions.
A motion to recommit a conference report takes precedence over a motion to approve the report. But neither chamber can recommit a conference report after it has been approved by the other chamber, because
approval constitutes discharge of that chamber's conferees. In such cases,
a conference report can be recommitted only by a concurrent resolution.

Statements. House rules provide that all conference reports must
be accompanied by "a detailed statement sufficiently explicit to inform
the House what effect such amendments or propositions will have upon
the measures to which they relate." In the Senate, however, conferees
issue no written statements, and Members generally are given an informal oral explanation from the manager of the bill in conference.

In 1950, the Senate adopted a concurrent resolution that would
have required written statements to accompany conference reports in
both houses. The House, which already had such a procedure, did not
approve the resolution.

Dissent. There are no provisions for minority reports dissenting
from the conference committee decisions. Conferees who disagree with
their committe's report have no official vehicle for their views, except
refusal to sign the report. Frequently, however, they make their feelings
known before and during floor debate on the conference report. . . .

★ Rules of operation adopted by Consent Calendar Committee

THE FOLLOWING STATEMENT of rules of operation was first adopted by House Consent Calendar Committee members in the 89th Congress (1965). These rules were adopted substantially unchanged by the committees in 1967 and again in 1969:

On February 3 and February 8, respectively, the majority and minority floor leaders appointed their respective personnel of the objectors' committees: the gentleman from Oklahoma, Mr. Albert, appointed three members of his party and the gentleman from Michigan, Mr. Gerald R. Ford, appointed three members of his party. The objectors' committees are unofficial committees of the House of Representatives, existing at the request and at the pleasure of the respective floor leaders of the two parties who, in order to facilitate the proper screening of legislation which may be placed on the Consent Calendar, designate members of each side of the aisle charged with the specific responsibility of seeing to it that legislation passing by such procedure is in the interest of good government. The rule which is applicable to Consent Calendar procedure is clause 4 of Rule XIII, [found] in section 746 of the *Rules of the House of Representatives*. The operation of such procedure is described in Cannon's *Procedures in the House of Representatives*.

For several sessions now objectors on both sides of the aisle have followed certain rules for consideration of Consent Calendar bills which they have made known to the members at the beginning of a session. These rules are not publicized at this time to establish hard-and-fast procedures but rather to advise the members of the House as to the manner in which the committee plans to operate throughout the 89th Congress.

The members of the committees feel that generally no legislation should pass by unanimous consent which involves an aggregate expenditure of more than $1 million; second, that no bill which changes national policy or international policy should be permitted to pass on the Consent Calendar but rather should be afforded the opportunity of open and extended debate; third, that any bill which appears on the Consent Calendar, even though it does not change national or international policy, or does not call for an expenditure of more than $1 million, should not be approved without the membership being fully informed of its contents, providing it is a measure that would apply to the districts of a majority of the members of the House of Representatives, in which case the minimum amount of consideration that should be given such a bill would be clearance by the leadership of both parties being brought before the House on the Consent Calendar.

It has been the policy of the objectors on the Consent Calendar heretofore to put such a bill over without prejudice one or more times to give an opportunity to the members to become fully informed as to the contents of such a bill, and the Consent Calendar objectors for the 89th Congress wish to follow like procedure; fourth, that if a bill has been placed on the Consent Calendar and the members of the committee having jurisdiction over the legislation show that it has not been cleared by the Bureau of the Budget, by the respective departments affected by such legislation, or that such reports from the committee or from the department show that the legislation is not in accord with the President's program, it should not pass on the Consent Calendar but that the chairman of the House committee having jurisdiction over the legislation should either call it up under suspension of the rules with the permission of the Speaker or should go to the Rules Committee for a rule for such legislation. While the members of the objectors' committees feel that a report from the Bureau of the Budget is necessary before a bill should be placed upon the Consent Calendar, they do not wish to take the position that the report from the Bureau of the Budget must necessarily show the approval of such legislation by the Bureau. However, if such approval is not shown, then in the consideration of the legislation, even if considered on the Consent Calendar, the chairman reporting the bill, or the sponsor of the bill, should be willing to accept the responsibility of stating to the members the action of the Bureau of the Budget and the reasons for such action.

The members of the Consent Calendar objectors' committee also feel it fair to state to the membership that it is not their purpose to obstruct legislation or to object to bills or pass them over without prejudice because of any personal objection to said bill or bills by any one member or all of the members of the Consent Calendar objectors' committee, but rather that their real purpose, in addition to expediting legislation, is to protect the membership against having bills passed by unanimous consent which, in the opinion of the objectors, any member of the House might have objection to.

The members of the Consent Calendar objectors' committee earnestly request that the chairman of the standing committees of the House having the responsibility for bringing legislation before the House take into consideration the contents of this statement before placing bills on the Consent Calendar. While it is not absolutely necessary that the sponsors of bills appearing on the Consent Calendar contact the various members of the Consent Calendar objectors' committee, nevertheless, in the interest of saving time and avoiding the possibility of having bills laid over unnecessarily, it is good practice to do so; and the objectors welcome the continuance of the procedure of getting in touch with them at least twenty-four hours before the legislation is called up under the regular Consent Calendar procedure. In many instances such thoughtfulness on the part of the sponsors will clear away questions which the objectors have and consequently will make for the expeditious handling of legislation.

Wayne N. Aspinall
John J. McFall
Edward P. Boland
Majority Objectors
Thomas M. Pelly
Durward G. Hall
Albert W. Johnson
Minority Objectors

★ Example of the open rule

House Calendar No. 266

89th CONGRESS
2D SESSION

H. RES. 906

[Report No. 1680]

IN THE HOUSE OF REPRESENTATIVES

JUNE 30, 1966

Mr. BOLLING, from the Committee on Rules, reported the following resolution; which was referred to the House Calendar and ordered to be printed

RESOLUTION

1   *Resolved,* That upon the adoption of this resolution it
2 shall be in order to move that the House resolve itself into
3 the Committee of the Whole House on the State of the Union
4 for the consideration of the bill (H.R. 15750) to amend
5 further the Foreign Assistance Act of 1961, as amended,
6 and for other purposes. After general debate, which shall
7 be confined to the bill and shall continue not to exceed five
8 hours, to be equally divided and controlled by the chairman
9 and ranking minority member of the Committee on Foreign
10 Affairs, the bill shall be read for amendment under the five-
11 minute rule. At the conclusion of the consideration of the
12 bill for amendment, the Committee shall rise and report the

[*page*]
2

1 bill to the House with such amendments as may have been
2 adopted, and the previous question shall be considered as
3 ordered on the bill and amendments thereto to final passage
4 without intervening motion except one motion to recommit.

★ Summary of the Legislative Reorganization Act of 1970

DURING SEPTEMBER and October, 1970, the House and Senate completed action on the Legislative Reorganization Act of 1970. Providing for the first comprehensive reorganization since 1946, the Act includes sections dealing with the committee system, fiscal controls, sources of information, and Congress as an institution. The House voted 326 to 19 to approve the Act, H.R. 17654, on September 17 (after 11 days of debate over a two-month period), and the Senate voted 59 to 5 for passage with minor amendments on October 6. Following is a summary of the Act (as passed by the House) prepared by Walter Kravitz, of the Legislative Reference Service:

Major features by title

TITLE I. THE COMMITTEE SYSTEM

1. Revised procedures to democratize the proceedings of committees, including: (a) a method whereby a majority of a committee may call special meetings; (b) adequate time for the filing of minority or additional views to committee reports; (c) the timely filing of committee reports; (d) reasonable notice of committee hearings; (e) right of the minority to have its witnesses heard; (f) subcommittees to be subject to the authority of their parent committees;

(g) availability of committee reports and hearings a reasonable time before floor consideration of a measure.

2. Make the details of roll-call votes in committee available to the public.

3. Authorize televising and radio broadcasting of committee hearings in both Houses.

4. Prohibit general proxies in committees, but permit specific proxies under certain conditions.

5. Encourage House committees to adopt more extensive written rules.

6. Redefinition of congressional oversight, and provision for annual oversight reports by committees.

7. Equal division of time for debate on conference reports between the two major parties.

8. Revision of many House floor procedures, including: (a) to permit the recording of names in teller votes; (b) separate votes and 40 minutes of debate on non-germame amendments attached to House-passed bills; (c) limitations on the power of House conferees; (d) availability of conference reports 3 days before floor consideration; (e) an accelerated method for counting a quorum; (f) authorization for electronic voting; (g) under certain conditions, guaranteed time for debate on amendments in Committee of the Whole.

9. Entitle the minority on a committee to one-third of the funds authorized for temporary and investigative staff.

TITLE II. FISCAL CONTROLS

1. Increase the availability to Congress of several types of budgetary and fiscal data.

2. By law, direct the GAO to provide committees with cost-effectiveness analysts upon request.

3. Provide for GAO assistance to committees in analyzing on-going Government programs.

4. Provide that the Appropriations Committees of both Houses shall hold hearings, early in each session, on the budget as a whole, the transcript of such hearings to be transmitted to every Member of their respective Houses.

5. By various means, provide for the presentation of 5-year cost estimates on both current programs and proposed programs.

6. Involve the Comptroller General, as an agent of Congress, in the development in the executive branch of a standard classification system for Government programs and activities.

TITLE III. SOURCES OF INFORMATION

1. Direct the Legislative Reference Service (renamed the Congressional Research Service) in the Library of Congress to assist all committees on a regular and continuing basis in the analysis of legislative proposals and alternatives to them.

2. Reconstitute the Joint Committee on the Library as a Joint Committee on the Library and Congressional Research, with expanded membership from the two Houses at large as well as from the two Administration Committees; bipartisan, evenly divided between the two parties; provided with professional and clerical staff; required to supervise the Library and the CRS, and to make annual reports on its activities. (*Eliminated by Senate amendment.*)

3. Give to minority members on committees their own minimum staff as a matter of right, in the Senate without restriction as to hiring and firing, in the House subject to approval by the majority of the whole committee.

4. Authorize committees to employ consultants and research organizations, subject to approval by the relevant House.

5. Authorize committees to assist their staffs in obtaining specialized training, without loss of employment rights and other employee benefits.

6. Provide for updating the compilation of the precedents of the House every 5 years; have the Parliamentarian of the House

prepare and have published at the beginning of every Congress an up-to-date condensed version of currently useful House precedents.

TITLE IV. CONGRESS AS AN INSTITUTION

1. Create a Joint Committee on Congressional Operations, with 5 members from each House, to make a continuing study of congressional organization and operations, to identify court actions of interest to the Congress; and to supervise an Office of Placement and Office Management.

2. Abolish the Joint Committee on Immigration and Nationality Policy.

3. Establish a Capitol Guide Service for the purpose of providing free tours of the Capitol, and making tour guides congressional employees.

4. Convert House employees' pay, and also the pay of employees of the Architect of the Capitol, from a basic to a gross system.

5. Provide an August recess for Congress.

6. Authorize the planning, site procurement, and construction of a dormitory and school building for pages and for their future supervision.

7. Authorize modernization of the House visitors' galleries.

TITLE V. OFFICE OF THE HOUSE LEGISLATIVE COUNSEL

Revises the basic statute of the Office of the Legislative Counsel in the House of Representatives.

Summary by section

[NOTE.—Only provisions applicable to the House of Representatives are described. Numbers and letters in parentheses indicating those parts of the sections containing such House language may change in the Act's final print.]

TITLE I—THE COMMITTEE SYSTEM

Section 102. Calling of Committee Meetings

(b) Each standing committee shall fix regular meeting days (at least 1 per month); chairman may call additional meetings; a majority may call a special meeting within 7 calendar days after filing a written request; authority of ranking majority member to preside in the absence of the chairman.

Section 103. *Open Committee Business Meetings*

(b) Business meetings shall be open except when the committee by majority vote determines otherwise.

Section 104. *Public Announcement of Committee Votes*

(b) The result of each roll-call vote in committee, including the names of those voting for and against, whether in person or by proxy, shall be made available for public inspection.

Section 105. *Filing of Committee Reports*

(b) Reports must be filed within 7 calendar days (exclusive of days when the House is not in session) after a majority of the committee files a written request. Exempts Rules Committee with respect to House rules, order of business and joint rules.

Section 106. *Proxy Voting*

(b) Prohibits proxy voting in committees except when a committee, by written rule, permits them, in which case proxies must be in writing, designate the person who is to execute them, and be limited to a specific measure or matter and any amendments or motions pertaining thereto.

Section 107. *Supplemental, Minority, and Additional Views*

(b) Right of committee members, if notice is given at the time of a measures' approval, to not less than 3 calendar days in which to file supplemental, minority, or additional views, which views shall be printed in the same volume as the committee report. Rules Committee is exempted.

Section 108. *Availability of Committee Reports Before House Consideration*

(b), (c) No measure (including appropriation bills) may be considered by the House unless the committee report thereon has been available to Members at least 3 calendar days (excluding Satturdays, Sundays, and legal holidays); no general appropriation bill shall be considered until printed hearings have been available at least 3 calendar days (excluding Saturdays, Sundays, and legal holidays); other committees shall make every reasonable effort to have printed hearings available; not applicable to declarations of war or emergency, or to legislative veto procedures. Exempts Rules, House Administration, and Standards of Official Conduct Committees.

Section 109. Motions for Consideration by the House of Measures Previously Made in Order . . .

Speaker given discretionary authority to recognize a committee authorized Member for the purpose of calling up a bill previously made in order by a resolution.

Section 110. Committee Funds

(b) Committee expenditures from the contingent fund shall be authorized by 1 primary expense resolution, which may not be considered by the House until the report on the resolution has been available to Members for at least 1 calendar day. The report shall specify the amount of total funds requested and the amounts for each committee activity. Additional expense resolutions shall be subject to same conditions, plus statement of reasons for failure to procure funds in primary expense resolution. If they so request, the minority party on any committee shall be entitled to one-third of the funds authorized for temporary and investigative staff. Exempts Appropriations Committee.

Section 111. Public Notice of Committee Hearings

(b) Requires 1 week's public notice of committee hearings unless committee determines otherwise, in which case requires notice at earliest possible date. Notice is to be published in The Daily Digest. Exempts Rules Committee.

Section 112. Open Committee Hearings

(b) Hearings shall be open to the public, except when committee by a majority vote determines otherwise.

Section 113. Statements of Witnesses at Committee Hearings

(b) Requires submission by witnesses of written statements in advance of oral testimony, so far as practicable.

Section 114. Calling of Witnesses Selected by the Minority ...

(b) Entitles majority of minority party members on a committee to call witnesses during at least 1 day of a hearing.

Section 115. Points of Order With Respect to Committee Hearing
    Procedure

(b) Points of order in the House against a measure with respect to violations of hearings procedure may be made only by a member of the committee reporting the measure, and only if such point was timely raised in the committee "and improperly overruled or not properly considered."

Section 116. Broadcasting of Committee Hearings

(b) Permits televising, radio broadcasting and still photographing of House committee hearings, when authorized by majority vote of the committee, *provided that* The committee adopts written rules to the effect that: live broadcast coverage is to be uninterrupted and without commercial sponsorship; conduct of the hearing conforms to acceptable standards of behavior; no subpoened witness shall be photographed, televised or broadcast against his will; coverage by television to be limited to 4 fixed cameras not obstructing committee proceedings; equipment to be installed prior to hearing; lighting shall be at lowest level possible for adequate coverage; not more than 5 still photographers, who shall not come between witness and committee members during hearing; broadcast and photography personnel shall be orderly and unobtrusive.

Section 117. Committee Meetings During Sessions of the Houses of
    Congress

(b) Committees may sit during House sessions except when a measure is being considered for amendment under the 5-minutes rule. Exempts from prohibition for sitting during proceedings under the 5-minutes rule the Committee on Appropriations, Government Operations, Internal Security, Rules, and Standards of Official Conduct.

Section 118. Legislative Review by Standing Committees

(b) Revises definition of oversight function for committees; requires annual reports by committees of their review activities. Exempts Committees on Appropriations, House Administration, Rules, and Standards of Official Conduct.

Section 119. Debate time on printed amendments

Provides 10 minutes debate in Committee of the Whole on amendments printed in the Record after the reporting of a bill but at least 1 day prior to the amendment's floor consideration, the time to be equally divided for and against the amendment, *provided* that no debate shall be allowed when the offering of the amendment is dilatory.

Section 120. Recording teller votes

Provides for tellers with clerks, upon request supported by one-fifth of a quorum, in which the names of those voting on each side of a question and the names of absentees, will be recorded by the clerks or by electronic device, and entered in the Journal.

Section 121. Electronic recording of roll calls and quorum calls

Authorizes use of appropriate electronic equipment for recording roll calls and quorum calls in the House.

Section 122. Expeditious conduct of quorum calls

Permits a non-debatable motion to dispense with further proceedings under a quorum call, once a sufficient number, whether in Committee of the Whole or in the House, has been recorded. For 30 minutes thereafter Members may have their presence recorded on tally sheets.

Section 123. Debate on motions to recommit with instructions

Permits 10 minutes debate on the motion to recommit with instructions. After the previous question has been ordered, the time to be equally divided for and against the motion.

Section 124. Copies of amendments

In Committee of the Whole, 5 copies of each amendment offered shall be sent to the majority and minority tables and at least 1 copy to the majority and minority cloak rooms.

Section 125. Conference reports

(b) Explanatory statement on conference report shall be prepared jointly by conferees of the 2 Houses. Time allotted for debate on conference report shall be equally divided between majority and minority party. A substitute reported by House conferees shall not include matter not committed to the conference by either House. Furthermore, their report shall not include modifications that are beyond the scope of the issues committed to the conference. Conference reports may not be considered until 3 days (excluding Saturdays, Sundays, and legal holidays) after having been printed in the Congressional Record (not applicable during the last 6 days of the session). Copies of the report and accompanying statement must be available on the floor.

Section 126. Non-germane amendments

Permits separate votes on non-germane amendments to House-passed measures, with 40 minutes debate equally divided for and against the amendment at issue. No such amendment shall be agreed to by House conferees without specific prior authority from the House by a vote of the House on every such amendment.

Section 127. Reading of the Journal of the House

Removes necessity for reading the House Journal unless the Speaker so orders. If he does not, one motion shall be in order that the Journal be read and such motion shall be determined without debate.

Section 128. Clarification of Certain Provisions and Elimination of Obsolete Language in Certain House Rules

Rules of the House apply to committees and subcommittees; committees may adopt additional rules not inconsistent with House rules; committee rules apply to their subcommittees. Strikes obsolete language from several rules referring to delegations from Alaska and Hawaii, and makes technical changes in other rules.

TITLE II—FISCAL CONTROLS

Part 1

Section 201. Budgetary and Fiscal Data Processing System

Directs Secretary of the Treasury and Director, Office of Management and Budget, to develop, establish, and maintain a standardized information and data processing system for budgetary and fiscal data, in cooperation with the Comptroller General.

Section 202. Budget Standard Classifications

Directs Treasury Secretary and OMB Director to develop, establish and maintain standard classifications of Federal agency programs, activities, receipts, expenditures, in cooperation with the Comptroller General, and to submit progress reports thereon.

Section 203. Availability to Congress of Budgetary, Fiscal, and Related Data

Upon request, Treasury Secretary and OMB Director shall supply committees with information on the location and nature of data on Federal agency programs, activities, receipts, and expenditures, and, to the extent feasible, prepare summary tables of such data.

Section 204. Assistance to Congress by General Accounting Office

Comptroller General shall upon request of either House or a committee of jurisdiction, review and analyze results of existing Government programs and activities. He shall also make available to committees upon request employees expert in analyzing cost benefit studies.

Section 205. Power and Duties of Comptroller General . . .

Authorizes Comptroller General to organize the GAO as he considers necessary to carry out functions imposed on him in this title, and to report annually to Congress on the performance of those functions.

Section 206. Preservation of Existing Authorities . . .

Preserves functions of Treasury Secretary, OMB Director, and Comptroller General under other statutes.

Section 207. Definition

Defines "Federal agency" for the purpose of this title.

Part 2

Section 221. Supplemental Budget Information

In his annual budget, the President shall inform Congress of the amounts proposed for appropriation and expenditure in the up-coming fiscal year, and estimated amounts for the ensuing 4 fiscal years, on each of his proposals for legislation creating a new program or changing any existing one.

On or before June 1, the President shall send Congress up-dated figures on the budget for the ensuing fiscal year.

On or before June 1, the President shall send to Congress up-dated estimates of expenditures for the 4 fiscal years following the next fiscal year, and summaries of estimated expenditures of balances carried over to those fiscal years.

Part 3

Section 231. Assistance by General Accounting Office . . .

Upon request, Comptroller General shall explain and discuss any GAO report with interested committees.

Section 232. Delivery by General Accounting Office to Congressional Committees of Reports to Congress

The Comptroller General shall deliver copies of GAO reports to Congress to the Appropriations Committees, the Government Operations Committees, and any other committee which has requested information about any program or Federal agency dealt with in the report.

Section 233. Furnishing . . . of Its Reports Generally

Upon request, Comptroller General shall send a copy of any GAO report to any committee.

Section 234. Furnishing to Committees and Members . . . by General Accounting Office of Monthly and Annual Lists of Its Reports . . .

Directs Comptroller General to furnish committees and Members with monthly and annual lists of GAO reports and, upon request, copies of such reports.

Section 235. Assignment of GAO Employees to Committees

Comptroller General may not assign any GAO employee to full-time duty with any committee for any period of more than 1 year. In his annual report he shall give detailed information about GAO employees assigned to committees, including cost to GAO.

Part 4

Section 242. Hearings on the Budget by Committees on Appropriations of Senate and House

(g) Appropriations Committee shall hold public hearings on the budget as a whole within 30 days after its transmittal to Congress each year, taking testimony from Treasury Secretary, OMB Director, and Chairman of Council of Economic Advisers, among others. Transcript of hearings to be printed and furnished to each Member.

Part 5

Section 252. Cost Estimates in Reports of . . . House Committees Accompanying Certain Legislative Measures

(b) Committee reports on bills shall contain estimates of costs for the current and next 5 fiscal years. On measures affecting revenues, requires only a 1-year estimate of gain or loss in revenues. For this provision, members of the Joint Committee on Atomic Energy are to be considered a House committee. The Committees on Appropriations, House Administration, Rules, and Standards of Official Conduct are exempted.

Section 253. Appropriations on Annual Basis

(c) Each committee shall "endeavor to insure" that all continuing Government programs and activities are appropriated for

annually. From time to time, committees shall review programs under their jurisdictions to ascertain whether they can be shifted to
annual appropriations.

TITLE III—SOURCES OF INFORMATION

Part 1.
Section 302. Increase of Professional Staffs of House Standing Com-
     mittees; House Minority Professional and Clerical Staffs; Fair
     Treatment for House Minority Staffs

(b) Increases permissible number of standing committees'
permanent professional staff from 4 to 6. A majority of a committee's minority party members may select no more than 2 of the 6
for assignment to the minority. "The committee shall appoint any
persons so selected whose character and qualifications are acceptable to a majority of the committee." Minority may continue
to select until their choices are appointed. Any staff may be fired
by majority vote of a committee. Minority may select 1 of a committee's 6 permissible permanent clerical staff under same conditions. Committees on Appropriations and Standards of Official
Conduct are exempted.

(c) When no vacancies exist for minority staff, appointments
shall nevertheless be made, upon request and subject to above procedures, to be paid from contingent fund. These shall move into
vacancies in permanent staff as they occur. Permanent minority staff
shall be accorded equitable treatment on pay, work facilities, and
accessibility to committee records. Minority shall not, as a matter of
right, be entitled to additional staff if the permissible number is
already employed.

(d) If a committee is already authorized more than 6 professional and/or 6 clerical staff, nothing in this section shall be
construed to require a reduction in such staff, or in any of them
assigned to the minority.

(e) The addition of 2 permanent professional staff authorized in (b) above shall be in addition to any professional staff now authorized to a committee.

*Section 303. Procurement of Temporary or Intermittent Services of
    Consultants for . . . House Standing Committees*

Authorizes standing committees to hire consultants and consultative organizations, subject to House Administration Committee approval and pertinent resolutions.

*Section 304. Specialized Training for Professional Staffs of . . .
    House Standing Committees*

Authorizes standing committees to assist professional staff in obtaining specialized training useful in their official duties.

Part 2

Section 321. Congressional Research Service

Legislative Reference Service is redesignated the Congressional Research Service, and its duties, administration, and relationships with Congress and with the Library of Congress are comprehensively redefined.

New duties:

(1) Assist committees in analyzing, appraising, and evaluating advisability of enacting legislative proposals and alternatives thereto and estimating their probable results; maintain continuous liaison with committees.

(2) Inform committees of programs and activities scheduled to expire in current Congress.

(3) Provide committees with lists of subjects and policy areas suitable for analysis in depth.

(4) Upon request, prepare concise legislative histories of measures upon which committee hearings are to be held.

New authority:

(1) Require Government agencies to produce data.

(2) Hire or contract for temporary services of experts, consultants, and research organizations.

(3) Allot research personnel to supergrade positions without reference to statutory quotas, subject to approval by Joint Committee on the Library and Congressional Research.

Section 322. Repeal of Obsolete Law Relating to . . . Office of Coordinator of Information

Repeals statutory authority for the defunct Office.

Part 3

Section 331. Joint Committee on the Library and Congressional Research

Retitles the Joint Committee on the Library as the Joint Committee on the Library and Congressional Research, with a bipartisan membership expanded to 12 of which 2 in the House shall be from House Administration Committee. Chairmanship and vice chairmanship to be held by different parties. House members to be selected by Speaker. Jurisdiction over the Library generally and the operations of the Congressional Research Service. Authorized professional and clerical staff appointed by majority vote of the Joint Committee. (*Eliminated by Senate amendment.*)

Section 332. Related Changes in Existing Law

Makes necessary changes in law to reflect change in name of the Joint Committee on the Library and Congressional Research.

Part 4

Section 341. Periodic Compilation of Parliamentary Precedents of the House of Representatives

The House Parliamentarian is directed, 5 years after completion of the currently authorized revision of the House precedents, to prepare and have printed new compilations every 5th year thereafter.

Section 342. Perodic Preparation by House Parliamentarian of Condensed and Simplified Versions of House Precedents

The House Parliamentarian is directed to prepare and have printed, at the beginning of each Congress commencing with the 93rd, a condensed and, insofar as practicable, up-to-date version of all precedents of current use and application in the House, together with informative text.

TITLE IV—CONGRESS AS AN INSTITUTION

Part 1

Section 401. Joint Committee on Congressional Operations

Creates a Joint Committee on Congressional Operations to consist of five members from each House, three from the majority and two from the minority.

Section 402. Joint Committee . . . Duties

The Joint Committee on Congressional Operations is to 1) conduct continuing study of congressional organization and operations and recommend improvements; 2) identify and call to the attention of Congress court actions and proceedings of vital interest to the Congress; 3) supervise the Office of Placement and Office Management. The Joint Committee may not make recommendations concerning the rules, parliamentary procedure, practices or precedents of either House.

Section 404. Joint Committee . . . Staff

The Joint Committee on Congressional Operations is authorized a permanent staff of six professional and six clerical employees. It may also retain temporary consultants.

Section 406. Office of Placement and Office Management

Establishes central office to assist in filling personnel and office management requirements in the Congress.

Part 2

Section 421. Abolishment of Joint Committee on Immigration and Nationality Policy

Part 3

Section 431. Authority of Officers of the Congress Over Congressional Employees

Authorizes officers of Congress to determine whether prospective employees possess necessary qualifications for jobs to be assigned to them, and to remove or otherwise discipline employees, thereby clarifying authority of officers over patronage employees.

Part 4

Section 441. Establishment and Operation of the Capitol Guide Service

Establishes a Capitol Guide Service, under the supervision of a Board composed of the Architect of the Capitol, the Sergeants at Arms of the 2 Houses, an employee appointed by the Senate minority leader, and an employee appointed by the House minority leader. The Service is to furnish free tours of the Capitol and assist Capitol Police on special occasions.

Part 6

Section 461. Summer recess for Congress

Unless otherwise provided by Congress, the two Houses shall either adjourn *sine die* not later than July 31 or provide for an adjournment of at least 30 days ending the second day after Labor Day.

Part 7

Section 467. House employee salary system

Converts pay system for all House employees, including individual members' and committee staff personnel, from the *basic* to the *gross* salary system.

Part 8

Section 471. Modernization of House Galleries

Directs the Speaker to appoint a bipartisan 5 member commission to study, develop a program for, and put into effect, with the aid of the Architect of the Capitol, improvements in the House galleries that will include glassing them in and providing facilities that will permit spectators to hear floor proceedings while receiving explanations of those proceedings.

Part 9
Sections 491 and 492. Senate and House Pages
Provide that Pages shall be between 16 and 18 years of age; and that a dormitory and school building is authorized.

TITLE V—OFFICE OF THE LEGISLATIVE COUNSEL
[Extensively revises duties and functions of this office]

Bibliography

★ Bibliography: Studies of Congress

JOHN F. MANLEY, *University of Wisconsin*

THIS BIBLIOGRAPHY PRESENTS some of the major works on Congress that may be of interest to Congressmen, teachers of American politics, students, and others concerned with understanding how Congress—and especially the House of Representatives—performs its functions. Part I of the Bibliography contains books and articles that focus primarily on the Congress—its history, functions, internal organization, and operation. Part II contains studies that describe and, in some instances, evaluate the role of the Congress in the American system.

The works listed represent several different approaches by political scientists to the study of Congress. Some scholars, for example, combine an interest in understanding Congress with a penchant for reforming it. Works by some of the best-known critics of Congress—along with opposing arguments by equally distinguished scholars—appear in Part II of the Bibliography under the heading, "Congress: Criticism and Dissent." Another prolific group of scholars is more concerned with describing accurately how Congress *does* work and less concerned with prescribing how it *ought* to work. Distinguished by dependence on extensive interviews with members of Congress and other participants in the legislative process (or on analysis of roll-call voting data and of party, constituency, and informal characteristics), the work of these scholars appears throughout the Bibliography; a substantial number of such books and articles on the House appears in Part I.

Also listed in this Bibliography are commentaries by close observers of the congressional scene who are not political scientists. Among the most valuable of these are writings by members of Congress, which constitute a rich and largely unmined source of information. For the political scientist, these books are full of suggestions for research. For practitioners of the art of congressional politics, they contain useful information about the folkways of the two chambers, the elements of political influence, and the traditions governing effective participation in the legislative process. Perhaps of greatest interest, first-hand accounts by veteran legislators show how U.S. Representatives as different as Jerry Voorhis and Joseph Martin have found ways of shaping a legislative career in a complex political system. Each member must, on the basis of his personal temperament and goals, decide how he is going to take part in the life of Congress. Knowledge of the ways in which others have fared with their choices may not be an infallible guide to the right selection, but it will, at a minimum, expose the risks and rewards of the alternatives.

In recent years, there has been a resurgence of interest in congressional scholarship; the books and articles listed below are only a small part of the total volume of works on Congress. (For a more extensive bibliography, see Charles O. Jones and Randall B. Ripley, *The Role of Political Parties in Congress* [Tucson, Ariz.: University of Arizona Press, 1961].) Renewed interest in Congress places one more demand on the time of the Congressman and his office staff, as they are called upon with increasing frequency to grant interviews to political scientists. The product of recent research suggests, however, that cooperation between the academic community and the practitioner of congressional politics pays off in the development of a body of knowledge helpful to those who are concerned with maintaining—or strengthening—its place in our democratic system.

I. Congress and Its Functions

BAILEY, STEPHEN K. *Congress in the Seventies.* New York: St. Martin's Press, 1970.

———. *Congress Makes a Law.* New York: Columbia University Press, 1950.

BERMAN, DANIEL M. *A Bill Becomes a Law: The Civil Rights Act of 1960.* New York: Macmillan, 1962.

BIBBY, JOHN F. and ROGER H. DAVIDSON. *On Capitol Hill.* New York: Holt, Rinehart & Winston, 1967.

CONGRESSIONAL QUARTERLY SERVICE. *Congress and the Nation.* Vol. I: *1945–1964.* Vol. II: *1965–1968.* Washington, D.C.: Congressional Quarterly Service, 1964, 1969.

DE GRAZIA, ALFRED, coord. *Congress: The First Branch of Government.* Washington, D.C.: American Enterprise Institute, 1966.

EIDENBERG, EUGENE and ROY O. MOREY. *An Act of Congress: The Legislative Process and the Making of Education Policy.* New York: W. W. Norton, 1967.

GALLOWAY, GEORGE B. *The Legislative Process in Congress.* New York: Thomas Y. Crowell, 1953.

GRIFFITH, ERNEST S. *Congress: Its Contemporary Role.* 3rd ed. New York: New York University Press, 1961.

GROSS, BERTRAM M. *The Leglislative Struggle.* New York: McGraw-Hill, 1953.

JEWELL, MALCOLM E. and SAMUEL C. PATTERSON. *The Leglislative Process in the United States.* New York: Random House, 1966.

KEEFE, WILLIAM J. and MORRIS S. OGUL. *The American Legislative Process: Congress and the States.* Englewood Cliffs, N.J.: Prentice-Hall, 1968.

LOWI, THEODORE J., ed. *Legislative Politics, U.S.A.* Boston: Little, Brown, 1965.

ROBINSON, JAMES A. *Congress and Foreign Policy-Making: A Study in Legislative Influence and Initiative.* Homewood, Ill.: The Dorsey Press, 1967.

ROCHE, JOHN P., and LEONARD W. LEVY. *The Congress.* New York: Harcourt, Brace & World, 1964.

TRUMAN, DAVID B., ed. *The Congress and America's Future.* Englewood Cliffs, N.J.: Prentice-Hall, 1965 .

YOUNG, ROLAND. *The American Congress.* New York: Harper & Bros., 1958.

The Senate

HARRIS, JOSEPH P. *The Advice and Consent of the Senate.* Berkeley: University of California Press, 1953.

HAYNES, GEORGE H. *The Senate of the United States.* 2 vols. Boston: Houghton Mifflin, 1938.

HUITT, RALPH K. "Democratic Party Leadership in the Senate," *American Political Science Review,* LV (June 1961), 333–345.

————. "The Morse Committee Assignment Controversy: A Study in Senate Norms," *American Political Science Review,* LI (June 1957), 313–329.

————. "The Outsider in the Senate: An Alternative Role," *American Political Science Review,* LV (September 1961), 566–575.

————. "The Internal Distribution of Influence: The Senate," in *The Congress and America's Future,* ed. DAVID B. TRUMAN. Englewood Cliffs, N.J.: Prentice-Hall, 1965. Pp. 77–101.

MATTHEWS, DONALD R. *U.S. Senators and Their World.* Chapel Hill: University of North Carolina Press, 1960.

PRESTON, NATHANIEL STONE, ed. *The Senate Institution.* New York: Van Nostrand Reinhold, 1969.

RIPLEY, RANDALL B. *Power in the Senate.* New York: St. Martin's Press, 1969.

ROTHMAN, DAVID J. *Politics and Power: The United States Senate, 1869–1901.* Cambridge: Harvard University Press, 1966.

WHITE, WILLIAM S. *Citadel.* New York: Harper & Bros., 1957.

The House

ALEXANDER, DE ALVA S. *History and Procedure of the House of Representatives.* Boston: Houghton Mifflin, 1916.

CLAPP, CHARLES E. *The Congressman: His Work as He Sees It.* Washington, D.C.: The Brookings Institution, 1963.

FENNO, RICHARD F. "The Internal Distribution of Influence: The House," in *The Congress and America's Future*, ed. DAVID B. TRUMAN. Englewood Cliffs, N.J.: Prentice-Hall, 1965. Pp. 52–76.

GALLOWAY, GEORGE B. *History of the United States House of Representatives*. New York: Thomas Y. Crowell, 1962.

MACNEIL, NEIL. *Forge of Democracy*. New York: David McKay, 1963.

PEABODY, ROBERT L., and NELSON W. POLSBY. *New Perspectives on the House of Representatives*. 2nd ed. Chicago: Rand McNally, 1969.

POLSBY, NELSON W. "The Institutionalization of the U.S. House of Representatives," *American Political Science Review*, LXII (March 1968), 144–168.

The Representative

DAVIDSON, ROGER H. *The Role of the Congressman*. New York: Pegasus, 1969.

DEXTER, LEWIS ANTHONY. "The Job of the Congressman," in *Readings in American Political Behavior*, ed. RAYMOND E. WOLFINGER. Englewood Cliffs, N.J.: Prentice-Hall, 1966. Pp. 5–26.

———. "What Do Congressmen Hear?," in *Politics and Social Life*, ed. NELSON W. POLSBY, ROBERT A. DENTLER, and PAUL A. SMITH. Boston: Houghton Mifflin, 1963. Pp. 485–495.

———. "The Representative and His District," in *Politics and Social Life*, pp. 495–512.

———. *The Sociology and Politics of Congress*. Chicago: Rand McNally, 1970.

BOOKS BY HOUSE MEMBERS

BLOOM, SOL. *The Autobiography of Sol Bloom*. New York: Putnam's, 1948.

BOLLING, RICHARD. *House Out of Order*. New York: Dutton, 1965.

———. *Power in the House*. New York: Dutton, 1968.

CELLER, EMANUEL. *You Never Leave Brooklyn*. New York: John Day, 1953.

COFFIN, FRANK. *Witness for Aid*. Boston: Houghton Mifflin, 1964.

EVINS, JOE L. *Understanding Congress*. New York: Clarkson N. Potter, 1963.

KIRWIN, MICHAEL. *How to Succeed in Politics*. New York: Macfadden, 1964.

LAGUARDIA, FIORELLO H. *The Making of an Insurgent*. Philadelphia: Lippincott, 1948.

LA FOLLETTE, ROBERT M. *La Follette's Autobiography*. Madison: University of Wisconsin Press, 1960.

LUCE, ROBERT. *Congress: An Explanation*. Cambridge: Harvard University Press, 1926.

MARTIN, JOE. *My First Fifty Years in Politics* (as told to Robert J. Donovan). New York: McGraw-Hill, 1960.

MILLER, CLEM. *Member of the House*. New York: Scribner's, 1962.

NORRIS, GEORGE W. *Fighting Liberal: The Autobiography of George W. Norris*. New York: Macmillan, 1945.

SMITH, FRANK. *Congressman from Mississippi*. New York: Pantheon, 1964.

SMITH, T. V. *The Legislative Way of Life*. Chicago. University of Chicago Press, 1940.

VOORHIS, JERRY. *Confessions of a Congressman*. Garden City, N.Y.: Doubleday, 1947.

WELTNER, CHARLES L. *Southerner*. New York: Lippincott, 1966.

WRIGHT, JIM. *You and Your Congressman*. New York: Coward-McCann, 1965.

PARTY, CONSTITUENCY, AND VOTING

CHERRYHOLMES, CLEO H. and MICHAEL J. SHAPIRO, *Representatives and Roll Calls*. Indianapolis and New York: Bobbs-Merrill, 1969.

FROMAN, LEWIS A., JR. *Congressmen and Their Constituencies*. Chicago: Rand McNally, 1963.

MARWELL, GERALD. "Party, Region and the Dimensions of Conflict in the House of Representatives, 1949–1954," *American Political Science Review*, LXI (June 1967), 380–399.

MAYHEW, DAVID R. *Party Loyalty Among Congressmen: The Difference Between Democrats and Republicans, 1947–1962*. Cambridge: Harvard University Press, 1966.

MILLER, WARREN, and DONALD STOKES. "Constituency Influence in Congress," *American Political Science Review*, LVII (March 1963), 45–57.

PENNOCK, J. ROLAND. "Party and Constituency in Postwar Agricultural

Price-Support Legislation," *Journal of Politics,* XVIII (May 1956), 167–210.

RIESELBACH, LEROY N. "The Demography of the Congressional Vote on Foreign Aid, 1939–1958," *American Political Science Review,* LVIII (September 1964), 577–588.

RIKER, WILLIAM H., and DONALD NIEMI. "Stability of Coalitions on Roll Calls in the House of Representatives," *American Political Science Review,* LVI (March 1962), 58–65.

SHANNON, WAYNE W. *Party, Constituency, and Congressional Voting.* Baton Rouge: Louisiana State University Press, 1968.

TRUMAN, DAVID B. *The Congressional Party.* New York: John Wiley, 1959.

TURNER, JULIUS. *Party and Constituency: Pressures on Congress.* Baltimore: The Johns Hopkins Press, 1951.

URICH, THEODORE. "The Voting Behavior of Freshmen Congressmen," *Southwestern Social Science Quarterly* (March 1959).

CONGRESSIONAL OFFICE STAFF

BUTLER, WARREN H. "The Role of the Staff," *Public Administration Review,* XXVI (March 1966), 3–13.

The Speakership

BROWN, GEORGE ROTHWELL. *Speaker of the House.* New York: Brewer, Warren and Putnam, 1932.

BUSBEY, L. WHITE. *Uncle Joe Cannon.* New York: Holt, 1927.

CHIU, CHANG-WEI. *The Speaker of the House of Representatives Since 1896.* New York: Columbia University Press, 1928.

CLARK, CHAMP. *My Quarter Century of American Politics.* 2 vols. New York: Harper & Bros., 1920.

DORROW, C. DWIGHT. *Mr. Sam.* New York: Random House, 1962.

FOLLET, MARY P. *The Speaker of the House of Representatives.* New York: Longmans, Green, 1896.

ROBINSON, WILLIAM A. *Thomas B. Reed: Parliamentarian.* New York: Dodd, Mead, 1930.

TUCHMAN, BARBARA W. "Czar of the House," *American Heritage,* XIV (December 1962), 32ff.

Party organizations and leadership

FROMAN, LEWIS A. JR., and RANDALL B. RIPLEY. "Conditions for Party Leadership: The Case of the House Democrats," *American Political Science Review,* LIX (March 1965), 52–63.

GALLOWAY, GEORGE B. "Leadership in the House of Representatives," *Western Political Quarterly,* XII (June 1959), 417–441.

JONES, CHARLES O. *Party and Policy Making: The House Republican Policy Committee.* New Brunswick, N.J.: Rutgers University Press, 1965.

————. "Joseph G. Cannon and Howard W. Smith: An Essay on the Limits of Leadership in the House of Representatives," *Journal of Politics,* XXX (August 1968), 617–646.

————. *The Minority Party in Congress.* Boston: Little, Brown, 1970.

————. "The Minority Party and Policy-Making in the House of Representatives," *American Political Science Review,* LXII (June 1968), 481–493.

PEABODY, ROBERT L. "Party Leadership Changes in the United States House of Representatives," *American Political Science Review,* LXI (September 1967), 675–693.

RIPLEY, RANDALL B. *Party Leadership in the House of Representatives.* Washington, D.C.: The Brookings Institution, 1967.

————. *Majority Party Leadership in Congress.* Boston: Little, Brown, 1967.

Rules and procedures

FROMAN, LEWIS A., JR. *The Congressional Process: Strategies, Rules and Procedures.* Boston: Little, Brown, 1967.

RIDDICK, FLOYD M. *The United States Congress: Organization and Procedure.* Manassas, Va.: National Capitol Publishers, 1949.

The committee system

HUITT, RALPH K. "The Congressional Committees: A Case Study," *American Political Science Review,* XLVII (June 1954), 340–365.

GALLOWAY, GEORGE B. "Development of the Committee System in the House of Representatives," *American Historical Review,* LXV (October 1959), 17–30.

GAWTHORP, LOUIS C. "Changing Membership Patterns in House Committees," *American Political Science Review,* LX (June 1966), 366–373.

KAPLAN, LEWIS A. "The House Un-American Activities Committee and Its Opponents: A Study in Congressional Dissonance," *Journal of Politics,* XXX (August 1968), 647–671.

MORROW, WILLIAM L. *Congressional Committees.* New York: Scribners, 1967.

RIPLEY, RANDALL B. "Congressional Government and Committee Management," in *Public Policy,* ed. JOHN D. MONTGOMERY. Cambridge: Harvard University Press, 1965.

COMMITTEE ASSIGNMENTS

MASTERS, NICHOLAS. "Committee Assignments in the House of Representatives," *American Political Science Review,* LV (June 1961), 345–357.

SWANSON, WAYNE R. "Committee Assignments and the Nonconformist Legislator: Democrats in the U.S. Senate," *Midwest Journal of Political Science,* XIII (February 1969), 84–94.

INDIVIDUAL COMMITTEE STUDIES

CARR, ROBERT K. *The House Committee on Un-American Activities, 1945–1950.* Ithaca: Cornell University Press, 1952.

FENNO, RICHARD F., JR. *The Power of the Purse.* Boston: Little, Brown, 1966.

GOODMAN, WALTER. *The Committee.* New York: Farrar, Straus & Giroux, 1968.

JONES, CHARLES O. "Representation in Congress: The Case of the House Agriculture Committee," *American Political Science Review,* LV (June 1961), 358–367.

MANLEY, JOHN F. *The Politics of Finance: The House Committee on Ways and Means.* Boston: Little, Brown, 1970.

WESTPHAL, ALBERT C. F. *The House Committee on Foreign Affairs.* New York: Columbia University Press, 1942.

THE COMMITTEE ON RULES

AMERICAN ENTERPRISE INSTITUTE. *History and Powers of the House Committee on Rules.* Washington, D.C.: American Enterprise Institute, 1963.

PEABODY, ROBERT L. "The Enlarged Rules Committee," in *New Perspectives on the House of Representatives,* ed. ROBERT L. PEABODY and NELSON W. POLSBY. Chicago: Rand McNally, 1963. Pp. 129–164.

PRICE, H. DOUGLAS. "Race, Religion, and the Rules Committee: The Kennedy Aid to Education Bills," in *The Uses of Power,* ed. ALAN F. WESTIN. New York: Harcourt, Brace & World, 1962.

ROBINSON, JAMES A. *The House Rules Committee.* Indianapolis and New York: Bobbs-Merrill, 1963.

SUBCOMMITTEES

GOODWIN, GEORGE. "Sub-Committees: The Miniature Legislatures of Congress," *American Political Science Review,* LVI (September 1962), 596–604.

JONES, CHARLES O. "The Role of the Congressional Subcommittee," *Midwest Journal of Political Science,* VI (November 1962), 327–344.

SELECT AND JOINT COMMITTEES

GREEN, HAROLD, and ALAN ROSENTHAL. *Government of the Atom.* New York: Atherton, 1963.

VARDYS, V. STANLEY. "Select Committees of the House of Representatives," *Midwest Journal of Political Science,* VI (August 1962), 247–265.

THE CONFERENCE COMMITTEE

McGOWN, ADA C. *The Congressional Conference Committee.* New York: Columbia University Press, 1927.

STEINER, GILBERT Y. *The Congressional Conference Committee.* Urbana, Ill.: University of Illinois Press, 1951.

COMMITTEE STAFFING

COCHRANE, JAMES D. "Partisan Aspects of Congressional Committee Staffing," *Western Political Quarterly,* XVII (June 1964), 338–348.

KAMMERER, GLADYS. *The Staffing of the Committees of Congress.* Lexington: University of Kentucky Press, 1949.

————. "The Record of Congress in Committee Staffing," *American Political Science Review*, XLV (December 1951), 1126–1136.

KAMPLEMAN, MAX. "The Legislative Bureaucracy: Its Response to Political Change," *Journal of Politics*, XVI (August 1954), 539–550.

KOFMEHL, KENNETH. *Professional Staffs of Congress.* West Lafayette, Ind.: Purdue University Press, 1962.

MANLEY, JOHN F. "Congressional Staff and Public Policy-Making: The Joint Committee on Internal Revenue Taxation," *Journal of Politics*, XXX (November 1968), 1046–1067.

The seniority system

CELLER, EMANUEL. "The Seniority Rule in Congress," *Western Political Quarterly*, XIV (March 1961), 160–167.

GOODWIN, GEORGE, JR. "The Seniority System in Congress," *American Political Science Review*, LIII (June 1959), 412–436.

HINCKLEY, BARBARA. "Seniority in the Committee Leadership Selection of Congress," *Midwest Journal of Political Science*, XIII (November 1969), 613–630.

POLSBY, NELSON W., MIRIAM GALLEHER, and BARRY SPENCER RUNDQUIST. "The Growth of the Seniority System in the U.S. House of Representatives," *American Political Science Review*, LXIII (September 1969), 787–807.

WOLFINGER, RAYMOND E., and JOAN HEIFETZ. "Safe Seats, Seniority, and Power in Congress," *American Political Science Review*, LIX (June 1965), 337–349.

Informal groups

FIELLIN, ALAN. "The Functions of Informal Groups in Legislative Institutions," *Journal of Politics*, XXIV (February 1963), 72–91.

KESSEL, JOHN H. "The Washington Congressional Delegation," *Midwest Journal of Political Science*, VIII (February 1964), 1–21.

KOFMEHL, KENNETH. "The Institutionalization of a Voting Bloc," *Western Political Quarterly*, XVII (June 1964), 256–272.

The politics of change

ATKINSON, CHARLES. *The Committee on Rules and the Overthrow of Speaker Cannon.* New York: Columbia University Press, 1911.

CUMMINGS, MILTON C., JR., and ROBERT L. PEABODY. "The Decision to Enlarge the Committee on Rules: An Analysis of the 1961 Vote," in *New Perspectives on the House of Representatives,* ed. ROBERT L. PEABODY and NELSON W. POLSBY. Chicago: Rand McNally, 1963. Pp. 167–194.

DAVIDSON, ROGER, DAVID KOVENOCK, and MICHAEL O'LEARY. *Congress in Crisis: Politics and Congressional Reform.* Belmont, Calif.: Wadsworth Publishing Co., 1966.

FISHEL, JEFF. "Party, Ideology, and the Congressional Challenger," *American Political Science Review,* LXIII (December 1969), 1213–1232.

JONES, CHARLES O. *Every Second Year: Congressional Behavior and the Two-Year Term.* Washington, D.C.: The Brookings Institution, 1967.

MACKAYE, WILLIAM R. *A New Coalition Takes Control: The House Rules Committee Fight of 1961.* New York: McGraw-Hill, 1963. Eagleton Institute Case No. 29.

PEABODY, ROBERT L. *The Ford-Halleck Minority Leadership Contest, 1965.* New York: McGraw-Hill, 1966. Eagleton Institute Case No. 40.

POLSBY, NELSON W. "Two Strategies of Influence: Choosing a Majority Leader, 1962," in *New Perspectives on the House of Representatives,* ed. ROBERT L. PEABODY and NELSON W. POLSBY. Chicago: Rand McNally, 1963. Pp. 237–270.

SALOMA, JOHN S., III. *Congress and the New Politics.* Boston: Little, Brown, 1969.

II. *Congress and the American System*

BAUER, RAYMOND A., ITHIEL DE SOLA POOL, and LEWIS ANTHONY DEXTER. *American Business and Public Policy: The Politics of Foreign Trade.* New York: Atherton, 1963.

CATER, DOUGLASS. *Power in Washington,* New York: Random House, 1964.

CLEAVELAND, FREDERIC N., and associates. *Congress and Urban Problems*. Washington, D.C.: The Brookings Institution, 1969.

COHEN, BERNARD C. *The Political Process and Foreign Policy*. Princeton, N.J.: Princeton University Press, 1957.

HERRING, E. PENDLETON. *Presidential Leadership*. New York: Holt, Rinehart & Winston, 1940.

KEY, V. O., JR. *Public Opinion and American Democracy*. New York: Alfred A. Knopf, 1961.

————. *Politics, Parties and Pressure Groups*. New York: Thomas Y. Crowell Co., 1958.

LIPSET, SEYMOUR M. *Political Man*. New York: Doubleday, 1960.

MUNGER, FRANK J., and RICHARD F. FENNO, JR. *National Politics and Federal Aid to Education*. Syracuse: Syracuse University Press, 1962.

NEUSTADT, RICHARD E. *Presidential Power*. New York: John Wiley, 1960.

RANNEY, AUSTIN, and WILMORE KENDALL. *Democracy and the American Party System*. New York: Harcourt, Brace & World, 1956.

ROSSITER, CLINTON L. *The American Presidency*. New York: Harcourt, Brace & World, 1960.

SORAUF, FRANK J. *Party Politics in America*. Boston: Little, Brown, 1968.

SUNDQUIST, JAMES L. *Politics and Policy: The Eisenhower, Kennedy, and Johnson Years*. Washington, D.C.: The Brookings Institution, 1968.

TRUMAN, DAVID B. *The Governmental Process*. New York: Knopf, 1951.

WILDAVSKY, AARON. *The Politics of the Budgetary Process*. Boston: Little, Brown, 1964.

Congress: Criticism and dissent

AGAR, HERBERT. *The Price of Union*. Boston: Houghton Mifflin Co., 1950.

BAILEY, STEPHEN K. *The Condition of Our National Political Parties*. New York: Fund for the Republic, 1959.

BURNS, JAMES MACGREGOR. *The Deadlock of Democracy: Four Party Politics in America*. Englewood Cliffs, N.J.: Prentice-Hall, 1963.

CLARK, JOSEPH S. *Congress: The Sapless Branch*. New York: Harper & Row, 1964.

―――. *Congressional Reform: Problems and Prospects*. New York: Thomas Y. Crowell, 1965.

DE GRAZIA, ALFRED, ed. *Congress: The First Branch of Government*. New York: Doubleday, 1967.

HERRING, E. PENDLETON. *The Politics of Democracy*. 1st ed. 1940. New York: W.W. Norton, 1965.

MC INNIS, MARY, ed. *We Propose: A Modern Congress. Selected Proposals by the House Republican Task Force on Congressional Reform and Minority Staffing*. New York: McGraw-Hill, 1966.

RANNEY, AUSTIN. *The Doctrine of Responsible Party Government*. Urbana: University of Illinois Press, 1962.

SCHATTSCHNEIDER, E. E. *Party Government*. New York: Farrar & Rinehart, 1942.

WILSON, WOODROW. *Congressional Government*. Cleveland: World, 1886; Meridian Books, 1956.

Executive-Legislative relations

BINKLEY, WILFRED E. *President and Congress*. 3rd rev. ed. New York: Vintage Books, 1962.

CARROLL, HOLBERT N. *The House of Representatives and Foreign Affairs*. Pittsburgh: University of Pittsburgh Press, 1958.

CHAMBERLAIN, LAWRENCE H. *The President, Congress and Legislation*. New York: Columbia University Press, 1946.

COOPER, JOSEPH, and GARY BOMBARDIER. "Presidential Leadership and Party Success," *Journal of Politics*, XXX (November 1968), 1012–1027.

DAHL, ROBERT A. *Congress and Foreign Policy*. New York: Harcourt, Brace, 1950.

FREEMAN, J. LEIPER. *The Political Process: Executive Bureau-Legislative Committee Relations*. New York: Random House, 1965.

HARRIS, JOSEPH P. *Congressional Control of Administration*. Washington, D.C.: Brookings Institution, 1964.

PIPE, G. RUSSELL. "Congressional Liaison: The Executive Branch Consolidates Its Relations with Congress," *Public Administration Review*, XXVI (March 1966), 14–24.

POLSBY, NELSON W. *Congress and the Presidency.* Englewood Cliffs, N.J.: Prentice-Hall, 1964.

SALOMA, JOHN S., III. *The Responsible Use of Power: A Critical Analysis of the Congressional Budget Process.* Washington, D.C.: American Enterprise Institute, 1964.

SCHLESINGER, ARTHUR M., JR., and ALFRED DE GRAZIA. *Congress and the Presidency.* Washington, D.C.: American Enterprise Institute, 1967.

TAYLOR, TELFORD. *Grand Inquest: The Story of Congressional Investigation.* New York: Simon and Schuster, 1955.

WALLACE, ROBERT. *Congressional Control of Federal Spending.* Detroit: Wayne State University Press, 1960 .

WESTERFIELD, H. BRADFORD. *Foreign Policy and Party Politics.* New Haven, Conn.: Yale University Press, 1955.

Congress and the courts

MORGAN, DONALD G. *Congress and the Constitution.* Cambridge: Harvard University Press, 1966.

MURPHY, WALTER F. *Congress and the Court.* Chicago: University of Chicago Press, 1962.

PRITCHETT, C. HERMAN. *Congress Versus the Supreme Court, 1957–1960.* Minneapolis: University of Minnesota Press, 1961.

Interest groups

BLAISDELL, DONALD C. *American Democracy Under Pressure.* New York: Ronald Press, 1957.

BUNZEL, JOHN H. *The American Small Businessman.* New York: Alfred A. Knopf, 1962.

CALKINS, FAY. *The CIO and the Democratic Party.* Chicago: University of Chicago Press, 1952.

CELLER, EMANUEL. "Pressure Groups in Congress," *The Annals of the American Academy of Political and Social Science,* CCCXIX (September 1958), 1–9.

COHEN, BERNARD C. *The Influence of Non-Governmental Groups on Foreign Policy-Making.* Boston: World Peace Foundation, 1959.

DEXTER, LEWIS ANTHONY. *How Organizations Are Represented in Washington.* New York: Bobbs-Merrill, 1969.

ENGLER, ROBERT. *The Politics of Oil*. New York: The Macmillan Co., 1961.

GABLE, RICHARD W. "NAM: Influential Lobby or Kiss of Death?" *Journal of Politics*, XV (May 1953), 254–273.

HERRING, E. PENDLETON. *Group Representation Before Congress*. Baltimore: The Johns Hopkins Press, 1929.

KEY, V. O., JR. "The Veterans and the House of Representatives," *Journal of Politics*, V (February 1943), 27–40.

LATHAM, EARL. *The Group Basis of Politics*. Ithaca: Cornell University Press, 1952.

MAASS, ARTHUR. *Muddy Waters: The Army Engineers and the Nation's Rivers*. Cambridge: Harvard University Press, 1951.

MILBRATH, LESTER W. *The Washington Lobbyists*. Chicago: Rand McNally, 1963.

RIGGS, FRED. *Pressures on Congress: A Study of the Repeal of Chinese Exclusion*. New York: Columbia University Press, 1950.

SCHATTASCHNEIDER, E. E. *Politics, Pressures and the Tariff*. New York: Prentice-Hall, 1935.

SOMIT, ALBERT, and JOSEPH TANENHAUS. "The Veteran in the Electoral Process: The House of Representatives," *Journal of Politics*, XIX (May 1957), 184–201.

SURREY, STANLEY S. "The Congress and the Tax Lobbyist—How Special Tax Provisions Get Enacted," *Harvard Law Review*, LXX (May 1957), 1145–1182.

ZEIGLER, HARMON. *Interest Groups in American Society*. Englewood Cliffs, N.J.: Prentice-Hall, 1963.

The electorate

BERELSON, BERNARD, PAUL LAZARSFELD, and WILLIAM McPHEE. *Voting*. Chicago: University of Chicago Press, 1954.

BURDICK, EUGENE, and ARTHUR J. BRODBECK, eds. *American Voting Behavior*. Glencoe, Ill.: Free Press, 1959.

CAMPBELL, ANGUS, PHILIP E. CONVERSE, WARREN E. MILLER, and DONALD E. STOKES. *The American Voter*. New York: John Wiley & Sons, 1960.

CAMPBELL, ANGUS, GERALD GURIN, and WARREN E. MILLER. *The Voter Decides*. Evanston, Ill.: Row, Peterson & Co., 1954.

CONVERSE, PHILIP E., AAGE R. CLAUSEN, and WARREN E. MILLER. "Electoral Myth and Reality: The 1964 Election," *American Political Science Review*, LIX (June 1965), 321–336.

CUMMINGS, MILTON C. *Congressmen and the Electorate: Elections for the U.S. House and the President, 1920–1964.* New York: The Free Press, 1966.

JONES, CHARLES O. "Inter-Party Competition for Congressional Seats," *Western Political Quarterly*, XVII (September 1964), 461–476.

KEY, V. O., with the assistance of MILTON C. CUMMINGS, JR. *The Responsible Electorate.* Cambridge: The Belknap Press, 1966.

LAZARSFELD, PAUL F., BERNARD R. BERELSON, and HAZEL GAUDET. *The Peoples Choice.* 2nd ed. New York: Columbia University Press, 1948.

McPHEE, WILLIAM N., and WILLIAM A. GLASER, eds. *Public Opinion and Congressional Elections.* New York: Free Press, 1962.

The press

CATER, DOUGLAS. *The Fourth Branch of Government.* Boston: Houghton Mifflin, 1959.

CHESTER, EDWARD W. *Radio, Television and American Politics.* New York: Sheed and Ward, 1969.

COHEN, BERNARD C. *The Press and Foreign Policy.* Princeton: Princeton University Press, 1963.

DUNN, DELMAR D. *Public Officials and the Press.* Reading, Mass.: Addison-Wesley, 1969.

MAC NEIL, ROBERT. *The People Machine: The Inflence of Television on American Politics.* New York: Harper & Row, 1968.

NIMMO, DAN D. *Newsgathering in Washington.* New York: Atherton Press, 1964.

RESTON, JAMES. *The Artillery of the Press: Its Influence on American Foreign Policy.* New York and Evanston: Harper & Row, 1966.

RIVERS, WILLIAM L. *The Opinion Makers.* Boston: Beacon Press, 1965.

―――. *The Adversaries: Politics and the Press.* Boston: Beacon Press, 1970.

Index

★ Index